Nissan's Business Japanese

Plus

Nissan's Business Japanese *Plus*

A Complete Intermediate Course in Business Japanese

ビジネスを成功させる日本語

Hajime Takamizawa

Chief Instructor
Japan Field School
U.S. State Department

Published by Passport Books
in Association with Nissan Motor Co., Ltd.

PASSPORT BOOKS
a division of *NTC Publishing Group*
Lincolnwood, Illinois USA

1993 Printing

This edition first published in 1991 by Passport Books,
a division of NTC Publishing Group, 4255 West Touhy Avenue,
Lincolnwood (Chicago), Illinois 60646-1975 U.S.A.
Originally published by Nissan Motor Co., Ltd.
© Copyright by the International Division of Nissan Motor Co., Ltd.
Manufactured in the United States of America.

3 4 5 6 7 8 9 VP 9 8 7 6 5 4 3 2

ACKNOWLEDGMENTS

It has been a privilege to contribute to the *Business Japanese* Project, which fills such an important need in two-way communication between Japan and the rest of the world. I find it especially rewarding to know that a textbook that was originally designed for diplomats is now being used by educational and business communities alike, and that this textbook is playing such a vital role in popularizing the study of Japanese throughout the world.

Like its predecessor, *Business Japanese PLUS* aims to improve speaking ability; also like its predecessor, it provides dialogues and vocabulary targeted at business people in Japan and overseas. On the assumption that more advanced students will take a greater interest in the written language, we have also included **kanji** for all appropriate Japanese terms throughout the book, with **hiragana** in small type inserted over each character for your reading convenience. In order not to impede your progress in mastering the spoken language, however, we have relegated special reading practice of **kana** and **kanji** to the Appendix (II).

I am deeply indebted to the management of Nissan Motor Co., Ltd., without whose vision and support *Business Japanese* would never have been realized, much less introduced to such a wide audience. I am especially grateful to the staff of the International Division for their guidance in the production of this second edition.

I am grateful also to Mr. Yuji Nakazato and Mr. Masaaki Nakamori for their assistance in preparing the language sections of this book, and to Ms. Mizuko Saga for her helpful advice. Finally, I wish to express my special thanks to Ms. Madalena Velasquez, Mr. Hayato Yoshida and the other staff members of Asian Advertisers, Inc., for their contributions and their cooperation throughout this project.

Hajime Takamizawa
Chief Instructor
Japan Field School
U.S. State Department

PREFACE

We are very pleased to present this edition of *Business Japanese PLUS*.

In the our years since the *Business Japanese* project was launched, the textbooks and cassette tapes in the series have become international best-sellers. The series has been heralded as a timely contribution by schools, governmental and private organizations, as well as by individual businessmen and women. In fact, *Business Japanese* is now a key textbook in courses offered by a number of institutions in Japan and overseas.

As an international company with business activities in over 150 countries, Nissan is of course pleased and gratified that *Business Japanese* has been so well received everywhere. We feel that our *Business Japanese* Project helps to fill one more gap in the exchange of information between East and West. We are proud to have played a part in furthering worldwide business communication, and reaffirm our commitment to promote international understanding about Japan, its language and its customs.

Business Japanese PLUS , like its predecessor, was a group effort. We would like to acknowledge in particular the contributions of Professor Hajime Takamizawa, Chief Instructor at the U.S. State Department Japan Field School, who authored the language sections; and Ms. Madalena Velasquez of Asian Advertisers, Inc., who wrote the *"Business Information"* sections and assisted Nissan's International Division in compiling the information for these sections.

We also take this opportunity to thank the hundreds of readers who sent comments and suggestions about *Business Japanese* and who so kindly shared their professional experiences in Japan with us so we in turn could provide timely and pertinent advice in the *"Business Information"* sections. We have incorporated many of your suggestions in this volume and welcome any additional ideas you may have for the improvement of *Business Japanese* in the future.

We wish you much enjoyment in your study of Japanese and continued success in your business activities in Japan.

Yutaka Kume
President
Nissan Motor Co., Ltd.

CONTENTS

Acknowledgements
Preface
Introduction

Lesson	Language Section	Page	Business Information	Page
21	Arranging a Meeting	1	A Visit from the Head Office	13
22	Describing the Company	15	Making Presentations	27
23	Explaining the Product	29	Preparing the Interpreter	41
24	Price and Quantity	43	Reading Financial Statements	53
25	Payment and Delivery	59	Giving Gifts	70
26	At the Bank	73	Checks and Savings	85
27	A Price Reduction	87	Advanced Negotiations	98
28	At the Office II	101	Hiring and Training Staff	112
29	At a Business Gathering	115	Finding an Office	125

Lesson	Language Section	Page	Business Information	Page
30	At the Factory	127	Business Proverbs	139
31	More Technical Discussions	141	Negotiating Parlance	153
32	Service and Maintenance	155	Maintaining the Long-Term Relationship	168
33	Planning a Celebration	171	Socializing	184
34	Technical Trouble	187	Handling Problems	201
35	Clearing Up Misunderstandings	203	Joining a Japanese Firm	215

Appendix I	1. Verb Inflections	218
	2. Suru Verb List	222
	3. Adjective Chart	225
	4. Copula Chart	225
Appendix II	1. Katakana	226
	2. Hiragana	227
	3. Kanji	229
Index		239

INTRODUCTION

Objective

BUSINESS JAPANESE offers a new orientation to the study of the Japanese language. Unlike the generalized approach of most Japanese textbooks, the aim of *BUSINESS JAPANESE* is to help the foreign business person meet his or her specific needs in everyday business situations in Japan:

BUSINESS JAPANESE will assist you in mastering all fundamentals of grammar and vocabulary essential for normal business activities.

BUSINESS JAPANESE will equip you with a wealth of background information about Japanese companies, local business protocol, customs, etc. to enable you to understand, and operate with confidence in, your new business environment.

Organization of the Text

1 **Lessons:** *BUSINESS JAPANESE II*, which picks up where BUSINESS JAPANESE left off, starts with Lesson 21. The volume is divided into fifteen lessons, each with the same easy-to-follow format:

   a. Statement of lesson objectives.
   b. List of target expressions and grammatical points to master.
   c. Description of business situation to be covered.
   d. Dialogue utilizing target expressions in business situations. New vocabulary you should pay particular attention to is listed before every conversation, and also written in Japanese for your reference.
   e. Full dialogue provided in Japanese writing, for reference.
   f. Related and additional useful expressions for business situation.
   g. Notes on grammar and vocabulary introduced in the dialogue.
   h. Practices, exercises, and self-testing.
   i. "Business Information": Background information pertaining to the business situation.

2 **Appendices:**
   a. Appendix I
       Verb Chart: shows inflections of all verbs which appear in this volume.
       "Suru" Verb Chart: indicates all verbs and nouns in this volume which can be used as the stems in compound **-suru** verbs.
       Adjective Chart: shows inflections of all adjectives which appear in this volume.
   b. Appendix II
       Reading Section: introduces all **katakana** and **hiragana** as well as 100 of the most frequently used **kanji** (Chinese characters), based on *A Study of Uses of Chinese Characters in Modern Newspapers* (published by The National Language Research Institute, 1976.)

Special Features

In *BUSINESS JAPANESE*, the level of language skills is closely coordinated with that of the business activities being described in order to provide the most coherent structure for the gradual acquisition of business-related skills:

a. As the narrative proceeds from relatively simple business situations, such as making appointments, to more complex ones like contract negotiations and mechanical problems, the student is taught correspondingly more sophisticated expressions and grammatical patterns.

b. Grammar rules and new terminology are introduced systematically so that each new chapter reinforces and expands the skills covered in the previous one.

c. Alternate expressions and uses are provided wherever possible to allow the student maximum opportunity to tailor newly-acquired skills to his/her individual needs.

d. Each dialogue in the text is based on a single business situation in Japan. Each lesson can therefore also serve as a handy phrase-book for the student when searching for specific words, expressions, etc. appropriate for a given business situation.

This integrated format ensures that, by the end of the course, the student will not only have mastered the fundamentals of Japanese grammar, but will also be self-sufficient in basic, daily conversation with his Japanese affiliates and familiar with the idiosyncracies of his new working environment.

How to Use This Text

BUSINESS JAPANESE has been designed so that even a busy professional can learn Japanese either in class or at home, with a minimum of preparation and review. Students are of course recommended to proceed at their own pace, as best suits their individual schedules and skills. The following guidelines, however, have been provided for your benefit to ensure through and rapid mastery of the material covered in this volume:

Step1: Introduction to the Dialogue
1) Instructor explains new target expressions, grammar and vocabulary (with reference to Notes as necessary)
2) Student practices pronunciation of new vocabulary.
3) Student practices the dialogue.
4) Role-playing exercises based on the dialogue to develop initial familiarity with new words and patterns.

Step 2: Introduction to Related Expressions
1) Instructor explains related and additional expressions (with reference to Notes as necessary) for systematic expansion and enrichment of core expressions.
2) Student practices pronunciation.
3) Role-playing exercises as in Step 1.
   [Please note that instead of routinely memorizing new expressions, etc., students are encouraged to acquire mastery over them through repeated use and varied application.]

Step 3: Practices and Exercises
1) Completion of all practices and exercises provided.
2) Exercises also draw upon preceding lessons in order to ensure depth of understanding. Thorough comprehension of each exercise is recommended before proceeding to the next.

Step 4: Applied Conversation
1) Rewording and adaptation of exercises, etc., to relate target expressions as much as possible to student's own experiences.
2) Students are encouraged to request additional drills from the instructor to tailor new expressions to their personal business needs.

Step 5: Review
Review of the business dialogue and *Business Information* to place narrative into broader perspective.

Step 6: Preparation for Next Lesson
Students are encouraged to read notes on grammar, idiomatic expressions and *Business Information* prior to the actual lesson.

If these guidelines are faithfully observed, most students will spend about 8 hours on each lesson and complete *BUSINESS JAPANESE II* in a total of approximately 120 hours. Even at a pace of only 5 hours a week, or one hour per working day, the course may be completed in 24 weeks, or under 6 months.

Optional: Reading Section (Appendix II)

Section 1 Katakana: Practice reading and writing the **katakana** syllabary in the chart. Then repeat the *Reading Practice* until you develop a feel for the Japanese pronunciation of foreign words and can read all **katakana** fluently.

Section 2 Hiragana: Practice reading and writing the **hiragana** syllabary in the chart, column by column. Then repeat the *Reading Practice* for each column until you can read all **hiragana** fluently.

Section 3 Kanji:*

    Step 1) Study the readings, meaning and usages of each **kanji** listed in the chart.
    Step 2) Repeat the *Reading Practice* until you can read the characters fluently.
    Step 3) Review each sentence to be sure you understand its meaning.

* The 100 **kanji** presented here are intended only as an introduction. Advanced students may eventually like to obtain a guide to reading and writing the 1,945 Standard-Use (**jooyoo**) **kanji**. Each of the following books is excellent and widely available:

    1) Kanji & Kana, W. Hadamitzky, ed. (Charles E. Tuttle), ¥3,200.–
    2) Essential Kanji, P.G. O'Neill, ed. (Weatherhill), ¥1,600.–
    3) A Guide to Reading & Writing Japanese, F. Sakade, ed. (Charles E. Tuttle), ¥1,500.–

Special Note Concerning Self-Study

It is of course preferable that a teacher be available to explain to you the more tricky aspects of grammar and other special characteristics of the Japanese language. However, for those who will be studying the course on their own, the following are recommended in addition to the standard guidelines:

    1) Careful study of the "Table of Japanese Sounds" provided on the following pages. If possible, students should also practice listening and pronunciation with the help of *BUSINESS JAPANESE* casstte tapes.
    2) Close reading of the dialogue and additional expressions for *basic* comprehension. Heavy reliance on the English translations is not recommended, as Japanese expressions frequently have no real equivalent in any other language. Wherever possible, literal (if awkward) translations have been provided to facilitate comprehension.
    3) Careful study of all notes on grammar and vocabulary.
    4) Diligence in completing all practices, exercises and drills. Repetition of key exercises is strongly recommended for the independent student, and you should not move on the the next exercise until absolutely confident of the preceding one. Model answers have been provided for most exercises for your guidance.

Note: All company names, except for Nissan Motor Co., Ltd., and all personal names used in this text are purely fictional. Any coincidences with real-life companies or personalities are unintentional.

A TABLE OF JAPANESE SOUNDS

Showing the Katakana and Hiragana syllabaries

The romanization system used in this text is basically the system used in ordinary dictionaries (i.e. the Hepburn system). The letters **a**, **i**, **u**, **e**, and **o** represent the five basic vowels in Japanese, pronounced as follows, with crisp, short breaths: **a** as in B*a*ch, **i** as in p*i*ano, **u** as in h*u*la, **e** as in b*e*t, and **o** as in h*o*pe. Vowels can be doubled, resulting in almost exactly twice the length of the same sound as the single short vowel. However, note that, in this text, there are the following three exceptions to the Hepburn system:

1. Doubled (long) vowels are indicated as **aa**, **ii**, **uu**, **ee**, and **oo**, instead of ā, î, ū, ē, and ō.

Examples:

Hepburn System	This Text	Meaning
Kachō	**Kachoo**	'Manager'
Tōkyō	**Tookyoo**	'Tokyo'

The vowel cluster **ei** is represented as the doubled (long) vowel, **ee**.

Example:

Hepburn	This Text	Meaning
Keiyaku	**Keeyaku**	'contract'

a あ / ア B*a*ch	**i** い / イ p*i*ano	**u** う / ウ h*u*la	**e** え / エ b*e*t	**o** お / オ h*o*pe
ka か / カ	**ki** き / キ	**ku** く / ク	**ke** け / ケ	**ko** こ / コ
sa さ / サ	**shi** し / シ	**su** す / ス	**se** せ / セ	**so** そ / ソ
ta た / タ	**chi** ち / チ	**tsu** つ / ツ	**te** て / テ	**to** と / ト
na な / ナ	**ni** に / ニ	**nu** ぬ / ヌ	**ne** ね / ネ	**no** の / ノ
ha は / ハ	**hi** ひ / ヒ	**hu** ふ / フ	**he** へ / ヘ	**ho** ほ / ホ
ma ま / マ	**mi** み / ミ	**mu** む / ム	**me** め / メ	**mo** も / モ
ya や / ヤ		**yu** ゆ / ユ		**yo** よ / ヨ
ra* ら / ラ	**ri*** り / リ	**ru*** る / ル	**re*** れ / レ	**ro*** ろ / ロ
wa わ / ワ	**n** ん / ン			

ga が / ガ	
za ざ / ザ	
da だ / ダ	

ba ば / バ	
pa ぱ / パ	

«Doubled

aa

* The Japanese "r" sound is the only consonant that does not closely correspond to any English consonant. It is pronounced by flicking the tip of the tongue against the roof of the mouth, to produce a sound resembling the English "d".

2. The consonant **n**, when it is pronounced as an independent syllable preceding a **y** or a vowel within a word, is indicated as **n**' for additional clarity.

Examples:

Hepburn	This Text	Meaning
honya	**hon'ya**	'bookstore'

When three or more vowels follow each other, an apostrophe is used to indicate word formation.

Example: **Kee'eegaku** 'business administration'

3. **Fu**, the "fricative *h*", is indicated as **hu**.

Examples:

Hepburn	This Text	Meaning
Furansu	**Huransu**	'France'
fune	**hune**	'ship'

KEY

Katakana → ス / **su** / す — Hiragana — Romanization

gi ぎ ギ	**gu** ぐ グ	**ge** げ ゲ	**go** ご ゴ
ji じ ジ	**zu** ず ズ	**ze** ぜ ゼ	**zo** ぞ ゾ
		de で デ	**do** ど ド

bi び ビ	**bu** ぶ ブ	**be** べ ベ	**bo** ぼ ボ
pi ぴ ピ	**pu** ぷ プ	**pe** ぺ ペ	**po** ぽ ポ

(long) Vowels»

ii	**uu**	**ee**	**oo**

kya きゃ キャ	**kyu** きゅ キュ	**kyo** きょ キョ
gya ぎゃ ギャ	**gyu** ぎゅ ギュ	**gyo** ぎょ ギョ
hya ひゃ ヒャ	**hyu** ひゅ ヒュ	**hyo** ひょ ヒョ
bya びゃ ビャ	**byu** びゅ ビュ	**byo** びょ ビョ
pya ぴゃ ピャ	**pyu** ぴゅ ピュ	**pyo** ぴょ ピョ
nya にゃ ニャ	**nyu** にゅ ニュ	**nyo** にょ ニョ
rya りゃ リャ	**ryu** りゅ リュ	**ryo** りょ リョ
sha しゃ シャ	**shu** しゅ シュ	**sho** しょ ショ
ja じゃ ジャ	**ju** じゅ ジュ	**jo** じょ ジョ
cha ちゃ チャ	**chu** ちゅ チュ	**cho** ちょ チョ

Special Symbols:

(   )   in the English version indicates: (a) words which do not actually appear in the Japanese, but are provided for a more natural translation; (b) words that further clarify English translation; (c) references to other parts of the text; (d) a description/clarification of the business situation. (exception: the word 'it,' when used in idiomatic expressions about time, weather, etc. is not found in parentheses.)

(   )   in the Japanese version indicates words that are not always necessary, and that may be dropped depending either on the context or on the style of the individual speaker.

[lit.   ]   indicates literal translation.

[imp.]   indicates implied meaning.

«   »   indicates general category or person/thing/grammatical term etc. to be inserted.

/   /   indicates: (a) terms pertaining to grammar; (b) cue(s) to be used in the following Practice.

...   indicates that the sentence is incomplete, and requires the insertion of a word, phrase, or clause for completion.

-      clarifies the formation of words, and does not affect pronunciation. In this text, "-" has been inserted in the following cases:

         a) between a personal name and **san/sama**/job title.
            Example: Yamada-san
         b) preceding "counters."
            Example: ichi-dai
         c) between noun and **suru/dekiru.**
            Example: benkyoo-suru
         d) compound words.
            Example: Nihon-muke

Lesson 21

Arranging a Meeting

OBJECTIVES

1   to use the Potential form.

2   to make an appointment.

3   to describe the weather and temperature.

TARGET EXPRESSIONS AND PATTERNS

1   I can do X.   **Watakushi wa <X> ga... rareru.**

2   X named Y   **<Y> to iu <X>**

3   as (much) as possible   **narubeku (ooku)**

SITUATION

USM, Ltd. is an American industrial robot manufacturer trying to sell its latest models to Japanese firms for the first time. Mr. William Brown of P&C, Ltd., USM's agent in Japan, receives a telex saying that a USM sales engineer named Stephen Jones will be arriving in Tokyo to assist in P&C's negotiations with Nissan Motor Co., Ltd. Mr. Brown calls Mr. Ohyama, General Manager of the Purchasing Department at Nissan Motor Co., Ltd. and arranges an appointment.

21/Arranging a Meeting

DIALOGUE

Ohyama

1	(This) is Ohyama.	**Ooyama desu.**

Brown

2	Mr. Ohyama, (this) is Brown of P&C, Ltd.	**Ooyama-san, Pii-ando-shii no Buraun desu.**

	as usual	**aikawarazu,** あいかわらず
Ohyama	(is) hot	**atsui,** 暑い

3	Oh, Mr. Brown, it's hot as usual.	**Aa, Buraun-san, aikawarazu, atsui desu nee.**

	certainly, really	**mattaku,** まったく
	cannot stand	**yarikirenai,** やりきれない
	tomorrow	**asu,** あす
	person named Jones	**Joonzu to iu hito,** ジョーンズという人
Brown	to visit Japan	**rainichi-suru,** 来日する

4	Yes, (it) certainly is. (I) can hardly stand it. By the way, (I) just received a telex that says a person named Jones from USM is visiting Japan tomorrow.	**Ee, mattaku atsukute yarikiremasen ne. Tokoro de, ima terekkusu ga hairi-mashita ga, asu Yuu-esu-emu kara Joonzu to iu hito ga rainichi-suru soo desu.**

Ohyama

5	Is that so? Mr. Jones. What kind of person is he?	**Soo desu ka. Joonzu-san desu ne. Don-na kata desu ka.**

Brown	sales engineer	**seerusu-enjinia,** セールス・エンジニア

6	(He)'s a sales engineer.	**Seerusu-enjinia desu.**

	question	**shitsumon (-suru),** 質問(する)
	to answer	**kotaeru,** 答える
Ohyama	can answer	**kotaerareru,** 答えられる

| **7** | Then, (he) can answer technical questions, too. | **Jaa, gijutsuteki na shitsumon ni mo kotaeraremasu ne.** |

| **Brown** | moreover | **sore ni,** それに |

| **8** | Moreover, it seems (he) will be bringing various data on the new products. | **Sore ni, shinseehin ni tsuite no shiryoo mo iroiro motte kuru yoo desu.** |

| | our company | **toosha,** 当社 |
| **Ohyama** | can come | **korareru,** 来られる |

| **9** | Well then, when could (you) come to our office? | **De wa, toosha no hoo e wa itsu korare-masu ka.** |

| | (is) early, soon | **hayai,** 早い |
| **Brown** | as soon as possible | **narubeku hayaku,** なるべく早く |

| **10** | (We) would like to meet (you) as soon as (you) are free. How about the day after tomorrow? | **Narubeku hayaku oai-shitai n desu ga, asatte wa ikaga desu ka.** |

Ohyama

| **11** | That's fine, but in the morning (I) have something to do [lit. a schedule], so how about two o'clock in the afternoon? | **Kekkoo desu ga, gozen-chuu wa chotto yotee ga arimasu kara, gogo ni-ji goro wa doo deshoo ka.** |

| **Brown** | Mr. Jones | **Joonzu-shi,** ジョーンズ氏 |

| **12** | In that case, (I)'ll call on (you) with Mr. Jones the day after tomorrow at two o'clock. | **De wa, asatte ni-ji ni Joonzu-shi to issho ni ukagaimasu.** |

21/Arranging a Meeting

JAPANESE WRITING

1 大山： 大山です。

2 ブラウン： 大山さん、ピー・アンド・シーのブラウンです。

3 大山： ああ、ブラウンさん、あいかわらず、暑いですねえ。

4 ブラウン： ええ、まったく暑くてやりきれませんね。ところで、今テレックスが入りましたが、あすユー・エス・エムから ジョーンズという人が 来日する そうです。

5 大山： そうですか。ジョーンズさんですね。どんな方ですか。

6 ブラウン： セールス・エンジニアです。

7 大山： じゃあ、技術的な質問にも 答えられますね。

8 ブラウン： それに、新製品についての資料も いろいろ持って来るようです。

9 大山： では、当社の方へは いつ来られますか。

10 ブラウン： なるべく早くお会いしたいんですが、あさっては いかがですか。

11 大山： 結構ですが、午前中は ちょっと予定がありますから、午後二時ごろは どうでしょうか。

12 ブラウン： では、あさって二時に ジョーンズ氏といっしょに 伺います。

ADDITIONAL USEFUL EXPRESSIONS

1 At the office

day(s)	**hi,**	日
hot day(s)	**atsui hi,**	暑い日
to continue	**tsuzuku,**	続く
unpleasant	**iya/na/,**	いや（な）

A:	It's awful with this heat continuing day after day, isn't it?	**Mainichi, atsui hi ga tsuzuite, iya desu ne.**

	like this, to this extent	**konna ni,** こんなに

B:	It really is. Are Japanese summers always this hot?	**Hontoo desu nee. Nihon no natsu wa itsu mo konna ni atsui n desu ka.**

	(is) muggy	**mushiatsui,** むし暑い

A:	No. This year it's especially muggy.	**Iie. Kotoshi wa toku ni mushiatsui n desu yo.**

4

| B: | Oh, really. | **Soo desu ka.** |

| | (is) cool | **suzushii,** 涼^{すず}しい |

| A: | But Japanese autumns are cool and pleasant. | **Demo, Nihon no aki wa suzushikute ii desu yo.** |

2 After the business trip

| | Kansai (Area name) | **Kansai,** 関西^{かんさい} |

| A: | Last week, I went to Kansai. | **Senshuu Kansai e itte kimashita.** |

| B: | Was it a business trip? You had a hard time, didn't you? | **Shutchoo deshita ka. Taihen deshita ne.** |

| | last | **saigo,** 最後^{さいご} |
| | sight-seeing | **kenbutsu (-suru),** 見物^{けんぶつ}(する) |

| A: | (Yes,) but I was able to go sight-seeing in Kyoto on the last day. | **Demo, saigo no hi wa Kyooto-kenbutsu ga dekimashita kara…** |

| | weather | **tenki, otenki** (polite), 天気^{てんき}、お天気^{てんき} |

| B: | Oh, that was nice (for you). How was the weather? | **Sore wa yokatta desu ne. Otenki wa ikaga deshita ka.** |

	continuously	**zutto,** ずっと
	rain	**ame,** 雨^{あめ}
	to fall	**huru,** 降^ふる

| A: | Unfortunately, it was raining the whole time. | **Ainiku zutto ame ga hutte imashita.** |

3 At the office

| A: | Tomorrow, a friend from America is coming. | **Asu Amerika kara tomodachi ga kuru n desu.** |

5

21/Arranging a Meeting

	typhoon	**taihuu,**	台風

B:	Is that right? They say a typhoon is coming tomorrow.	**Soo desu ka. Ashita wa taihuu ga kuru soo desu yo.**

	to clear up	**hareru,**	晴れる

A:	Really? It was sunny this morning, but…	**Hontoo desu ka. Kesa wa harete imashita ga…**

	to become cloudy	**kumoru,**	曇る

B:	But it's already cloudy now.	**Demo, ima wa moo kumotte imasu yo.**

	Narita (Airport)	**Narita (Kuukoo),**	成田(空港)
	to meet	**mukaeru,**	迎える
	to go to meet	**mukae ni iku,**	迎えに行く

A:	Is that so? That's a problem, isn't it? I am going to Narita to meet (him,) but…	**Soo desu ka. Komarimashita nee. Narita e mukae ni iku n desu ga…**

REFERENCE

samui	寒い	(is) cold
atatakai	暖かい	(is) warm
ii tenki	いい天気	good weather
iya na tenki	いやな天気	bad weather
yuki ga huru	雪が降る	to snow
kaze ga huku	風が吹く	the wind blows/it is windy

NOTES

1 The Potential

Most Japanese verbs can be made into corresponding potential verbs meaning 'can do such-and-such'.
To form the potential:

A)   Class 1 verb (or **-ru** verb): Drop the final **-ru** and add **-rareru**.

Example: **taberu** 'to eat' — **abe*rareru*** 'can eat'

B)   Class 2 verb (or **-u** verb): Drop the final **-u** and add **-eru**.

Example: **hanasu** 'to speak' — **hanas*eru*** 'can speak'

C)   Class 3 verb (or **-aru** verb): Drop the final **-aru** and add **-areru**.

Example: **irassharu** 'to come' — **irassh*areru*** 'can come'

D)   Irregular verbs:

Examples: **kuru** 'to come' — *korareru* 'can come'
suru 'to do' — *dekiru* 'can do'

Note: Recently some young Japanese have begun to inflect Class 1 verbs (or **-ru** verbs) like Class 2 verbs (or **-u** verbs), for example, **tabereru** 'can eat.' However, you had better use the **taberareru** form as indicated in the examples above because the more recent trends in potential forms have not yet been fully accepted in Japanese society.

Examples: a) **Sumisu-san wa nihongo ga* hanas*emasu*.**
"Mr. Smith can speak Japanese."

b) **Ashita moo ichi-do *koraremasu* ka.**
"Can you come once more tomorrow?"

c) **Watakushi wa gijutsuteki na shitsumon ni wa kotae*raremasen*.**
"I cannot answer questions about technical matters."

d) **Kinoo Kawamoto-san wa Buraun-san ni a*emashita* ka.**
"Was Mr. Kawamoto able to meet Mr. Brown yesterday?"

* Like **-tai** form, the object (what one can do) of the potential verb is commonly indicated by the particle **ga** [Refer to *BUSINESS JAPANESE*, Lesson 9, Note **1**].

All potential verbs are themselves Class 1 verbs (or **-ru** verbs). The inflection of **hanaseru** 'can speak' is as follows:

Non-past	Non-past Negative	Past	Past Negative
hanas*eru*	**hanas*enai***	**hanas*eta***	**hanas*enakatta***
korar*eru*	**korar*enai***	**korar*eta***	**korar*enakatta***
deki*ru*	**deki*nai***	**deki*ta***	**deki*nakatta***

Note: There is an alternative form to express potential: non-past verb + **koto ga dekiru** 'be able to do' [Refer to *BUSINESS JAPANESE*, Lesson 18, Note **3**].

Compare: **Buraun-san wa nihongo ga hanasemasu.**
"Mr. Brown can speak Japanese."

and

Buraun-san wa nihongo o hanasu *koto ga dekimasu*.
"Mr. Brown is able to speak Japanese."

2 Gerund (**-te** form) of Reason

Gerunds are sometimes used to explain the reason for the main clause that follows. Thus,

> ***Atsukute* yarikiremasen.**
> "I cannot stand the heat [lit. It's very hot, so I cannot stand it]."

> **Jikan ga *nakute*, Buraun-san no paatii ni shusseki dekimasen deshita.**
> "I was busy [lit. (I) had no time], so I couldn't go to Mr. Brown's party."

> **Ooyama-san wa hisho ga byooki ni *natte*, komatte imasu.**
> "Mr. Ohyama is having a difficult time because his secretary got sick."

Note: This usage usually occurs when the cause-and-effect relationship between the first and the second clause is rather obvious or logical.

3 **<Y> to iu <X>** 'X named Y'

The combination Y **to iu** X is used to mean 'an X named Y' or 'an X called Y."
In this combination, Y is usually a name or designation.

Examples:		
Ooyama *to iu* buchoo		'a General Manager named Ohyama'
Nissan *to iu* kaisha		'a company called Nissan'
Yokohama *to iu* machi		'a city named Yokohama'
hisho *to iu* shigoto		'a secretary's job'
nan *to iu* hon		'what book [lit. a book named what]?'

4 **Narubeku** 'as much as possible'

Narubeku is usually followed by the **-ku** form of an adjective and forms an adverbial phrase meaning 'as … as possible'. Thus,

> ***Narubeku* yasu*ku* utte kudasai.**
> "Please sell it as cheap as you can."

> **Sonna hon o *narubeku* oo*ku* yomitai n desu.**
> "I want to read as many books of that kind as possible."

> ***Narubeku* yasashi*ku* hanashimashoo.**
> "I'll speak as simply as I can."

Narubeku sometimes occurs before an adjective modifying a noun. Thus,

> ***Narubeku* ookii chizu o katte kite kudasai.**
> "Please go and buy as large a map as possible."

PRACTICE

1 Communication Practice

Directions: Describe the temperature and the weather to the teacher using the following patterns.

Patterns:
a) **Kyoo wa totemo** (temperature) **desu ne.**

b) **Kinoo wa** (weather) **deshita ne.**

c) **Kyoo wa** (weather) **desu ne.**

d) **Koko no natsu wa hontoo ni** (temperature) **desu yo.**

e) (Your home town) **no ni-gatsu wa taitee** (weather) **desu yo.**

Examples:
a) **Kyoo wa totemo (samui) desu ne.**
"It's very (cold) today, isn't it?"

b) **Kinoo wa (iya na tenki) deshita ne.**
"The weather was (awful) yesterday, wasn't it?"

c) **Kyoo wa (ii tenki) desu ne.**
"It's (a nice day) [lit. good weather] today, isn't it?"

d) **Koko no natsu wa hontoo ni (suzushii) desu yo.**
"The summer here is really (cool)."

e) **(Shikago) no ni-gatsu wa taitee (iya na tenki) desu yo.**
"The weather (in Chicago) is usually bad in February."

Reference:

samui	(is) cold	**ii tenki**	good weather
atatakai	(is) warm	**iya na tenki**	bad weather
suzushii	(is) cool	**ame ga huru**	to rain
atsui	(is) hot	**yuki ga huru**	to snow
mushiatsui	(is) muggy	**kumoru**	to become cloudy
		hareru	to clear up

2 Response Practice

Examples: Teacher: **Iku tsumori* desu ka.**
"Do you plan to go?"

Student: **Ee, ikeru to omoimasu.**
"Yes, I think I can go."

* [Refer to *BUSINESS JAPANESE*, Lesson 19, Notes **7**]

a) **Ooyama-san ni au tsumori desu ka.**   **Ee, aeru to omoimasu.**

b) **Ashita kaeru tsumori desu ka.**   **Ee, kaereru to omoimasu.**

c) **Takada-san ni denwa-suru tsumori desu ka.**   **Ee, denwa-dekiru to omoimasu.**

d) **Konban, tegami o kaku tsumori desu ka.**   **Ee, kakeru to omoimasu.**

e)	Kore o shachoo ni miseru tsumori desu ka.	Ee, miserareru to omoimasu.
f)	Tanaka-san ni tanomu tsumori desu ka.	Ee, tanomeru to omoimasu.
g)	Nichiyoobi ni kuru tsumori desu ka.	Ee, korareru to omoimasu.
h)	Ano gakkoo ni hairu tsumori desu ka.	Ee, haireru to omoimasu.
i)	Bengoshi ni naru tsumori desu ka.	Ee, nareru to omoimasu.
j)	Ano hito o yatou tsumori desu ka.	Ee, yatoeru to omoimasu.

3 Communication Practice

Directions: Tell the teacher what you can/could do by using the following patterns.

Patterns:
- a) **Watakushi wa** (language) **ga hanasemasu**.
- b) **Watakushi wa** (name of food) **ga tsukuremasu**.
- c) **Mae wa** (sports) **ga dekimashita ga...**
- d) **Mada** (place) **e ikemasen**.
- e) **Watakushi wa** (language) **ga yomemasu**.
- f) (Person/persons) **ni wa nakanaka aemasen**.

Examples:
- a) **Watakushi wa (Supeingo) ga hanasemasu.**
  "I can speak (Spanish)."
- b) **Watakushi wa (suteeki) ga tsukuremasu.**
  "I can cook (a steak)."
- c) **Mae wa (sakkaa) ga dekimashita ga...**
  "I could play (soccer) before, but ..."
- d) **Mada (Chuugoku) e ikemasen.**
  "I cannot go to (China) yet."
- e) **Watakushi wa (Doitsugo) ga yomemasu.**
  "I can read (German)."
- f) **(Nakasone-san) ni wa nakanaka aemasen.**
  "We can hardly ever meet (Mr. Nakasone)."

4 Transformation Practice

Examples: Teacher: **Ano hito wa Joonzu to iimasu.**
  "That person is named Jones."

Student: **Joonzu to iu hito desu.**
  "He is a man named Jones."

a)	Ano kaisha wa Yuu-esu-emu to iimasu.	Yuu-esu-emu to iu kaisha desu.
b)	Sono kuruma wa Purinsu to iimasu.	Purinsu to iu kuruma desu.
c)	Ano hisho wa Yamada to iimasu.	Yamada to iu hisho desu.
d)	Kono shinbun wa Mainichi to iimasu.	Mainichi to iu shinbun desu.
e)	Sono biiru wa Kirin to iimasu.	Kirin to iu biiru desu.

10

5 Expansion practice

Examples: Teacher: **Oai-shitai n desu. /hayaku/**
"I would like to see you." /soon/

Student: **Narubeku hayaku oaishitai n desu.**
"I would like to see you as soon as possible."

a) **Kitai n desu. /osoku/**   **Narubeku osoku kitai n desu.**

b) **Uritai n desu. /takaku/**   **Narubeku takaku uritai n desu.**

c) **Ryokoo-suru tsumori desu. /ooku/**   **Narubeku ooku ryokoo-suru tsumori desu.**

d) **Kakimashita. /omoshiroku/**   **Narubeku omoshiroku kakimashita.**

e) **Katarogu o motte kite kudasai. /takusan/**   **Narubeku takusan katarogu o motte kite kudasai.**

6 Comprehension Practice

Directions: The teacher reads aloud the following passage and then asks the student questions about it.

Pii-ando-shii no Nihon no shisha ni Detoroito no honsha kara terekkusu ga hairimashita. Yuu-esu-emu kara Joonzu to iu seerusu-enjinia ga ashita Nihon e kuru koto ni natta soo desu. Buraun-san wa Nissan no Ooyama-buchoo ni denwa o kakete, sono koto o hanashimashita. Joonzu-shi wa gijutsuteki na shitsumon ni mo kotaerareru hazu desu kara, Ooyama-buchoo mo yorokonde imasu. Buraun-san wa narubeku hayaku Ooyama-buchoo to soodan-shitai no de, asatte no gogo ni-ji ni Joonzu-shi to issho ni Nissan e iku koto ni shimashita.

Questions:

1 **Doko kara terekkusu ga hairimashita ka.**
2 **Dare ga Amerika kara kimasu ka.**
3 **Sono hito no shigoto wa nan desu ka.**
4 **Sono hito wa Pii-ando-shii no hito desu ka. De wa doko no hito desu ka.**
5 **Dare ga gijutsuteki na shitsumon ni kotaeraremasu ka.**
6 **Buraun-san wa itsu Nissan e iku koto ni shimashita ka.**
7 **Hitori de ikimasu ka.**
8 **Buraun-san to Joonzu-shi wa Nissan e itte, nani o shimasu ka.**

EXERCISES

a) You have just come back from a business trip. Inform the teacher in Japanese of the following weather conditions.

1 It was very hot.
2 It rained every day.
3 It was really muggy.

4   It was warm and the weather was good.
5   It was cool.
6   You could not stand the cold.
7   It was snowing.
8   It was very windy.

b)   Inform the teacher in Japanese that:

1   You can introduce a good lawyer to Mr. Smith.
2   Mr. Kawamoto cannot go to JETRO's party.
3   Mr. Jones could answer Mr. Ohyama's technical questions.
4   Because you were very busy, you could not write a letter to Mr. Smith.

Model Answers:

a)   **1   Totemo atsukatta desu.**
      2   Mainichi ame ga hurimashita.
      3   Hontoo ni mushiatsukatta desu.
      4   Atatakakute, ii tenki deshita.
      5   Suzushikatta desu.
      6   Samukute yarikiremasen deshita.
      7   Yuki ga hutte imashita.
      8   Kaze ga totemo tsuyokatta desu.

b)   **1   Sumisu-san ni ii bengoshi o shookai dekimasu.**
      2   Kawamoto-san wa Jetoro no paatii ni ikemasen.
      3   Joonzu-san wa Ooyama-san no gijutsuteki na shitsumon ni kotaeraremashita.
      4   Totemo isogashikatta kara, Sumisu-san ni tegami ga kakenakatta n desu.

BUSINESS INFORMATION

A Visit from the Head Office

Important visitors from home can mean a trying time for the expatriate manager in Japan. Schedules have to be juggled around to accomodate them and special reports prepared for their scrutiny. You also have to help book flights and hotels, arrange for appropriate entertainment and, in general, put your own plans on hold for the duration of the visit.

If you are expecting a visit from the head office, you may find the following suggestions useful in making the business trip enjoyable and constructive both for your guest and yourself.

1 Advance Notice: When making the rounds of Japanese clients with your overseas visitor, you should bear in mind that there is no such thing in Japan as a pleasant surprise. To catch someone off guard is to cause **meewaku** (迷惑, trouble).

Consequently, you should let your associates know as soon as you can about arriving technicians or executives, as Mr. Brown does in the DIALOGUE. Be sure to explain the intention of the proposed visit to the client, as well as the specific personnel your boss or technician would like to see. Information about your visitor's company – if different from your own – its industry ranking and other pertinent data are also helpful. If these are not readily available, be sure at least to indicate the visitor's title and position since your client will do his utmost to arrange for staff of comparable rank to appear at the meeting. Finally, a detailed agenda for the meeting should be submitted ahead of time as this will not only allow your client to be better prepared, but also assure that your guest will get as many answers as possible to his or her questions within the limited time available.

2 Meishi Readiness: Exchanging business cards is an indispensable formality in Japan (See *BUSINESS JAPANESE Business Information 1*). Visitors should therefore have an abundant supply of meishi–printed with all appropriate information in both English and Japanese–waiting for them when they arrive. If the information on the cards you had prepared turns out to be erroneous, you should have a new set made since scribbling "corrections" on one's meishi prior to exchange is considered very bad form. For unexpected or last-minute visits, there are special stationers who can print "emergency meishi" in under two hours. Certain large hotels also provide overnight or same-day meishi service.

3 Schedule Control: Once your Japanese associates have been advised of a visiting business "dignitary", they may want to provide "Airport-to-Airport" service, i.e. pick the guest up at the terminal, attend to his every need while in town, and then see him off at the airport once again when he departs. This is mostly to be hospitable, to be sure, but sometimes it is also to prevent the visitor from meeting with local competition during his stay. Consequently, you should not hesitate to take the initiative for your visitor's schedule, as otherwise he may find his time thoroughly monopolized day and night by one exceedingly generous, but overly possessive, company.

4 Not-So-Great Expectations: If your boss is accustomed to straight talk and quick action, he should probably be warned to lower his expectations for the trip. A business transaction will not necessarily materialize any faster because of his personal intervention; decision-making will not necessarily speed up because he and the top management of your client firm have finally met face-to-face. As mentioned before, Japanese directors can be quite removed from the daily business of their company (*BUSINESS JAPANESE Business Information 17*), and may show up for the meeting with your boss more for **aisatsu** (挨拶 , paying respects) than for active discussion and problem solving. He who appears to be your boss's equal in title may not be his equal in decision-making responsibility, especially in large corporations. Thus your boss should not expect the same kind of leverage from management in Japan as in the West–nor, of course, the same results.

5 Reciprocating: Japanese businessmen tend to pull out all the stops when entertaining important overseas visitors. Lunches and dinners can be lavish, followed by sprees in exclusive clubs on the Ginza. Neither you nor your guest need feel obliged to reciprocate in kind during his limited stay, however. Instead, your guest could later just send a personal letter thanking all levels of staff for their hospitality, and perhaps also a "typical" present from the home country to the individual(s) who took care of him most frequently during his visit. More elaborate entertainment can be arranged when it is the Japanese company's turn to go on business to your country.

6 Japanese National Holidays: The list of public holidays below is provided for the visitor's reference. You should also note that many offices in Japan are closed for 4-5 days over the New Year, during the first week of May ("Golden Week") and for several days in mid-August for **Obon**, or the Festival of Souls. Most Japanese also take their summer vacations in August.

January 1:	New Year's Day (お正月/元日 , **Oshoogatsu/Ganjitsu**)
January 15:	Coming of Age Day (成人の日 , **Seejin No Hi**)
February 11:	Founding of the Nation Day (建国記念の日 , **Kenkoku Kinen No Hi**)
Around March 20:	Spring Equinox (春分の日 , **Shunbun No Hi**)
April 29:	The Emperor's Birthday (天皇誕生日 , **Tennoo Tanjoobi**)
May 3:	Constitution Day (憲法記念日 , **Kenpoo Kinenbi**)
May 5:	Children's Day (子供の日 , **Kodomo No Hi**)
September 15	Respect for the Aged Day (敬老の日 , **Keeroo No Hi**)
Around September 20:	Autumn Equinox (秋分の日 , **Shuubun No Hi**)
October 10:	National Fitness Day (体育の日 , **Taiiku No Hi**)
November 3:	Culture Day (文化の日 , **Bunka No Hi**)
November 23:	Thanksgiving Day (勤労感謝の日 , **Kinroo Kansha No Hi**)

Lesson 22

Describing the Company

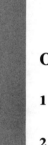

OBJECTIVES

1   to explain one's own company: history, main products, number of employees, financial status, etc.

2   to tell more about the weather.

TARGET EXPRESSIONS AND PATTERNS

1	It is expected that ...	... **mitooshi da.**
2	as \<X\>	**\<X\> to shite**
3	more than \<X\>	**\<X\> ijoo**
4	less than \<X\>	**\<X\> ika**

SITUATION

Mr. Brown and Mr. Jones arrive together at the Purchasing Department of Nissan. After Mr. Brown has introduced Mr. Jones to Mr. Ohyama, Mr. Ohyama asks questions about USM, Ltd.

22/Describing the Company

DIALOGUE

	sky	sora, 空
	trip	tabi, 旅
Ohyama	flight	sora no tabi, 空の旅

> **1** Mr. Jones, how was the flight?
>
> Joonzu-san, sora no tabi wa ikaga deshita ka.

Jones	comfortable	kaiteki/na/, 快適(な)

> **2** The weather was fine and (the flight) was comfortable.
>
> Tenki mo yokute, kaiteki deshita.

	(is) terrible	hidoi, ひどい
Ohyama	storm	arashi, 嵐

> **3** Is that right? Yesterday, Tokyo was terribly stormy, (but...)
>
> Soo desu ka. Kinoo Tookyoo wa hidoi arashi deshita ga...

	airport	kuukoo, 空港
	to arrive (at)	tsuku, 着く
Jones	to be surprised	bikkuri-suru, びっくりする

> **4** That's right. When I arrived at the airport, (I) was surprised it was raining so hard.
>
> Soo desu ne. Watakushi mo kuukoo e tsuita toki, ame ga hidoku hutte ita no de, bikkuri-shimashita.

	last night	sakuban, 昨晩
Ohyama	to sleep	nemuru, 眠る

> **5** Did (you) sleep well last night?
>
> Sakuban wa yoku nemuremashita ka.

	(sleep) like a log	gussuri, ぐっすり
Jones	completely	sukkari, すっかり

> **6** Yes, thank you. (I) slept like a log until nine o'clock, so (I)'m completely refreshed.
>
> Ee, okagesama de. Ku-ji made gussuri nemurimashita kara, sukkari genki ni narimashita.

	as a maker	**meekaa to shite,**	メーカーとして
	old days	**mukashi,**	昔
Ohyama	famous, well known	**yuumee/na/,**	有名(な)

7	Well, (I) would like to ask a little bit about your company, but USM has been well-known as a machine tool maker for a long time, hasn't it?	**De wa, onsha ni tsuite sukoshi ukagaitai n desu ga, Yuu-esu-emu wa koosakuki-kai no meekaa to shite mukashi kara yuumee desu ne.**

Jones	foundation	**sooritsu (-suru),**	創立(する)

8	Yes, next year is going to be (our) 90th anniversary, so (we) have (quite) a history.	**Hai, rainen ni wa sooritsu kyuujuu-nen ni narimasu kara, rekishi no aru kaisha desu.**

	automatic machine tool	**jidoo-koosakuki,**	自動工作機
Brown	first	**saisho,**	最初

9	The company that first made automatic machine tools was USM, too.	**Jidoo-koosakuki o saisho ni tsukutta no mo Yuu-esu-emu desu yo.**

Ohyama

10	Is that right [lit. Was that so]? (I) didn't know.	**Soo deshita ka. Shirimasen deshita.**

	sales	**uriage,**	売り上げ
Brown	"No. 1" in America	**Amerika ichi,**	アメリカ一

11	Last year, their robot sales were also the highest in America.	**Kyonen mo robotto no uriage wa Amerika ichi deshita.**

	per year	**nenkan,**	年間
Ohyama	to produce	**seesan-suru,**	生産する

12	Is that so? How many robots do (you) produce per year?	**Soo desu ka. Nenkan nan-dai gurai robotto o seesan-shite imasu ka.**

| | more than | ijoo, 以上 |
| Jones | prospect | mitooshi, 見通し |

13 (We produced) about 3,000 units last year, but (we) expect to produce over 3,500 units this year. | **Kyonen wa sanzen-dai gurai deshita ga, kotoshi wa sanzen gohyaku-dai ijoo ni naru mitooshi desu.**

Ohyama

14 That's very good, isn't it? | **Sore wa kekkoo desu ne.**

JAPANESE WRITING

1 大山： ジョーンズさん、空の旅はいかがでしたか。

2 ジョーンズ： 天気も良くて、快適でした。

3 大山： そうですか。きのう東京はひどい嵐でしたが…

4 ジョーンズ： そうですね。私も空港へ着いた時、雨がひどく降っていたので、びっくりしました。

5 大山： 昨晩はよく眠れましたか。

6 ジョーンズ： ええ、おかげさまで。9時までぐっすり眠りましたから、すっかり元気になりました。

7 大山： では、御社について少し伺いたいんですが、ユー・エス・エムは工作機械のメーカーとして昔から有名ですね。

8 ジョーンズ： はい、来年には創立九十年になりますから、歴史のある会社です。

9 ブラウン： 自動工作機を最初に作ったのもユー・エス・エムですよ。

10 大山： そうでしたか。知りませんでした。

11 ブラウン： 去年もロボットの売り上げはアメリカ一でした。

12 大山： そうですか。年間何台ぐらいロボットを生産していますか。

13 ジョーンズ： 去年は3,000台ぐらいでしたが、今年は3,500台以上になる見通しです。

14 大山： それは結構ですね。

ADDITIONAL USEFUL EXPRESSIONS

1 At the office

	establishment	**setsuritsu (-suru),** 設立（する）

A:	When was your company established?	**Onsha no setsuritsu wa itsu desu ka.**

B:	It was established in 1950.	**Sen kyuuhyaku gojuu-nen ni setsuritsu-shimashita.**

	capital	**shihonkin,** 資本金
	around how much?	**dono kurai,** どのくらい

A:	Around how much is (your) capital?	**Shihonkin wa dono kurai desu ka.**

	to increase the capital	**zooshi-suru,** 増資する

B:	Originally it was 3 million yen, but last year we increased it to 10 million yen.	**Hajime wa sanbyaku-man-en deshita ga, kyonen zooshi-shite, issen-man-en ni narimashita.**

	employee(s)	**juugyooin,** 従業員

A:	Around how many employees are there?	**Juugyooin wa nan-nin gurai imasu ka.**

	in all	**awasete,** 合わせて

B:	There are about 150 including the head office and the factories.	**Honsha to koojoo, awasete hyakugo-juunin gurai desu.**

2 Talking with a friend

	shareholder	**kabunushi,** 株主
	general shareholders' meeting	**kabunushi-sookai,** 株主総会

A:	When does your company hold its general shareholders' meeting?	**Anata no kaisha no kabunushi-sookai wa itsu desu ka.**

22/Describing the Company

the first ten days of a month	joojun, 上旬
the middle of a month	chuujun, 中旬
the last ten days of a month	gejun, 下旬

B:	It is (held) toward the end of March.	San-gatsu no gejun desu.

settlement of accounts	kessan, 決算

A:	Accounts are settled once a year, aren't they?	Kessan wa ichi-nen ni ichi-do desu ne.

B:	That's right. Only in March.	Soo desu. San-gatsu dake desu.

business	jigyoo, 事業
contents	naiyoo, 内容
business (results)	jigyoo-naiyoo, 事業内容

A:	It looks like business is very good this year, doesn't it?	Kotoshi wa jigyoo-naiyoo ga ii yoo desu ne.

dividend	haitoo, 配当
to increase	hueru, 増える

B:	Thanks (to you), it looks like (we) can also increase (our) dividends.	Okagesama de, haitoo mo sukoshi hueru yoo desu.

your company (in this case)	otaku, お宅
stock, share	kabu, 株
yield, interest	rimawari, 利回り
(is) low	hikui, 低い

A:	I think your company's stock (price) is expensive, so the yield is low, isn't it?	Otaku no kabu wa ima takai desu kara rimawari wa hikui deshoo.

less than	ika, 以下

B:	Yes, it's under 3 percent.	Ee, san-paasento ika desu.

3 At the office

	to go to bed	**neru,** 寝る

A:	About what time do you usually go to bed?	**Taitee nan-ji goro nemasu ka.**

	to get up	**okiru,** 起きる

B:	I usually go to bed at about ten and get up at about six.	**Taitee juu-ji goro nete, roku-ji goro oki-masu.**

NOTES

1 **... to shite** 'as ...'

To shite usually follows a noun, and its English equivalents are 'as ...' or 'for ...'

Examples:
a) **Yamada-san wa hisho *to shite* hataraite imasu.**
"Ms. Yamada is working as a secretary."

b) **Kono okane wa boonasu *to shite* moraimashita.**
"I received this money as a bonus."

c) **Buraun-san wa shishachoo *to shite* rainichi-shimashita.**
"Mr. Brown came to Japan as the President of the branch office."

The noun + **to shite** pattern may be used with the particle **wa** to single out an item or characteristic for general comparison.

Kikai-meekaa *to shite wa* chiisai kaisha desu.
"As a machine maker, it's small [lit. it's a small company]."

Kore wa robotto *to shite wa* kanari takai mono desu.
"This is quite expensive for a robot."

2 **ijoo** and **ika**

Ijoo, occurring immediately after a number, or a number plus a counter, means 'more than,' 'over' or 'above.'
However, the number + **ijoo** pattern is frequently inclusive of that number. For example, **gojuu ijoo** may mean 'fifty or more' or 'over fifty.' In some cases, the meaning is ambiguous and can only be determined from the context of the sentence.

Examples:
go-jikan *ijoo*
'five hours or more' or 'more than five hours'

sen-en *ijoo* no hon
'a book costing one thousand yen or more' or 'a book costing over a thousand yen'

22/Describing the Company

The opposite of **ijoo** is **ika** 'less than', 'under', 'below.' The combination of a number + **ika** may also mean either:'(the number) or less' or 'not more than (the number).' Therefore, **gojuu ika** may mean 'fifty or less, not more than fifty' or 'less than fifty.'

Examples: **juu-nin** *ika*
'ten people or less' or 'under ten people'

gojuuman-en *ika* **no kyuuryoo**
'a salary of 500,000 yen or less' or 'a salary of under 500,000 yen'

3   ... mitooshi da

Mitooshi is a noun meaning 'prospect', 'forecast', 'estimate.' It is often used in the following pattern.

Sentence or Phrase	+	**mitooshi da.**
Ano kaisha wa rainen zooshi-suru	+	*mitooshi desu*.
It is expected (that) +		that company will increase its capital next year.
[lit. The forecast is (that) + ...]		

In this pattern, the preceding clause indicates what is being forecasted or expected.

Examples: a) **Robotto no kakaku wa chikai uchi ni yasuku naru** *mitooshi desu*.
"It is expected that the price of the robot will go down soon."

b) **Kongetsu no jidoosha seesan wa nijuuman-dai ni naru** *mitooshi desu*.
"It is estimated that the car production this month will amount to 200,000 units."

4 Notes on Usage

A) **No** 'the one(s)' in **jidoo-koosakuki o saisho ni tsukutta** *no* **wa** "The one that first made automatic machine tools was..."
In this case, **no** is used instead of **kaisha** 'company' [Refer to *BUSINESS JAPANESE*, Lesson 7, Note **3**].

B) Place name, + **ichi**
A place name or an organization name + **ichi** is the Japanese equivalent of 'the best in (the place)', or 'the best in (the organization).' Thus,

Kono sushiya wa *Nihon ichi* **desu yo.**
"This sushi shop is the best in Japan."

C) Don't confuse **neru** 'to sleep/to go to bed' with **nemuru** 'to sleep.'

Examples: a) Takahashi-san wa taitee juu-ichi-ji goro *nemasu*.
"Mr. Takahashi usually goes to bed around 11 o'clock."

b) **Takahashi-san wa taitee hachi-jikan gurai** *nemurimasu/nemasu*.
"Mr. Takahashi usually sleeps for eight hours."

22/Describing the Company

PRACTICE

1 Communication Practice

Directions: Describe your company to the teacher using the following patterns.

Patterns: a) **Kaisha no setsuritsu wa** (year) **desu.**

b) **Kaisha no shihonkin wa** (amount in yen/dollars/etc.) **desu.**

c) **Juugyooin wa** (number) **gurai imasu.**

d) **Kessan wa** (month) **desu.**

e) **Kyonen no uriage wa** (amount in yen/dollars/etc.) **gurai deshita**

f) **Kotoshi no uriage wa** (amount in yen/dollars/etc.) **ni naru mitooshi desu.**

Examples: a) **Kaisha no setsuritsu wa (1915-nen) desu.**
"Our company was established in (1915)."

b) **Kaisha no shihonkin wa (500-man-doru) desu.**
"Our company capital is (5,000,000 dollars)."

c) **Juugyooin wa (1,500-nin) gurai imasu.**
"As for employees, we have about (1,500 people)."

d) **Kessan wa (san-gatsu) desu.**
"The settlement of accounts is (in March)."

e) **Kyonen no uriage wa (12-oku-en) gurai deshita.**
"Last year's sales were about (1.2 billion yen)."

f) **Kotoshi no uriage wa (15-oku-en) ni naru mitooshi desu.**
"It is expected that sales this year will be (1.5 billion yen)."

2 Expansion Practice

Example: Teacher: **Yuu-esu-emu wa yuumee desu. /koosaku-kikai no meekaa/**
"USM, Ltd. is famous." /a machine tool maker/

Student: **Yuu-esu-emu wa koosaku-kikai no meekaa to shite yuumee desu.**
"USM, Ltd. is famous as a machine tool maker."

a) **Kono heya o tsukatte imasu. /jimusho/**　　**Kono heya o jimusho to shite tsukatte imasu.**

b) **Ano kaisha ni tsutomete imashita. /jimuin/**　　**Ano kaisha ni jimuin to shite tsutomete imashita.**

c) **Takada-san wa totemo ii hito desu. /tomodachi/**　　**Takada-san wa tomodachi to shite totemo ii hito desu.**

d) **Kono katarogu o okurimasu. /shiryoo/**　　**Kono katarogu o shiryoo to shite okurimasu.**

e) **Ano hito o yatoimasu. /hisho/**　　**Ano hito o hisho to shite yatoimasu.**

22/Describing the Company

3 Response Practice

Example: Teacher: **Kotoshi no seesan wa sanzen-dai gurai desu ka.** /ijoo/
"Is this year's production (amount) about 3,000 units?" /more than/

Student: **Iie, sanzen-dai ijoo desu.**
"No. It's more than 3,000 units."

a) **Kyuuryoo wa yonjuu-man gurai desu ka.** /ika/   **Iie, yonjuu-man ika desu.**

b) **Shain wa gohyaku-nin gurai desu ka.** /ijoo/   **Iie, gohyaku-nin ijoo desu.**

c) **Robotto wa nijuu-dai gurai irimasu ka.** /ijoo/   **Iie, nijuu-dai ijoo irimasu.**

d) **Otaku kara koko made ichi-jikan gurai kakarimasu ka.** /ijoo/   **Iie, ichi-jikan ijoo kakarimasu.**

e) **Kongetsu no uriage wa gohyaku-man gurai desu ka.** /ika/   **Iie, gohyaku-man ika desu.**

4 Transformation Practice

Example: Teacher: **Yuu-esu-emu ga jidoo-koosakuki o saisho ni tsukutta kaisha desu.**
"USM, Ltd. was the first company to produce automatic machine tools."

Student: **Jidoo-koosakuki o saisho ni tsukutta no wa Yuu-esu-emu desu.**
"The first one that produced automatic machine tools was USM, Ltd."

a) **Yamada-san ga kono shorui o kaita hito desu.**   **Kono shorui o kaita no wa Yamada-san desu.**

b) **Kinyoobi ga boku no tsugoo ga ii hi desu.**   **Boku no tsugoo ga ii no wa kinyoobi desu.**

c) **Ano ginkoo ga Tanaka-san ga hataraite iru tokoro desu.**   **Tanaka-san ga hataraite iru no wa ano ginkoo desu.**

d) **Kono hon ga kinoo katta hon desu.**   **Kinoo katta no wa kono hon desu.**

e) **Ano hito ga robotto no setsumee o suru hito desu.**   **Robotto no setsumee o suru no wa ano hito desu.**

5 Response Practice

Example: Teacher: **Kotoshi seesan wa hueru to omoimasu ka.**
"Do you think the production will increase this year?"

Student: **Ee, hueru mitooshi desu.**
"Yes, it's expected to increase."

a) Kongetsu no uriage wa hueru to   Ee, hueru mitooshi desu.
    omoimasu ka.

b) Kono kabu wa takaku naru to omoima-   Ee, takaku naru mitooshi desu.
    su ka.

c) Kono kikai wa ureru to omoimasu ka.   Ee, ureru mitooshi desu.

d) Ano kaisha wa zooshi-suru to omoimasu Ee, zooshi-suru mitooshi desu.
    ka.

e) Keeki ga yoku naru to omoimasu ka.   Ee, yoku naru mitooshi desu.

6 Comprehension Practice

Directions: The teacher reads aloud the following passage and then asks the student
                    questions about it.

Yuu-esu-emu no Joonzu-san wa kinoo rainichi-shimashita. Tenki ga yokatta no de,
sora no tabi wa taihen kaiteki deshita. Shikashi, Narita ni tsuita toki, arashi datta no
de, bikkuri-shimashita. Narita kara Tookyoo no hoteru e tsuite, sugu nemashita. Kesa
ku-ji made gussuri nemuremashita kara, kyoo wa totemo genki desu. Gogo wa Buraun-san to issho ni Nissan e itte, Ooyama-buchoo ni atte, Yuu-esu-emu no koto ya
robotto no koto o setsumee suru koto ni natte imasu.

Questions:

1   Joonzu-san wa itsu Nihon e kimashita ka.
2   Joonzu-san no tabi wa ikaga deshita ka.
3   Nihon e tsuita toki, tenki wa doo deshita ka.
4   Joonzu-san wa kyoo genki desu ka. Doo shite desu ka.
5   Joonzu-san wa kyoo gogo nani o shimasu ka.
6   Joonzu-san wa hitori de Nissan e ikimasu ka.
7   Nissan de dare ni au hazu desu ka.
8   Nissan de nan ni tsuite setsumee-shimasu ka.

EXERCISES

a) Inform the teacher of the following in Japanese:

    1   The time you went to bed yesterday.
    2   The time you got up this morning.
    3   Whether or not you slept well last night.
    4   The time you usually go to bed.
    5   The time you usually get up.

22/Describing the Company

b)   Inform the teacher in Japanese that:

1   It is expected that sales at Mr. Tanaka's company will increase considerably.
2   Mr. Smith, the President of P & C, Ltd. plans to increase its capital this summer.
3   Mr. Brown will go back to Detroit soon because he wants to attend the general meeting of shareholders of P & C, Ltd.
4   In the case of Mr. Suzuki's company, the price of shares has become very expensive, so the return is not very good.
5   Mr. Kawamoto's father is very famous as a lawyer.

Model Answers:

a)   1   Kinoo wa ...ji ni nemashita.
2   Kesa wa ...ji ni okimashita.
3   Kinoo wa yoku nemuremashita/neraremashita (or nemuremasen/neraremasen deshita).
4   Taitee ...ji goro nemasu.
5   Taitee ...ji goro okimasu.

b)   1   Tanaka-san no kaisha no uriage wa kanari hueru mitooshi desu.
2   Pii-ando-shii no shachoo no Sumisu-san wa kono natsu zooshi-suru tsumori desu.
3   Buraun-san wa Pii-ando-shii no kabunushi-sookai ni shusseki-shitai no de, chikaiuchi ni Detoroito e kaerimasu.
4   Suzuki-san no kaisha no baai, kabu no nedan ga taihen takaku natta no de, rimawari wa amari yoku arimasen.
5   Kawamoto-san no otoosan wa bengoshi to shite taihen yuumee desu.

BUSINESS INFORMATION

Making Presentations

Collecting the data for business presentations in Japan is like preparing for **omiai** (お見合 , an arranged meeting between a prospective bride and groom). Just as the go-between for **omiai** thoroughly investigates the two families to assure a suitable match, so too, Japanese companies probe deeply into one another's background before doing business together. First-time presentations covering all the "right" information can therefore go a long way to put your prospective client's mind at ease as to your respectability and reliability, and convince him that the business you propose does indeed have all the ingredients for a lasting and fruitful partnership.

1 What To Present: The More The Better.

Most Japanese businessmen attend presentations not to pass judgment but simply to learn as much as possible. Moreover, the decision-making apparatus in Japanese companies usually receives input from employees at various levels and departments to ensure company-wide consensus. Consequently, presentations should include something for everyone. The more you provide–and the more different *types* of information you provide–the more people will be acquainted with your proposal ... and the better the prospects for true company-wide involvement. It is of course best to mail all this information to your prospective client prior to your arrival in Japan (See *BUSINESS JAPANESE II Business Information 21*). But since not all those attending the meeting will have had the time to translate and read it, you should also take care to bring along plenty of extras for the actual presentation.

Standard materials for Japanese presentations include detailed product descriptions, of course, but also information about company capital, history, facilities, number of employees, main shareholders and customers and banks, marketing strategies, technical know-how, educational and professional background of management, and other data which Westerners would normally consider excessive or irrelevant. Questions about your personal background may also arise. Occasionally, Japanese firms will inquire about technical specifications which you consider strictly proprietary. This is not so much to snoop on your company, as you may think, but often just motivated by genuine interest or by anxiety to improve their own product line. The underlying notion here, as with marriages, is that both parties have to show willingness to help each other and not just get their money's worth. Consequently, you should not be unduly alarmed or indignant upon being asked such "intrusive" questions, but rather feel around for the real motive behind them and give what information you can without jeopardizing your own position.

2 How To Present: The Local Touch, The "Soft Sell"

As with the business luncheon (See *BUSINESS JAPANESE Business Information 10*), the form of presentations can be as important as their content. For example, many businessmen have found that parading one's achievements, however impressive, before a Japanese audience seldom produces the desired effect. Nor will meticulous accounts of your successes everywhere else in the world necessarily make the Japanese anxious to

27

climb onto your product bandwagon themselves. This is because there are actually few success stories overseas that have been repeated *verbatim* in Japan. Too much emphasis on global exploits may suggest that you haven't done your homework vis-a-vis the specialized *Japanese* market and are simply–or smugly–relying on your accomplishments elsewhere to carry you through. In addition, you risk offending the more conservative members of your audience who prefer to think that the Japanese are indeed a breed apart and therefore deserve a unique approach, and not something that just happened to succeed in other countries.

In contrast to the West, secondly, successful presentations in Japan are not always direct or logical, nor do they revolve primarily around a product's merits. Instead, a Japanese sales presentation is often rambling, ambiguous and full of "unrelated" information about the product's (or company's) on-going contributions to society and mankind–or what we in the West sometimes jokingly refer to as "hearts and flowers." This is partly because self-praise and straight talk are considered unsophisticated in Japan, as anyone familiar with the evocative soft sell of local commercials will already know. Also, in the same way that a bride's ancestry is traditionally valued more highly than her physical appearance and talents, so too in business, the pros and cons of a specific product can be outweighed by corporate philosophies and goals which may have little to do with the product itself, but which are also bound to outlast that product and are therefore more meaningful in the consideration of a long-term relationship.

Finally, as with marriages, mutual interest and cooperation are essential to ensure the on-going success of a business partnership. You should consequently view your presentation not so much as an opportunity to extol your own products but as a time for listening, gathering information and establishing rapport. Advance investigation about your prospective client's corporate culture, management and power structure, industry ranking, business transactions in progress (or in abeyance), etc., may of course clue you in as to its needs and priorities. Even more important, such preparedness will indicate your sincere interest in the firm as a business partner and thus also increase your chances for a successful match in this all-important business **omiai**.

Lesson 23

Explaining the Product

OBJECTIVES

1 to explain one's products.

2 to elaborate on an explanation.

3 to ask for and give permission.

TARGET EXPRESSIONS AND PATTERNS

1	It means that …	**…wake da.**
2	Does it mean that…?	**…wake desu ka.**
3	Even if …	**…te mo**
4	May (I do) …?	**…te mo ii desu ka.**
5	(It) has been done.	**…te aru.**
6	No matter (what) it is…	**(nan) de mo**
7	(It) is worth doing…	**…suru kachi ga aru.**

SITUATION

While at Nissan, Mr. Jones explains to Mr. Ohyama certain features of USM's new robots that could be particularly useful in automobile production.

23/Explaining the Product

DIALOGUE

| | new type | **shingata,** 新型 (しんがた) |
| **Ohyama** | special characteristic(s) | **tokuchoo,** 特徴 (とくちょう) |

| **1** | What special characteristic(s) does USM's new robot have? | **Yuu-esu-emu no shingata robotto ni wa donna tokuchoo ga arimasu ka.** |

	a kind (of), a type (of)	**is-shu,** 一種 (いっしゅ)
	intelligence	**chinoo,** 知能 (ちのう)
	intelligent robot	**chinoo-robotto,** 知能ロボット (ちのう)
	high level	**koodo,** 高度 (こうど)
	sensor	**sensaa,** センサー
	function	**kinoo (-suru),** 機能(する) (きのう)
Jones	work, operation	**sagyoo (-suru),** 作業(する) (さぎょう)

| **2** | This is one type of intelligent robot with an advanced sensor function, so it can perform various operations. | **Kore wa is-shu no chinoo-robotto de, koodo no sensaa-kinoo ga arimasu no de, iron na sagyoo ga dekimasu.** |

	that is, in short	**tsumari,** つまり
	(work) for several units	**suu-dai-bun,** 数台分 (すうだいぶん)
Ohyama	that means	**wake da,** わけだ

| **3** | In short, that means one robot can do the work of several, doesn't it? | **Tsumari, ichi-dai de suu-dai-bun no shigoto ga dekiru wake desu ne.** |

	list, chart	**hyoo,** 表 (ひょう)
	kind, type	**shurui,** 種類 (しゅるい)
	eight types	**has-shurui,** 八種類 (はっしゅるい)
	assembly, assembling	**kumitate,** 組み立て (くた)
Jones	assembling operations	**kumitate-sagyoo,** 組み立て作業 (くたさぎょう)

| **4** | Yes, it's mentioned on this chart and it can perform eight types of assembling operations. | **Hai, kono hyoo ni kaite arimasu ga, has-shurui no kumitate-sagyoo ga dekimasu.** |

	present	**genzai,** 現在
	our company	**wagasha,** 我社
	automation	**jidooka (-suru),** 自動化(する)
	goal, objective	**kadai,** 課題
	to study, do research	**kenkyuu-suru,** 研究する
Ohyama	value	**kachi,** 価値

5 Presently, in our company, automation of assembling is (an important) objective, so it is worth studying, isn't it?

Genzai, wagasha de wa kumitate-sagyoo no jidooka ga kadai ni natte imasu kara, kenkyuu-shite miru kachi ga arimasu ne.

	(is) light	**karui,** 軽い
	(is) heavy	**omoi,** 重い
Jones	to attach	**toritsukeru,** 取り付ける

6 (We) certainly hope so. This robot can attach all (parts), large or small, light or heavy.

Zehi onegai-shimasu. Kono robotto wa ookii mono mo, chiisai mono mo, karui mono mo, omoi mono mo, nan de mo toritsukeraremasu kara…

Ohyama	car, automobile	**jidoosha,** 自動車

7 That means it is suitable for car factories, doesn't it?

Jidoosha-koojoo ni muite iru wake desu ne.

	(is) right, correct	**tadashii,** 正しい
	position	**ichi,** 位置
	to place	**oku,** 置く
Jones	in order to place	**oku no ni,** 置くのに

8 In particular, the sensor is convenient when placing heavy objects in correct positions.

Toku ni, omoi mono o tadashii ichi ni oku no ni, sensaa ga benri desu.

Ohyama	May I have (it)?	**itadaite mo ii,** (humble), いただいてもいい

9 (I) understand. By the way, may I have this chart?

Wakarimashita. Tokorode, kono hyoo wa itadaite mo ii desu ka.

23/Explaining the Product

	labor, work	**roodoo,** 労働
	labor union	**roodoo-kumiai,** 労働組合
	introduction	**doonyuu (-suru),** 導入（する）
Jones	to oppose	**hantai-suru,** 反対する

10 Yes, please. By the way, wouldn't the labor union object to introducing the robots in your company?	Ee, doozo. Tokoro de, onsha de wa, roodoo-kumiai ga robotto no doonyuu ni hantai-shimasen ka.

| | lay-off | **reiohu (-suru),** レイオフ（する） |
| **Ohyama** | to do, perform | **okonau,** 行う |

11 No. Even if (we) do introduce the robots, there would be no lay-offs, so (we) don't have to worry about that.	Ee, robotto o doonyuu-shite mo, reiohu wa okonaimasen kara, sonna shinpai wa arimasen.

| | union member | **kumiaiin,** 組合員 |
| **Jones** | disadvantageous | **huri /na/,** 不利（な） |

12 That means it will not be disadvantageous for union members.	Tsumari, kumiaiin ni huri ni naranai wake desu ne.

	only	**bakari,** ばかり
	not only that	**sore bakari de naku,** そればかりでなく
	(is) dangerous	**abunai,** 危ない
Ohyama	working conditions	**roodoo-jooken,** 労働条件

13 Not only that, but the robots handle dangerous operations, so that means working conditions will improve.	Sore bakari de naku, abunai sagyoo wa robotto ga suru no de, roodoo-jooken wa yoku naru wake desu.

| **Jones** | reason | **riyuu,** 理由 |

14 Then, there is no reason to oppose (the introduction of the robots).	Sore de wa, hantai-suru riyuu wa arimasen ne.

JAPANESE WRITING

1 大山： ユー・エス・エムの新型ロボットには どんな特徴がありますか。

2 ジョーンズ： これは 一種の知能ロボットで、高度のセンサー機能がありますので、いろんな作業ができます。

3 大山： つまり、一台で 数台分の仕事ができるわけですね。

4 ジョーンズ： はい、この 表に書いてありますが、八種類の組み立て作業ができます。

5 大山： 現在、我社では組み立て作業の自動化が課題になっていますから、研究してみる価値がありますね。

6 ジョーンズ： 是非お願いします。このロボットは大きいものも、小さいものも、軽いものも、重いものも、何でも取り付けられますから…

7 大山： 自動車工場に向いているわけですね。

8 ジョーンズ： 特に、重いものを正しい位置に置くのに、センサーが便利です。

9 大山： わかりました。ところで、この 表は いただいてもいいですか。

10 ジョーンズ： ええ、どうぞ。ところで、御社では、労働組合が ロボットの導入に反対しませんか。

11 大山： ええ、ロボットを導入しても、レイオフは 行いませんから、そんな心配はありません。

12 ジョーンズ： つまり、組合員に不利にならないわけですね。

13 大山： そればかりでなく、危ない作業はロボットがするので、労働条件はよくなるわけです。

14 ジョーンズ： それでは、反対する理由はありませんね。

ADDITIONAL USEFUL EXPRESSIONS

1 At the factory

A:	There are quite a lot of robots in this factory, aren't there?	**Kono koojoo wa zuibun robotto ga ooi desu nee.**
	all	zenbu, 全部
	about	bakari, ばかり

B:	Yes, (we) use about 30 units in all.	**Ee, zenbu de, sanjuu-dai bakari tsukatte imasu.**

23/Explaining the Product

dangerous	**kiken /na/,**	危険(な)
power	**chikara,**	力
heavy labor	**chikara-shigoto,**	力仕事

A:	That means, robots perform all dangerous operations and heavy labor, doesn't it?	**Tsumari, kiken na sagyoo ya chikara-shigoto wa zenbu robotto ga shite iru wake desu ne.**

this factory	**too-koojoo,**	当工場
efficiency	**kooritsu,**	効率
improvement in efficiency	**kooritsuka (-suru),**	効率化(する)
to make an effort	**chikara o ireru,**	力を入れる

B:	In this factory, we are making an effort to improve the efficiency of the operations, so…	**Too-koojoo de wa sagyoo no kooritsuka ni chikara o irete imasu kara…**

2 At the staff meeting

proposal	**teean (-suru),**	提案(する)

A:	What do you think about Mr. Tanaka's proposal?	**Tanaka-san no teean, doo omoimasu ka.**

economical efficiency	**keezaisee,**	経済性
advantageous	**yuuri /na/,**	有利(な)
to agree	**sansee-suru,**	賛成する

B:	Considering its efficiency, it may be advantageous, so I agree with it.	**Keezaisee o kangaeru to, yuuri deshoo kara, boku wa sansee-shimasu.**

safe, safety	**anzen /na/,**	安全(な)
safety	**anzensee,**	安全性

C:	I think there is a little problem regarding (its) safety.	**Watakushi wa anzensee no ten de mondai ga aru to omoimasu.**

3 Telephone conversation

A:	What time shall I call on you tomorrow?	**Ashita nan-ji ni ukagaimashoo ka.**

anytime	**nan-ji de mo,** 何時_{なんじ}でも

B:	Anytime is fine.	**Nan-ji de mo kekkoo desu.**

NOTES

1 **Wake da** 'it means that ...'

Wake, a noun meaning 'reason,' often occurs at the end of a sentence with the copula **desu/da** to indicate an explanation or clarification, and its English equivalent is 'I mean that ...' or 'it means that ...'

Clause or phrase	+	*wake da.*
Desu kara, roodoo-jooken ga yoku naru	+	*wake desu.*
So it means	+	that the working conditions will be improved.

When **wake desu ka** occurs at the end of a sentence, it indicates that the speaker is seeking confirmation or clarification. Its equivalent in English is 'Do you mean that ...?' or 'Does it mean that ...?'

Examples:
    a) **Wagasha de wa kumitate-sagyoo no jidooka ga juuyoo na kadai ni natte iru *wake desu.***
       "It means that in our company, automation of assembling operations is an important objective."

    b) **Isogashikute, sono paatii ni ikarenakatta *wake desu.***
       "I mean that I was busy and I couldn't go to that party."

    c) **Kono robotto wa kenkyuu-shite miru kachi ga nai *wake desu* ka.**
       "Do you mean that this robot is not worth studying?"

When the preceding clause or phrase ends with the informal non-past copula **da**, the expression **to iu** always occurs between the copula and **wake**. **To iu** is composed of the quotative **to** and the verb **iu** 'to say.' This combination **to iu** may also occur after verbs or adjectives without affecting the meaning of the sentence.

Examples:
    a) **da + to iu**
       Nihonsee no robotto no hoo ga benri *da to iu* wake desu ka.
       "Do you mean the Japanese robot is more convenient?"

    b) **verb + (to iu)**
       Kono kikai wa uchi no koojo ni muite *iru (to iu)* wake desu.
       "It means this machine is suited for our factory."

    c) **adjective + (to iu)**
       Nan-ji de mo ii *(to iu) wake* desu ka.
       "Do you mean anytime is OK?"

2 Gerund + **mo**

A gerund + **mo** literally means 'even doing such-and-such,' 'even being such-and-such,' or 'even though (somebody/something) does such-and-such,' 'even though (somebody/something) is such-and-such.' Thus,

> **Ame ga *hutte mo*, iku tsumori desu.**
> "Even if it rains, I'll go."

> **Nedan ga *takakute mo*, kono hoo ga ii desu yo.**
> "Even though the price is high, this one is better."

This combination gerund + **mo** is often followed by **ii desu** '(it) is good' or **kamaimasen** 'don't/won't mind,' and the pattern is used in requesting and granting permission.

Examples: a) **Kono taipuraitaa o tsuka*tte mo ii desu* ka.**
> "May I use this typewriter [lit. Is it all right (even) if I use this type-writer]?"

> **Ee, tsuka*tte mo ii desu* yo.**
> "Yes, you may use it [lit. It's all right (even) if you use it]."

b) **Ashita ko*nakute mo kamaimasen* ka.**
> "Do you mind (even) if I don't come tomorrow?"

> **Ee, ko*nakute mo kamaimasen*.**
> "No, I don't mind (even) if you don't come."

Note: When you cannot allow the request, you should use the pattern **-te kudasai**. Thus,

> **Iie, tsukawana*ide kudasai*.**
> "No, please don't use it."

> **Iie, ki*te kudasai*.**
> "Yes, (I do mind), please come."
> [Refer to *BUSINESS JAPANESE*, Lesson 9, Note **4** and *BUSINESS JAPANESE II*, Lesson 26, Note **2** for use of *Hai/ Iie* in replying to 'negative' questions.]

3 Gerund + **aru**

The gerund of a transitive verb + **aru** is used to indicate the existing result of a previous action, like the gerund of an intransitive + **iru**, and means '(something) has been done' [Refer to *BUSINESS JAPANESE*, Lesson 13, Note **1**]. This combination implies that the action has already been performed by somebody (who may or may not be the speaker), and that its results are still being felt.

Compare: **Kono hyoo ni *kaite arimasu*.***
> "It has been written (by someone) in this chart [imp. ... and so, it can be read there]."

and

> **Joonzu-san wa ima Nihon ni *kite imasu*.**
> "Mr. Jones is in Japan [imp. Mr. Jones came to Japan and is still here]."

* The object of a transitive verb becomes the subject in the combination of the gerund + **aru**.

Carefully study the following sentences.

> **Tegami o kakimasu.**
> "I'll write a letter."
>> **Tegami**: object of transitive verb, **kakimasu**

> **Tegami o kaite imasu.**
> "I'm writing a letter."
>> **Tegami**: object of gerund of transitive verb, **kaite imasu**

> **Tegami ga kaite arimasu.**
> "A letter has been written."
>> **Tegami**: subject of gerund + **arimasu**

4 Interrogative + **de mo**

The combination of an interrogative word + **de mo** (i.e. the gerund of the copula **da** and the particle **mo** 'even') means 'no matter ... (something/someone) is' or 'any ... at all.' Thus,

Examples: *nan de mo*
Nan, 'what': 'no matter what it is', 'anything at all/everything'

itsu de mo
Itsu, 'when': 'no matter when it is', 'anytime at all/always'

dare de mo
Dare, 'who':'no matter who it is', 'anyone at all/everyone'

dokode mo
Doko, 'where': 'no matter where it is','anywhere at all/anywhere'

ikutsu de mo
Ikutsu, 'how many': 'no matter how many it is', 'any number/quantity at all'

5 Verb + **kachi ga aru** 'to be worth doing such-and-such'

When the phrase **kachi ga aru**, which literally means 'there is value,' is preceded by a verb, it means 'to be worth doing such-and-such.'

Examples: a)   **Kono hon wa ichi-do** *yomu kachi ga arimasu.*
"It's worth reading this book once."

b)   **Kono shigoto wa chikara o** *ireru kachi wa nai* **to omoimasu.**
"I think it is not worth putting effort into this job."

PRACTICE

1 Response Practice

Example: Teacher: **Kono robotto wa nani ga dekimasu ka.**
"What can this robot do?"

Student: **Nan de mo dekimasu.**
"It can do anything at all."

a) Kore wa doko de utte imasu ka.   Doko de mo utte imasu.

b) Dare ga kono shigoto o shimasu ka.   Dare de mo shimasu.

c) Itsu otaku ni imasu ka.   Itsu de mo imasu.

d) Nan-jikan matemasu ka.   Nan-jikan de mo matemasu.

e) Shain o nan-nin yatoimasu ka.   Nan-nin de mo yatoimasu.

2 Response Practice

Example: Teacher: **Kore o tsukatte mo ii desu ka.**
             "May I use this?"

             Student: **Ee, tsukatte mo ii desu yo.**
             "Yes, you may use it."

a) Kono shinbun o yonde mo ii desu ka.   Ee, yonde mo ii desu.

b) Ashita Kyooto e itte mo ii desu ka.   Ee, itte mo ii desu.

c) Kore o kenkyuu-shite mo ii desu ka.   Ee, kenkyuu-shite mo ii desu.

d) Robotto o doonyuu-shite mo ii desu ka. Ee, doonyuu-shite mo ii desu.

e) Koko ni kikai o oite mo ii desu ka.   Ee, oite mo ii desu.

3 Response Practice

Example: Teacher: **Ima kaette mo kamaimasen ka.**
             "May I go home now [lit. Do you mind even if I go home now]?"

             Student: **Iie, kaeranaide kudasai.**
             "No. Please don't go home."

a) Tanaka-san ni soodan-shite mo   Iie, soodan-shinaide kudasai.
    kamaimasen ka.

b) Gogo dekakete mo kamaimasen ka.   Iie, dekakenaide kudasai.

c) Koko de sagyoo o shite mo kamaimasen Iie, shinaide kudasai.
    ka.

d) Buchoo ni hanashite mo kamaimasen   Iie, hanasanaide kudasai.
    ka.

e) Sono shiryoo o mite mo kamaimasen ka. Iie, minaide kudasai.

4 Transformation Practice

Example: Teacher: **Robotto o doonyuu-shimasu. Rei-ohu wa okonaimasen.**
             "We introduce the robots. There will be no lay-offs."

             Student: **Robotto o doonyuu-shite mo, rei-ohu wa okonaimasen.**
             "Even if we introduce the robots, there will be no lay-offs."

a) Kumiai ga hantai-shimasu.   Kumiai ga hantai-shite mo, robotto o
    Robotto o doonyuu-shimasu.   doonyuu-shimasu.

b) Tsumaranai shigoto desu.
Kyuuryoo wa totemo ii n desu.

Tsumaranai shigoto de mo, kyuuryoo
wa totemo ii n desu.

c) Sensaa-kinoo ga arimasu.
Kono shigoto wa muzukashii desu.

Sensaa-kinoo ga atte mo, kono shigoto
wa muzukashii desu.

d) Ame ga hutte imasu.
Kyooto kenbutsu-suru tsumori desu.

Ame ga hutte ite mo, Kyooto kenbutsu-
suru tsumori desu.

e) Enjinia jaa arimasen.
Gijutsuteki na shitsumon ni
kotaeraremasu.

Enjinia jaa nakute mo, gijutsuteki
na shitsumon ni kotaeraremasu.

5 Response Practice

Example: Teacher: **Moo hyoo o kakimashita ka.**
"Have you already drawn the chart?"

Student: **Ee, moo kaite arimasu.**
"Yes, (it) has already been drawn."

a) Moo ano kikai o kaimashita ka.   Ee, moo katte arimasu.

b) Moo Yamada-san ni hanashimashita ka.   Ee, hanashite arimasu.

c) Moo shootaijoo o dashimashita ka.   Ee, moo dashite arimasu.

d) Moo kono hyoo o kare ni misemashita   Ee, moo misete arimasu.
ka.

e) Moo Joonzu-san ni oshiemashita ka.   Ee, moo oshiete arimasu.

6 Response Practice

Example: Teacher: **Kenkyuu-shimashoo ka.**
"Shall (I) study (it)?"

Student: **Ee, kenkyuu-suru kachi ga arimasu.**
"Yes, (it) is worth studying."

a) Robotto o doonyuu-shimashoo ka.   Ee, doonyuu-suru kachi ga arimasu.

b) Joonzu-san ni aimashoo ka.   Ee, au kachi ga arimasu.

c) Ano shiryoo o moraimashoo ka.   Ee, morau kachi ga arimasu.

d) Sugu seesan-shimashoo ka.   Ee, seesan-suru kachi ga arimasu.

e) Ano hito o yatoimashoo ka.   Ee, yatou kachi ga arimasu.

7 Comprehension Practice

Directions: The teacher reads aloud the following passage and then asks the student
questions about it.

**Joonzu-san wa Ooyama-buchoo ni Yuu-esu-emu no shingata robotto no tokuchoo o
setsumee-shimasu. Kono robotto wa is-shu no chinoo-robotto desu kara, koodo no
sensaa-kinoo o motte imasu. Sono sensaa-kinoo wa omoi mono o tadashii ichi ni oku**

sagyoo no baai benri desu. Mata, kono robotto wa ichi-dai de has-shurui no kumitate-sagyoo ga dekiru no de, iroiro na buhin o toritsukeru jidoosha-koojoo ni muite imasu. Sore bakari de naku, abunai sagyoo wa robotto ga suru kara, roodoo-jooken wa yoku naru wake desu.

Questions:

1   Joonzu-san wa dare ni nani o setsumee-shimasu ka.
2   Kono robotto no tokuchoo wa nan desu ka.
3   Sensaa-kinoo wa donna sagyoo no toki ni benri desu ka.
4   Kono robotto wa nan-shurui no kumitate-sagyoo ga dekimasu ka.
5   Kono robotto wa donna koojoo ni muite imasu ka.
6   Doo shite desu ka.
7   Koojoo no roodoo-jooken wa doo narimasu ka.

EXERCISES

Inform the teacher in Japanese that:

1   It has been decided that Mr. Tanaka's company will introduce two intelligent robots.
2   We have already finished the automation of assembling operations in this factory.
3   In the case of Mr. Okada's company, the labor union members oppose the introduction of the automatic machine tools.
4   Mr. Smith (the company President) thinks it is worth visiting Japan for the negotiations with Nissan.
5   General Manager Ohyama does not yet agree to Mr. Suzuki's proposal.
6   It is expected that even if the company introduces new NC machine tools, it will not be disadvantageous for employees.
7   Mr. Brown is studying how to negotiate [lit. the way of doing negotiations] with Japanese businessmen.

Model Answers:

1   Tanaka-san no kaisha wa chinoo-robotto o ni-dai doonyuu-suru koto ni natte imasu.
2   Kono koojoo no kumitate-sagyoo no jidooka wa moo owarimashita.
3   Okada-san no kaisha no baai, kumiaiin wa jidoo-koosakuki no doonyuu ni hantai-shite imasu.
4   Sumisu-shachoo wa Nissan to no shoodan no tame ni rainichi-suru kachi ga aru to omotte imasu.
5   Ooyama-buchoo wa Suzuki-san no teean ni mada sansee-shite imasen.
6   Kaisha ga shingata Enu-shii-koosakuki o doonyuu-shite mo, juugyooin ni huri ni naranai mitooshi desu.
7   Buraun-san wa Nihonjin bijinesuman to no kooshoo no shikata o kenkyuushite imasu.

BUSINESS INFORMATION

Preparing the Interpreter

Although the Japanese are among the world's most avid students of foreign languages, many businessmen are sadly lacking in English conversational ability or else too bashful to speak English in front of others (See *BUSINESS JAPANESE Business Information 17*). If you ever require the services of a professional interpreter, the following suggestions may come in handy.

1 Providing "Inside" Information: No matter how competent your interpreter seems, he or she is not a bilingual know-it-all. Whenever possible, therefore, you should reserve time before your business presentation to brief the interpreter about your line of business, your products and your expectations for the upcoming presentation. You should also explain all specialized terminology so that the interpreter will not have to lose time (and possibly face) stumbling over unfamiliar words later. During the actual presentation, moreover, you should be wary about using double negatives, e.g. "It is not entirely impossible that we will not make the deadline." Such awkward phrases are best avoided in any language, of course, but they are particularly troublesome in Japan where "yes" can mean "no" and vice versa (See *BUSINESS JAPANESE* Lesson 9, Note **4** ; *BUSINESS JAPANESE II* Lesson 26, Note **2**). You should also take care during the presentation to explain any colloquial or idiomatic expressions that crop up in your speech. Experienced interpreters may know expressions like "Time is money," but more esoteric literary references, however much they may enlighten an English-speaking audience, will leave both your Japanese hosts and interpreter in the dark.

2 Dealing with "Problematic" Politeness: The Japanese enjoy a worldwide reputation for courtesy and service. Unfortunately, when it comes to simultaneous interpretation, this polite streak can sometimes cause difficulties. Since direct or blunt statements can grate on the Japanese ear, you may find your interpreter "diluting" what you say into more acceptable–but more ambiguous and often longer–statements. For example, "Our product is respected around the world." is likely to become "It is said that our product is respected around the world." Sometimes the interpreter will also deliberately tone down your company's achievements so as to avoid boasting, which is offensive, and also to lower your position in relation to the client's, which is common courtesy in Japan. If you feel that certain facts should be conveyed in black and white for maximum effect, therefore, you should indicate so beforehand as otherwise your interpreter will automatically soften their impact out of respect for the Japanese listeners. On the other hand, you should not expect to get straight answers to your own questions, either. If you ask for a definite yes or no, for instance, the response will probably be "**Muzukashii**" or "It is difficult" (See *BUSINESS JAPANESE Business Information 20*). Again, rather than trying to evade the issue, your Japanese counterparts are just being polite. "It's difficult" is after all easier on the ear than plain old "No" and you, as the guest, must of course be spared the unpleasantness of such an abrupt and clumsy reply.

23/Explaining the Product

3 Missing Out On The Action: For all the convenience, using simultaneous interpreters is not without its disadvantages. Their services do not come cheaply, for one thing. Professional English interpreters cost upwards of ¥40,000 a day; those conversant in less-known languages charge more. If unexpected problems turn up and your negotiations drag on and on, as they often do, the investment can be considerable. And last but not least, being a Japanese himself and bound by certain social conventions, your interpreter may at times defer to your Japanese counterparts rather than to you who are in fact paying his wages. You may find, for example, that whole chunks of animated conversation go by without your interpreter volunteering any translation. This is not because he doesn't understand the conversation or because he is irresponsible. Often, the Japanese side will enter into a "private" discussion about your proposal, seizing on your ignorance of the language as an excuse *not* to transfer to another room. They will of course also instruct the interpreter to leave their conversation untranslated and he, being the polite Japanese that he is, will dutifully comply. Instead of interrupting or demanding immediate explanation, you should wait until the meeting is over and then "debrief" your interpreter about the action you missed. Even then, though, you will be dependent on his memory and cooperation. In the end, the only way to ensure that you are never left out in the cold is simply to set aside time for *BUSINESS JAPANESE*, and learn the language for yourself.

Lesson 24

Price and Quantity

OBJECTIVES

1   to discuss the price of a product and the size of an order.

2   to use terms concerning various kinds of costs.

TARGET EXPRESSIONS AND PATTERNS

1	depending on ...	**... ni yotte**
2	a respectful verb (to do)	**nasaru**
3	sometime (tomorrow)	**(ashita) juu ni**

SITUATION

After Mr. Jones and Mr. Ohyama finish discussing the technical features of the new USM robots, Mr. Ohyama asks Mr. Brown, President of USM's agency in Japan, about the price.

24/Price and Quantity

DIALOGUE

Ohyama

| 1 | Next, (I) would like to ask you about the price, (but...) | Tsugi ni kakaku ni tsuite ukagaitai n desu ga... |

	case	**baai,** 場合
	basic unit, body	**hontai,** 本体
	in addition	**hoka ni,** 他に
	attachment	**huzokuhin,** 付属品
	installation	**husetsu (-suru),** 付設(する)
	cost, expense	**hiyoo,** 費用
Brown	to cost	**kakaru,** かかる

| 2 | In the case of this new product, the basic unit is $40,000, but there are other expenses for attachments and installation. | Kono shingata no baai, hontai wa yon-man-doru desu ga, hoka ni huzokuhin ya husetsu no tame no hiyoo ga kakari-masu. |

Ohyama

| 3 | About how much would that cost? | Sore wa ikuragurai ni narimasu ka. |

	depending upon...	**...ni yotte,** ...によって
	installation cost	**husetsuhi,** 付設費
	overseas, foreign country	**kaigai,** 海外
Brown	per	**atari,** あたり

| 4 | As for the attachments, (the prices) differ depending on the type of operation, and the installation fee is $5,000 per unit in the case of foreign countries. | Huzokuhin wa sagyoo no naiyoo ni yotte chigaimasu ga, husetsuhi wa, kaigai no baai, ichi-dai atari gosen-doru ni natte imasu. |

	quantity	**suuryoo,** 数量
Ohyama	to discount	**nebiki-suru,** 値引きする

| 5 | Can you offer a discount depending on the size of the order? | Chuumon no suuryoo ni yotte, nebiki-dekimasu ka. |

	to do	**nasaru** (respectful), なさる
	to order	**gochuumon-nasaru** (respectful)
		ご注文なさる
	cost	**kosuto,** コスト
Brown	comparatively cheap	**wariyasu/na/,** 割安(な)

6	Yes, if (you) order more than five units, (we) can offer a five to seven percent discount. In addition, the installation costs will also become (comparatively) cheaper.	**Hai, hontai o go-dai ijoo gochuumon-nasaru baai wa go-paasento kara nana-paasento gurai no nebiki ga dekimasu. Sore ni, husetsu no kosuto mo wariyasu ni narimasu.**

Ohyama	estimate	**mitsumori,** 見積り

7	Then, could (you) prepare for us an estimate for an order of ten units?	**De wa, juu-dai chuumon-suru baai no mitsumori o tsukutte moraemasu ka.**

Brown

8	What shall (I) do about the attachments?	**Huzokuhin wa doo shimashoo ka.**

Ohyama	it's alright, (even) if you don't include (it)	**irenakute mo ii,** 入れなくてもいい

9	(You) don't have to include the attachments.	**Huzokuhin wa irenakute mo ii desu.**

	written estimate	**mitsumorisho,** 見積り書
Brown	to deliver	**todokeru,** 届ける

10	Then, (I) will discuss this with USM also and have the written estimate delivered sometime tomorrow.	**De wa, Yuu-esu-emu to mo soodan-shite, asu-juu ni mitsumorisho o oto-doke-shimasu.**

Ohyama

11	Then, please do so.	**Jaa, onegai-shimasu.**

24/Price and Quantity

JAPANESE WRITING

1　大山：　次に価格について 伺いたいんですが…

2　ブラウン：　この新型の場合、本体は4万ドルですが、他に付属品や付設のための費用が
　　　　　　　かかります。

3　大山：　それは いくらぐらいになりますか。

4　ブラウン：　付属品は 作業の内容によって違いますが、付設費は、海外の場合、1台あ
　　　　　　　たり 5,000ドルになっています。

5　大山：　注文の数量によって、値引きできますか。

6　ブラウン：　はい、本体を5台以上 ご注文なさる場合は 5パーセントから7パーセント
　　　　　　　ぐらいの 値引きができます。それに、付設のコストも割安になります。

7　大山：　では、10台 注文する場合の見積りを作ってもらえますか。

8　ブラウン：　付属品は どうしましょうか。

9　大山：　付属品は 入れなくてもいいです。

10　ブラウン：　では、ユー・エス・エムとも相談して、明日中に見積り書をお届けします。

11　大山：　じゃあ、お願いします。

ADDITIONAL USEFUL EXPRESSIONS

1 At business negotiations

charges, handling fees	**tesuuryoo,** 手数料

A:	Around how much is the handling fee?	**Tesuuryoo wa dono kurai desu ka.**

to claim, request, charge	**seekyuu-suru,** 請求する

B:	Ordinarily, our company charges eight percent of the sale, but…	**Hutsuu, wagasha wa uriage no hachi-paasento o seekyuu-shite imasu ga…**

to expect	**yosoo-suru,** 予想する

A:	Is (it) eight percent? It's a little high. We were expecting about five percent, but…	**Hachi-paasento desu ka. Chotto takai desu nee. Go-paasento gurai o yosoo-shite ita n desu ga…**

the first year	**ichi-nen-me,** 一年目

B:	Then how about six percent for the first year, and eight percent from the second year on?	**De wa, ichi-nen-me wa roku-paasento, ni-nenme kara hachi-paasento de wa ikaga deshoo ka.**

A:	That is fine.	**Kekkoo desu.**

2 At the office

last month	**sengetsu,** 先月
to order	**hatchuu-suru,** 発注する

A:	The products we ordered last month haven't been delivered yet, but have you heard anything [lit. was there any contact]?	**Sengetsu hatchuu-shita seehin ga mada todoite inai n desu ga, nani ka renraku ga arimashita ka.**

B:	Yes, there was a phone call [lit. contact by phone] this morning.	**Ee, kesa denwa de renraku ga arimashita.**

and, then	**sore de,** それで

A:	And, what did they say?	**Sore de nan te itte imashita ka.**

to be late	**okureru,** 遅れる
delivery of goods	**noohin (-suru),** 納品(する)
to be in time	**ma ni au,** 間に合う

B:	They say production is running late, so deliveries will not be (made) in time.	**Seesan ga okurete iru no de, noohin ga ma ni awanai soo desu.**

A:	How long did they say it would be delayed?	**Dono kurai okureru tte iimashita ka.**

B:	They said about one week.	**Is-shuukan gurai da soo desu.**

3 At the office

this term	**konki,** 今期
profit	**rieki,** 利益

A:	Around how much is that company's profit this term?	**Ano kaisha no konki no rieki wa dono gurai deshoo ka.**

24/Price and Quantity

hundred million	oku, 億
one hundred million	ichi-oku, 一億
surplus, black figure	kuroji, 黒字

B:	They say it's one hundred and fifty million in the black.	Ichi-oku gosen-man gurai no kuroji da soo desu.

the year before last	ototoshi, おととし
deficit, loss, red figure	akaji, 赤字

A:	They say they had been in the red until the year before last. However, recently they are doing a good job, aren't they?	Ototoshi made wa, akaji ga tsuzuite ita soo desu. Shikashi, konogoro wa gan-batte imasu ne.

NOTES

1 ... **ni yotte** 'depending on ...'

A noun + **ni yotte** is the equivalent of 'depending on such-and-such,' 'in accordance with such-and-such.' This combination is often followed by the verb **chigau** 'to be different.' Thus,

> **Kyuuryoo wa shigoto no naiyoo *ni yotte* chigaimasu.**
> "The salary differs depending on the type [lit. contents] of work."

Examples:
   a) **Iken wa hito *ni yotte* chigaimasu.**
   "The opinion is different depending on the person."

   b) **Shachoo no iken *ni yotte*, robotto o doonyuu-suru koto ni shimashita.**
   "(We) decided to introduce robots in accordance with the president's opinion."

2 A respectful verb: **nasaru**

Nasaru is the respectful form of **suru**. It is used both as an independent verb and as part of a compound verb (or **-suru** verb). Thus,

> **Anata ga kore o *nasaimashita* ka.**
> "Did you do this?"

> **Kyoo mo benkyoo-*nasaimasu* ka.**
> "Will you be studying today, too?"

3 **-juu ni** 'within ...'

A time word + **-juu** (i.e. **ashita-juu**) or **-chuu** means 'all ... long,' 'throughout.'

> **Konshuu-*chuu* uchi ni imasu.**
> "I'll be home all this week."

When the time word + **-juu** is followed by the particle **ni,** the combination means 'within ...,' 'before ... is over'or 'sometime ...' Thus,

kotoshi-*juu ni*	'within this year,' 'sometime this year'
raishuu-*chuu ni*	'within next week,' 'sometime next week'
kyoo-*juu ni*	'within today,' 'sometime today'

4 **-atari** 'per ...'

Atari which follows a number or a number + counter means 'per ...' or 'for each/ every ...'

Examples:

a) **Ano hito no kyuuryoo wa ichi-nichi-*atari* ichi-man-go-sen-en desu.**
"His salary is 15,000 yen per day."

b) **Kono robotto ichi-dai-*atari* no husetsuhi wa ikura desu ka.**
"How much is the installation cost for each robot [lit. per one unit of robot]?"

c) **Kono jimusho ni wa shain ni-ten-go-nin-*atari* ichi-dai no pasokon ga arimasu.**
"In this office, there is one personal computer for every 2.5 employees."

PRACTICE

1 Response Practice

Example: Teacher: **Huzokuhin wa ikura-gurai desu ka. /sagyoo no naiyoo/**
"Around how much do the attachments cost?" /type of work/

Student: **Sagyoo no naiyoo ni yotte chigaimasu.**
"(It) differs depending on the type of work."

a) **Konban minna hima desu ka. /hito/** **Hito ni yotte chigaimasu.**

b) **Koko ni aru pen wa minna onaji nedan desu ka. /shurui/** **Shurui ni yotte chigaimasu.**

c) **Anata wa itsumo kono jimusho ni imasu ka. /hi/** **Hi ni yotte chigaimasu.**

d) **Nebiki wa dono kaisha mo onaji desu ka. /kaisha/** **Kaisha ni yotte chigaimasu.**

e) **Husetsuhi wa ikura-gurai desu ka. /chuumon no suuryoo/** **Chuumon no suuryoo ni yotte chigaimasu.**

2 Level Practice

Example: Teacher: **Chuumon-shimasu ka.**
"Are you ordering (it)?" (Formal Plain)

Student: **Gochuumon-nasaimasu ka.**
"Will you be ordering (it)?" (Respectful)

24/Price and Quantity

a) **Kore wa dare ga shimasu ka.**   **Kore wa dare ga nasaimasu ka.**

b) **Nihongo o benkyoo-shimashita ka.**   **Nihongo o benkyoo-nasaimashita ka.**

c) **Kenkyuu-shite kudasai.**   **Kenkyuu-nasatte kudasai.**

d) **Shachoo ga setsumee-shimashita.**   **Shachoo ga setsumee-nasaimashita.**

e) **Bengoshi to soodan-shimasu ka.**   **Bengoshi to soodan-nasaimasu ka.**

3 Level Practice

Example: Teacher: **Mitsumori o tsukutte kudasai.**
"Please prepare a written estimate."

Student: **Mitsumori o tsukutte moraemasu ka.** (Polite Request)
"Could you prepare a written estimate for us?"

a) **Ashita mata kite kudasai.**   **Ashita mata kite moraemasu ka.**

b) **Kore o kentoo-shite kudasai.**   **Kore o kentoo-shite moraemasu ka.**

c) **Nebiki-shite kudasai.**   **Nebiki-shite moraemasu ka.**

d) **Anata no iken o oshiete kudasai.**   **Anata no iken o oshiete moraemasu ka.**

e) **Kono hito o yatotte kudasai.**   **Kono hito o yatotte moraemasu ka.**

4 Response Practice

Example: Teacher: **Husetsuhi wa ikura desu ka. /ichi-dai, go-sen-doru/**
"How much is the installation cost?" /1 unit, $5,000/

Student: **Ichi-dai-atari go-sen-doru desu.**
"(It) is 5,000 dollars per unit."

a) **Haizara wa ikura desu ka.**   **Hitotsu-atari rop-pyaku-en desu.**
/hitotsu, rop-pyaku-en/

b) **Jimusho no hiyoo wa ikura desu ka.**   **Ik-kagetsu-atari san-byaku-man-en**
/ik-kagetsu, san-byaku-man-en gurai/   **gurai desu.**

c) **Kono koojoo de dono kurai jidoosha o**   **Ichi-nichi-atari hap-pyaku-dai desu.**
seesan-shimasu ka.
/ichi-nichi, hap-pyaku-dai/

d) **Paatii no hiyoo wa dono gurai kakari-**   **Okyakusama hitori-atari go-sen-en**
mashita ka.   **deshita.**
/okyakusama hitori, go-sen-en/

e) **Onsha no kabu no haitoo wa donokurai**   **Hito-kabu*-atari juugo-en desu.**
desu ka.
/hito-kabu, juugo-en/

* one share

50

5 Response Practice

Example: Teacher: **Itsu todokete kuremasu ka. /ashita/**
"When can you deliver (it) for us ?" /tomorrow/

Student: **Ashita-juu ni todokemasu.**
"(I) will deliver (it) sometime tomorrow."

a)   **Itsu Oosaka e ikimasu ka. /raishuu/**   **Raishuu-chuu ni ikimasu.**

b)   **Itsu tegami o kakimasu ka. /kyoo/**   **Kyoo-juu ni kakimasu.**

c)   **Itsu Joonzu-san ga kimasu ka.**   **Kongetsu-chuu ni kimasu.**
/kongetsu/

d)   **Itsu aitai n desu ka./konban/**   **Konban-juu ni aitai n desu.**

e)   **Itsu robotto o doonyuu-shimasu ka.**   **Kotoshi-juu ni doonyuu-shimasu.**
/kotoshi/

6 Comprehension Practice

Direction: The teacher reads aloud the following passage and then asks the student questions about it.

Buraun-san wa Ooyama-san ni robotto no nedan ni tsuite setsumee-shimashita. Robotto no hontai wa yon-man-doru desu ga, hoka ni huzokuhin no hiyoo ya husetsuhi ga kakarimasu. Huzokuhin no hiyoo wa sono robotto ga suru sagyoo no naiyoo ni yotte chigaimasu ga, husetsuhi wa ichi-dai-atari go-sen-doru da soo desu. Mata go-dai-ijoo chuumon-suru baai, go-paasento kara nana-paasento gurai no nebiki o suru koto ni natte iru soo desu kara, Ooyama-san wa Buraun-san ni robotto juu-dai no mitsumori o tanomimashita. Buraun-san wa ashita-juu ni mitsumorisho o todokeru to iimashita.

Questions:

1   **Buraun-san wa Ooyama-san ni nan ni tsuite setsumee-shimashita ka.**
2   **Robotto no hontai wa ikura desu ka.**
3   **Huzokuhin wa.**
4   **Husetsuhi wa ichi-dai-atari ikura desu ka.**
5   **Nan-dai-ijoo chuumon-suru baai, nebiki ga arimasu ka.**
6   **Ooyama-san wa Braun-san ni nani o tanomimashita ka.**

EXERCISES

Inform the teacher in Japanese that:

1   As for this new product, you can not offer any discount.
2   You'll prepare a written estimate after consulting with your head office.
3   Even if (one) orders more than ten units, you cannot offer a ten percent discount.
4   The installation cost of machine tools differs depending on the size of the order.
5   You cannot deliver the products within this month because production is being delayed.

6   Delivery of the goods will be sometime next week.

7   Your company always charges eight percent as a commission.

8   In this period, the profit of your company is expected to be [lit. become] more than thirty million yen.

Model Answers:

1   **Kono shin-seehin wa nebiki-dekimasen.**

2   **Honsha to soodan-shite kara, mitsumorisho o tsukurimasu.**

3   **Juu-dai ijoo chuumon-shite mo, jup-paasento no nebiki wa dekimasen.**

4   **Koosaku-kikai no husetsuhi wa chuumon no suuryoo ni yotte chigaimasu.**

5   **Seesan ga okurete imasu kara, kongetsu-chuu ni seehin o todokeru koto wa dekimasen.**

6   **Noohin wa raishuu-chuu desu.**

7   **Wagasha wa itsumo tesuuryoo to shite hachi-paasento o seekyuu-shimasu.**

8   **Konki, wagasha no rieki wa sanzen-man-en ijoo ni naru mitooshi desu.**

BUSINESS INFORMATION

Reading Financial Statements

Most companies you contemplate doing business with will of course provide a cost estimate of products and services, along with other vital statistics. Occasionally, however, you may want to examine detailed financial statements of the company to get a more complete picture. In contrast to the West, such statements in Japan are normally presented in non-consolidated format in accordance with the Japanese Commercial Code. It is these non-consolidated statements that companies listed on the Tokyo Stock Exchange submit to their shareholders for approval at the annual shareholders' meeting, and on the basis of these statements too that securities firms and individuals generally base their investment decisions. According to the Securities and Exchange Act governing securities transactions, however, listed companies also have to submit to the Ministry of Finance an annual Marketable Securities Report (有価証券報告書, **Yuukashooken-hookoku-sho**) which includes detailed company and sales information in addition to the non-consolidated financial statements. Since 1977, companies have also been required to provide a *consolidated* financial statement in their Marketable Securities Report, but only as supplemental information.

The following non-consolidated data are excerpted from Nissan Motor Co., Ltd.'s annual report for fiscal 1984, ended March 31, 1985. If you come to just *recognize* most of the **kanji**, you will be able to hold your qwn in the reading and analysis of financial statements.

Note: (1) Under the Securities and Exchange Law of Japan, amounts of less than one million yen may be omitted. The totals shown in the following pages, therefore, do not necessarily agree with the sum of the individual amounts.
(2) For reasons of space, U.S. dollar amounts have not been included in the excerpted statements.

24/Price and Quantity

Millions of Yen

非連結貸借対照表 (Hi-renketsu* taishaku-taishoohyoo, NON-CONSOLIDATED BALANCE SHEETS)	
資産の部 (shisan no bu, ASSETS)	
流　動　資　産 (Ryuudoo-shisan, Current Assets)	1,105,737
現　金　預　金 (Genkin-yokin, Cash and Deposits)	174,252
受　取　手　形 (Uketori-tegata, Notes Receivable)	411,939
売　掛　金 (Urikake-kin, Accounts Receivable)	97,983
有　価　証　券 (Yuuka-shooken, Marketable Securities)	80,564
製　品 (Seehin, Finished Goods)	132,775
仕　掛　品 (Shikakari-hin, Unfinished Goods/Work in Process)	38,279
部　分　品 (Bubun-hin, Parts)	16,774
原　材　料 (Genzairyoo, Materials)	10,383
貯　蔵　品 (Chozoo-hin, Supplies)	8,818
前　払　金 (Maebarai-kin, Prepayments)	1,482
前　払　費　用 (Maebarai-hiyoo, Prepaid Expenses)	6,168
短　期　債　券 (Tanki-saiken, Short-Term Notes)	147,974
未　収　入　金 (Mishuunyuu-kin, Uncollected Balance)	9,774
貸　倒　引　当　金 (Kashidaore-hikiate-kin, Bad Debt Reserve)	−31,432
固　定　資　産 (Kotee-shisan, Fixed Assets)	1,381,133
有　形　固　定　資　産 (Yuukee-kotee-shisan, Tangible Fixed Assets)	608,804
建　物 (Tatemono, Buildings)	168,159
構　築　物 (Koochiku-butsu, Facilities)	29,721
機　械　装　置 (Kikai-soochi, Machinery and Equipment)	215,863
車　両　運　搬　具 (Sharyoo-unpan-gu, Vehicles and Other Transport Equipment)	6,657
工　具　器　具　備　品 (Koogu-kigu-bihin, Tools, Furniture and Fixtures)	39,023
土　地 (Tochi, Land)	111,159
建　設　仮　勘　定 (Kensetsu-karikanjyoo, Construction in Progress)	38,220
無　形　固　定　資　産 (Mukee-kotee-shisan, Intangible Fixed Assets)	1,777
施　設　利　用　権 (Shisetsu-riyoo-ken, Utility Rights)	1,080
その他の無形固定資産 (Sonota no mukee-kotee-shisan, Other Intangible Fixed Assets)	696
投　資　等 (Tooshi-too, Investments and Advances)	770,552
投　資　有　価　証　券 (Tooshi-yuuka-shooken, Investments in Securities)	169,770
子　会　社　株　式 (Kogaisha-kabushiki, Stock Investments in Subsidiaries)	287,383
子　会　社　出　資　金 (Kogaisha-shusshi-kin, Investments in Subsidiaries)	7,604
長　期　貸　付　金 (Chooki-kashitsuke-kin, Long-Term Loans Receivable)	304,756
長　期　前　払　費　用 (Chooki-maebarai-hiyoo, Long-Term Prepaid Expenses)	12,807
そ　の　他　の　投　資 (Sonota no tooshi, Other Investments)	2,192
貸　倒　引　当　金 (Kashidaore-hikiate-kin, Bad Debt Reserve)	−13,963
資　産　合　計 (Shisan-gookee, Total Assets)	**2,486,871**

* For reasons of space, the term **Hi-renketsu**, 'non-consolidated' will not be repeated in the following pages.

負債および資本の部	(Husai oyobi shihon no bu, LIABILITIES AND SHAREHOLDERS' EQUITY)	Millions of Yen
流　動　負　債	(Ryuudoo-husai, Current Liabilities)	974,276
支　払　手　形	(Shiharai-tegata, Bills Payable)	155,349
買　掛　金	(Kaikake-kin, Outstanding Balance of Credit and Purchase)	232,863
短　期　借　入　金	(Tanki-kariire-kin, Short-Term Loans)	144,164
一年以内返済の長期借入金	(Ichi-nen-inai-hensai no chooki-kariire-kin, Current Portion of Long-Term Loans)	17,912
一年以内償還の社債	(Ichi-nen-inai-shookan no shasai, Current Portion of Bonds)	23,363
未　払　金	(Miharai-kin, Accounts Payable)	11,771
未　払　費　用	(Miharai-hiyoo, Accrued Expenses)	215,255
未　払　法　人　税　等	(Miharai-hoojin-zee-too, Accrued Income Taxes)	54,988
前　受　金	(Maeuke-kin, Advances Received)	3,601
諸　預　り　金	(Sho-azukari-kin, Deposits Received)	4,730
従　業　員　預　り　金	(Jyuugyooin-azukari-kin, Employee's Deposits Receivable)	101,302
前　受　収　益　金	(Maeuke-shuueki-kin, Unearned Income)	8,923
割賦販売利益繰延金	(Kappu-hanbai-rieki-kurinobe-kin, Deferred Profits on Installment Sales)	52
固　定　負　債	(Kotee-husai, Long-Term Debt)	343,184
社　債	(Shasai, Notes and Bonds)	92,024
長　期　借　入　金	(Chooki-kariire-kin, Long-Term Loans)	164,682
長　期　預　り　金	(Chooki-azukari-kin, Other Long-Term Debt)	386
退　職　給　与　引　当　金	(Taishoku-kyuuyo-hikiate-kin, Reserve for Retirement Aloowance)	86,090
負　債　合　計	(Husai gookee, Total Liabilities)	**1,317,461**
(資　本　主　勘　定	Shihon-shukanjoo, SHAREHOLDERS' EQUITY)	
資　本　金	(Shihon-kin, Common Stock)	109,818
法　定　準　備　金	(Hootee-junbi-kin, Legal Reserves)	246,887
資　本　準　備　金	(Shihon-junbi-kin, Capital Reserves)	219,792
利　益　準　備　金	(Rieki-junbi-kin, Earned Legal Reserves)	27,094
剰　余　金	(Jooyo-kin, Retained Earnings)	812,703
資産買換差益積立金	(Shisan-kaikae-saeki-tsumitate-kin, Reserve from Marginal Profit of Replacement of Property)	3,522
研　究　開　発　積　立　金	(Kenkyuu-kaihatsu-tsumitate-kin, Reserve for Research and Development)	17,000
為　替　変　動　準　備　積　立　金	(Kawase-hendoo-junbi-tsumitate-kin, Reserve for Fluctuation of Foreign Exchange Rate)	4,000
海　外　投　資　等　損　失　積　立　金	(Kaigai-tooshi-too-sonshitsu-tsumitate-kin, Overseas Investments Reserve)	11,559
特　別　償　却　積　立　金	(Tokubetsu-shookyaku-tsumitate-kin, Special Depreciation Reserve)	3,488
別　途　積　立　金	(Betto-tsumitate-kin, Other Surplus Reserves)	684,342
当　期　未　処　分　利　益	(Tooki-mishobun-rieki, Unappropriated Retained Earnings)	88,791
（うち当期利益）	(Uchi-tooki-rieki, Current Period Net Income)	(74,276)
資　本　合　計	(Shihon gookee, Total Shareholders' Equity)	1,169,409
負　債・資　本　合　計	(Husai, Shihon gookee, Total Liabilities and Shareholders' Equity)	**2,486,871**

損 益 計 算 書 (**Son'eki-keesansho**, PROFIT AND LOSS STATEMENT)

Millions of Yen

(経 常 損 益 の 部) (**Keejoo-son'eki no bu**, RECURRING PROFIT AND LOSS)	
営 業 損 益 の 部 (**Eegyoo-son'eki no bu**, Operating Profit and Loss)	
営 業 収 益 (**Eegyoo-shuueki**, Revenue from Operations)	3,618,076
売 上 高 (**Uriage-daka**, Net Sales)	3,618,076
営 業 費 用 (**Eegyoo-hiyoo**, Operating Costs and Expenses)	3,555,330
売 上 原 価 (**Uriage-genka**, Cost of Sales)	2,784,402
販売費及び一般管理費 (**Hanbai-hi oyobi ippan-kanri-hi**, Selling and General Administrative Expenses)	770,928
割 賦 販 売 利 益 戻 入 前 営 業 利 益 (**Kappu-hanbai-rieki-modoshiire-mae-eegyoo-rieki**, Operating Income before Adjustment for Installment Sales)	62,746
割賦販売利益戻入額 (**Kappu-hanbai-rieki-modoshiire-gaku**, Adjustment for Installment Sales)	8,098
営 業 利 益 (**Eegyoo-rieki**, Operating Income)	70,845
営 業 外 損 益 の 部 (**Eegyoogai-son'eki no bu**, Non-Operating Profit and Loss)	
営 業 外 収 益 (**Eegyoogai-shuueki**, Non-Operating Income)	129,135
受取利息及び配当金 (**Uketori-risoku oyobi haitoo-kin**, Interest and Dividends Received)	107,486
その他の営業外収益 (**Sonota no eegyoogai-shuueki**, Other Income)	21,648
営 業 外 費 用 (**Eegyoogai-hiyoo**, Non-Operating Expenses)	51,796
支払利息及び割引料 (**Shiharai-risoku oyobi waribiki-ryoo**, Interest Expenses)	46,190
その他の営業外費用 (**Sonota no eegyoogai-hiyoo**, Other Expenses)	5,605
経 常 利 益 (**Keejyoo-rieki**, Recurring Income)	148,184
(特 別 損 益 の 部) (**Tokubetsu-son'eki no bu**, SPECIAL PROFITS AND LOSSES	
特 別 利 益 (**Tokubetsu-rieki**, Special Profits)	2,793
固 定 資 産 売 却 益 (**Kotee-shisan-baikyaku-eki**, Profits on the Sales of Fixed Assets)	1,229
投資有価証券売却益 (**Tooshi-yuuka-shooken-baikyaku-eki**, Profits on the Sales of Investments in Securities)	1,531
その他の特別利益 (**Sonota no tokubetsu-rieki**, Other Special Income)	32
特 別 損 失 (**Tokubetsu-sonshitsu**, Special Losses)	10,613
固 定 資 産 廃 却 損 (**Kotee-shisan-haikyaku-son**, Losses on Abandoned Fixed Assets)	5,976
投資・債権評価損 (**Tooshi, Saiken-hyooka-son**, Losses Resulting from Appraisal of Investments and Credit)	3,716
その他の特別損失 (**Sonota no tokubetsu-sonshitsu**, Other Special Losses)	921
税 引 前 当 期 利 益 (**Zeebiki-mae-tooki-rieki**, Income Before Taxes)	140,364
法 人 税 及 び 住 民 税 (**Hoojin-zee oyobi juumin-zee**, Income Taxes)	66,088
当 期 利 益 (**Tooki-rieki**, Net Income)	74,276
前 期 繰 越 利 益 (**Zenki-kurikoshi-rieki**, Retained Earnings)	30,129
中 間 配 当 額 (**Chuukan-haitoo-gaku**, Interim Dividends)	14,906
利益準備金積立額 (**Rieki-junbi-kin-tsumitate-gaku**, Legal Reserves)	707
当 期 未 処 分 利 益 (**Tooki-mishobun-rieki**, Unappropriated Retained Earnings)	88,791

利　益　処　分　(**Rieki-shobun**, DISTRIBUTION OF NET PROFIT) (Yen)

利　益　処　分	(**Rieki-shobun**, Distribution of Net Profit)	
当期未処分利益	(**Tooki-mishobun-rieki**, Unappropriated Retained Earnings)	88,791,456,293
資産買換差益積立金取崩額	(**Shisan-kaikae-saeki-tsumitate-kin-torikuzushi-gaku**, Disposition of Reserves for Deferred Gains on Fixed Assets Sold for Replacement)	8,532,783
海外投資等損失積立金取崩額	(**Kaigai-tooshi-too-sonshitsu-tsumitate-kin-torikuzushi-gaku**, Overseas Investments)	1,947,066,776
特別償却積立金取崩額	(**Tokubetsu-shookyaku-tsumitate-kin-torikuzushi-gaku**, Special Depreciation)	1,217,221,970
計	(**Kei**, Total)	**91,964,277,822**
これを次のとおり処分いたします。	(**Kore o tsugi no toori shobun-itashimasu**, Appropriation) [lit. This will be appropriated as follows.]	
利　益　準　備　金	(**Rieki-junbi-kin**, Surplus Reserve)	359,870,131
利　益　配　当　金	(**Rieki-haitoo-kin**, Dividends)	14,950,208,868
役　員　賞　与　金	(**Yakuin-shooyo-kin**, Bonus for Directors and Auditors)	350,000,000
資産買換差益積立金	(**Shisan-kaikae-saeki-tsumitate-kin**, Deferred Gains on Fixed Assets for Replacement)	1,223,517,198
海外投資等損失積立金	(**Kaigai-tooshi-too-sonshitsu-tsumitate-kin**, Reserves for Overseas Investments)	2,497,005,000
特別償却積立金	(**Tokubetsu-shookyaku-tsumitate-kin**, Special Depreciation)	217,148,599
別　途　積　立　金	(**Betto-tsumitate-kin**, General)	40,000,000,000
計	(**Kei**, Total)	**59,597,749,796**
次　期　繰　越　利　益	(**Jiki-kurikoshi-rieki**, Retained Earnings Carried Forward)	**32,366,528,026**

Selected Bibliography

The following works are listed for your reference should you require more in-depth information about financial reporting in Japan or about the financial status of Japanese companies.

Books

Financial Reporting in Japan
R. J. BALLON et al. (Kodansha International, 1976. ¥3,500)
An overview of financial reports and regulations, with various examples of Japanese annual reports provided together with brief analyses.

Japanese Finance: Markets and Institutions
Stephen BRONTE (Euromoney Publications, 1982. ¥28,900)
A review of major financial trends, institutions, regulations and reforms, the securities market, roles of government agencies and trading houses, etc.

24/Price and Quantity

Periodicals

[Note: Rates provided below are for domestic subscription only]

The Japan Stock Journal
(Japan Journal, Inc., Subscription ¥9,100)
Weekly newspaper for foreigners with information about listings on the Tokyo and Osaka Stock Exchanges, surveys on Japanese economy and individual companies.

The Nikko Quarterly Bulletin
(The Nikko Research Center, Ltd., Subscription ¥4,000)
Report for readers interested in Japanese securities market. Includes information on the economy, with brief survey of business, finance and major industries as well as statistics and data about companies on the Tokyo Stock Exchange.

The NRC Chartroom
(The Nikko Research Center, Ltd., Subscription ¥12,000)
A monthly guide for foreign investors in securities. Comprises data and analysis presented in graphs, and information on the Japanese economy and securities market.

The Securities Market in Japan, 1986
(Japan Securities Research Institute, Approx. ¥2,200)
Translation of biannual work by the Securities Bureau of the Ministry of Finance. Concise introduction to the Japanese securities market covering history, public corporation bond market, securities trading companies, taxation and regulations, etc. (Published end of each odd-numbered year)

Directories and Reference

Analysts' Guide 1985 (Every August)
(Daiwa Securities Research Institute, Daiwa Securities Co., Ltd., ¥20,000)
Compilation of data for foreign and domestic investors, including corporate financial statistics, stock prices, income amounts, profit, stock distribution, etc. of leading Japanese firms, as well as their industry rankings. Data is presented on non-consolidated basis.

Japan Company Handbook (Semiannual)
(The Oriental Economist, ¥8,400)
Listing of business firms on the first sections of the Tokyo, Osaka and Nagoya stock exchanges. Includes company synopsis, basic information about directors and employees, activities, products, performance and prospects.

Advanced Business English Dictionary
(Pacific Management Consultants, Inc., 1981, ¥15,000)
A revised and more handy version of the **Gendai Bijinesu Eego Daijiten** (現代ビジネス英語 大辞典) for Japanese businessmen. English-Japanese/Japanese-English, for foreign users who read **kanji**. Includes detailed definitions of financial terminology and appendix with a select list of Japanese companies in the first section of the Tokyo Stock Exchange.

Lesson 25

Payment and Delivery

OBJECTIVES

1   to engage in business talks.

2   to discuss trade terms.

3   to use the Conditional form.

4   to indicate that something has already been arranged, decided on.

TARGET EXPRESSIONS AND PATTERNS

1	If ...	...(shi)tara
2	It has been decided ...	... koto ni natte iru.
3	While ...	... nagara
4	both \<X\> and \<Y\>	\<X\> mo \<Y\> mo
5	the reason why ...	...(shita) no wa ... kara desu.

SITUATION

After receiving P&C's initial estimate, Mr. Ohyama asks Mr. Brown to come to Nissan once again to discuss details about payment terms and delivery.

25/Payment and Delivery

DIALOGUE

Ohyama

| 1 | Mr. Brown, thank you for (sending us) the estimate the other day. | Buraun-san, senjitsu wa mitsumori ari-gatoo gozaimashita. |

Brown   Oh, no   iya,   いや

| 2 | Oh, not at all. By the way, have (you) had a chance to look over that estimate? | Iya, tonde mo gozaimasen. Tokoro de, ano mitsumori wa gokentoo kudasai-mashita ka. |

	to contact	renraku o toru, 連絡を取る
	while (doing …)	…nagara, …ながら
	to go ahead	susumeru, 進める
Ohyama	a little more	moo sukoshi, もう少し

| 3 | Right now, (we) are going ahead with our review while keeping in contact with the Engineering Department, so please give us a little more time. | Ima, gijutsu-bu to renraku o torina-gara, kentoo o susumete imasu no de, moo sukoshi jikan o kudasai. |

Brown   if there is …   arimashitara,   ありましたら

| 4 | If there is any other material you need, (we) will prepare it, so… | Hoka ni mo nani ka hitsuyoo na shiryoo ga arimashitara, junbi-shimasu kara… |

| | to call (you) | oyobi-suru (respectful), お呼びする |
| **Ohyama** | to confirm | kakunin-suru, 確認する |

| 5 | Well no, as of now, there is no need for it. The reason (I) called you to-day is because (I) wanted to confirm some of the trade terms, so … | Iya, ima no tokoro, sono hitsuyoo wa arimasen. Kyoo oyobi-shita no wa tori-hiki-jooken ni tsuite, kakunin-shite oki-tai koto ga arimashite… |

Brown   yes   haa,   はあ

| 6 | Yes, what are they? | Haa, nan deshoo ka. |

	to hope for, prefer	**kiboo-suru,** 希望する
Ohyama	hope	**gokiboo** (respectful), ご希望

7	(You) prefer transactions in dollars, don't you?	**Keeyaku wa doru-date o gokiboo desu ne.**

	all	**subete,** すべて
	it is decided to (do)	**(suru) koto ni naru,** （する）ことになる
Brown	to pay	**shiharau,** 支払う

8	Yes, our policy is to conduct all of our transactions in dollar terms.	**Hai, watakushidomo wa subete no keeyaku o doru-date de suru koto ni natte imasu.**

	our side	**toohoo,** 当方
	as for us	**toohoo to shite wa,** 当方としては
Ohyama	if it is in yen terms	**en-date deshitara,** 円建でしたら

9	As for us, either dollars or yen would be fine, but if it is to be dollars, we would have to discuss the exchange (rate) also, so...	**Toohoo to shite wa doru-date de mo en-date de mo kamaimasen ga, doru-date deshitara, kawase-reeto ni tsuite mo soodan-suru hitsuyoo ga arimasu kara...**

Brown

10	In that case [lit. If it is so], let's go ahead with yens.	**Soo deshitara, en-date de ohanashi o susumemashoo.**

Ohyama

11	As for delivery terms, you did prefer FOB, didn't you?	**Shikiri-jooken wa ehu-oo-bii o gokiboo deshita ne.**

Brown

12	Yes, FOB New York.	**Hai, ehu-oo-bii Nyuuyooku desu.**

25/Payment and Delivery

Ohyama		payment	shiharai, 支払い

13 What is your opinion regarding payment terms? — **Shiharai-jooken wa doo okangae desu ka.**

		L/C	eru-shii, エル・シー
Brown		L/C at sight	eru-shii ichiran barai, エル・シー一覧払い

14 (We) prefer 100% L/C at sight, but as for the contract, I will consult further with USM, so… — **Hyaku-paasento eru-shii ichiran barai o kiboo-shimasu ga, keeyaku ni tsuite wa, Yuu-esu-emu to mo soodan shimasu kara…**

Ohyama

15 Well, (I)'ll consult with you again regarding these details later. — **Jaa, kuwashii jooken wa mata ato de soodan-shimasu.**

JAPANESE WRITING

1 大山： ブラウンさん、先日は見積り有り難うございました。

2 ブラウン： いや、とんでもございません。ところで、あの見積りは ご検討くださいましたか。

3 大山： 今、技術部と連絡を取りながら、検討を進めていますので、もう少し時間をください。

4 ブラウン： 他にも 何か必要な資料がありましたら、準備しますから…

5 大山： いや、今の所、その必要はありません。今日お呼びしたのは 取引条件について、確認しておきたいことがありまして…

6 ブラウン： はあ、何でしょうか。

7 大山： 契約は ドル建をご希望ですね。

8 ブラウン： はい、私共は すべての契約をドル建ですることになっています。

9 大山： 当方としては ドル建でも円建でもかまいませんが、ドル建でしたら、為替レートについても 相談する必要がありますから…

10 ブラウン： そうでしたら、円建で お話を進めましょう。

11 大山： 仕切条件はエフ・オー・ビーをご希望でしたね。

12 ブラウン： はい、エフ・オー・ビー ニューヨークです。

13 大山： 支払条件はどうお考えですか。

14 ブラウン： 100パーセント エル・シー一覧払いを希望しますが、契約については、ユー・エス・エムとも相談しますから…

15 大山： じゃあ、詳しい条件は またあとで相談します。

ADDITIONAL USEFUL EXPRESSIONS

1 At the office

floating exchange system	**hendoo-sooba-see,** 変動相場制
to stabilize	**antee-suru,** 安定する
management	**kee'ee(-suru),** 経営(する)

A:	In the case of companies like ours, stable management is rather difficult in the floating exchange rate system.	**Uchi no yoo na kaisha no baai wa, hendoo-sooba-see de wa antee-shita kee'ee wa muzukashiku narimasu.**

recently	**saikin,** 最近
foreign exchange rate	**kawase-sooba,** 為替相場
lower yen quotation	**en-yasu,** 円安

B:	Recently, the yen has been low on the foreign exchange, so...	**Saikin, kawase-sooba wa en-yasu ga tsuzuite imasu kara nee.**

before long	**sono uchi,** そのうち
higher yen quotation	**en-daka,** 円高

A:	I think the yen will go up before long, but...	**Maa, sono uchi en-daka ni naru to omoimasu ga...**

2 At the office

day off, holiday	**yasumi,** 休み

A:	What do you do on your holidays?	**Yasumi no hi wa nani o shite imasu ka.**

TV	**terebi,** テレビ

B:	I usually watch TV at home. And you?	**Boku wa taitee uchi de terebi o mite imasu. Anata wa.**

music	**ongaku,** 音楽

A:	I like reading books while listening to music, so...	**Boku wa ongaku o kikinagara, hon o yomu no ga suki desu kara...**

25/Payment and Delivery

	hobby	**shumi,** 趣味
B:	That's a good hobby, isn't it?	**Sore wa ii shumi desu ne.**

	lazy	**monogusa/na/,** ものぐさ（な）
A:	Not at all. I'm just lazy.	**Tondemo nai. Monogusa na dake desu yo.**

REFERENCE

jinkenhi	人件費	personnel expenses
genryoohi	原料費	material costs
koonetsuhi	光熱費	utilities expenses
kenkyuuhi	研究費	research expenses
koosaihi	交際費	entertainment expenses
sendenhi	宣伝費	advertising expenses
yusoohi	輸送費	transportation expenses
kaihatsuhi	開発費	development expenses
seezoohi	製造費	manufacturing expenses

NOTES

1 The Conditional

Japanese verbs and adjectives and the copula **da** have conditional forms, which may be translated: 'if such-and-such had happened/happens' or 'when such-and-such happened/has happened' or 'if so-and-so had done/does' or 'when so-and-so did/has done.' The conditional is formed by adding **ra** to the past tense of the verb, adjective or copula.

	Non-past	Past	Conditional
Verb	**aru**	**atta**	**atta*ra***
Adjective	**ii**	**yokatta**	**yokatta*ra***
Copula	**desu/da**	**deshita/datta**	**deshita*ra*/datta*ra***

The conditional itself is tenseless, and so the tense of the sentence is always determined by that of the final verb, adjective or copula.

Examples: a) **Okane ga *attara*, kuruma o kaimasu.**
"If I have (enough) money, I'll buy a car."

b) **Sono toki okane ga** *attara*, **kuruma o kaimashita ga...**
"If I had had money at that time, I'd have bought a car, but..."

c) **Jimusho e** *ittara*, **Takada-san ga imashita.***
"When I went to the office, Mr. Takada was there."

d) **Jooken ga** *yokattara*, **keeyaku-shimasu.**
"If the conditions are favorable, I'll make a contract (with you)."

e) **Ii jooken** *dattara*, **keeyaku-shimasu.**
"If (you can offer) good conditions, I'll make a contract (with you)."

* The conditional is sometimes used to indicate that two actions coincidentally occured at the same time. In this example, the speaker uses the conditional form to indicate that he went to the office without any expectation of seeing Mr. Takada there.

2 ... koto ni naru

Koto ni naru, following a verb in its citation form, means 'to be decided' or 'to be arranged.' Thus,

> **Amerika e iku** *koto ni narimashita.*
> "It was arranged that I would go to America."

When **koto** is preceded by a negative, the combination means 'to be arranged not to do such-and-such,' while **... koto ni (wa) naranai** means 'to be not arranged that ...' or 'to be not decided that ...'

Compare: **Ikanai** *koto ni narimashita.*
"It was decided that I wouldn't go."

and

Iku *koto ni narimasen deshita.*
"It didn't turn out [lit. wasn't decided] that I would go."

Examples: a) **Ashita Joonzu-san ga rainichi-suru** *koto ni natte imasu.***
"It has been arranged that Mr. Jones will come to Japan tomorrow."

b) **Nichiyoobi ni wa hatarakanai** *koto ni natte imasu.*
"It has been decided that we don't work on Sundays."

c) **Kotoshi-juu ni robotto o doonyuu-suru** *koto ni wa naranai deshoo.*
"It probably won't happen [lit. won't be decided] that we'll introduce robots within this year."

****Koto ni natte iru** is usually translated as '(it) has been arranged' or '(it) has been decided', and sometimes as '(it) is the custom/rule that.'

In *BUSINESS JAPANESE*, you learned that **... koto ni suru** 'to decide to do such-and-such' is used when the speaker wants to clearly indicate a decision. [Refer to *BUSINESS JAPANESE*, Lesson 19, Note 8]

Compare: **Amerika e iku** *koto ni shimashita.*
"I decided to go to America."

and

Amerika e iku *koto ni narimashita*.
"It was decided that I'd go to America."

3 -nagara

A verb stem (i.e. a verb **masu** form minus **masu**) + **nagara** means 'while doing such-and-such,' and this combination is used to indicate two actions being carried out simultaneously by someone or something.

Examples:

    a) **Koohii o nomi*nagara*, sono shiryoo o kentoo-shimashoo.**
       "Let's examine the data while drinking coffee."

    b) **Shachoo to soodan-shi*nagara*, kono mitsumorisho o tsukurimashita.**
       "While consulting with the President, I wrote this estimate
       [lit. prepared this written estimate]."

4 ... to shite wa

The combination of **to shite** + the particle **wa** is often used in the beginning of a sentence or phrase to emphasize the subject. It may be translated as: 'speaking from the standpoint of ...' or 'as for ...' Thus,

    Toohoo *to shite wa*, doru-date o kiboo-shimasu.
    "We prefer (transactions in) dollars." or "Speaking from our standpoint, we prefer (transactions in) dollars."

    Anata *to shite wa*, doonyuu ni sansee-dekinai wake desu ka.
    "On your side, do you mean you cannot agree to the introduction (of robots, etc.)?" or "As for your side, does this mean..."

5 Additional Use of no (wa)

No in **oyobi-shita no** in Dialogue **5**: In this sentence, a verb + **no** indicates an action which is then explained in the phrase that follows. The English equivalent of this pattern may be 'the reason ... is because ...' Thus,

    Keeyaku-shinakatta *no wa* nedan ga takakatta kara desu.
    "The reason we didn't finalize the contract is because the price was high."

    Paatii ni ikenakatta *no wa* isogashikatta kara desu.
    "The reason (I) wasn't able to go to the party is because (I) was busy."

PRACTICE

1 Response Practice

Example: Teacher: **Doru-date to en-date to dochira ga ii desu ka.**
                     "Which do you prefer, dollar terms or yen terms?"

             Student: **Doru-date de mo en-date de mo kamaimasen.**
                     "Either dollar terms or yen terms would be fine
                     [lit. I don't mind either dollar terms or yen terms]."

a) **Biiru to wain to dochira ga ii desu ka.** | **Biiru de mo wain de mo kamaimasen.**

b) **Ashita to asatte to dochira ga ii desu ka.** | **Ashita de mo asatte de mo kamaimasen.**

c) **Ehu-oo-bii to shii-ai-ehu to dochira ga ii desu ka.** | **Ehu-oo-bii de mo shii-ai-ehu de mo kamaimasen.**

d) **Nihon no ginkoo to Amerika no ginkoo to dochira ga ii desu ka.** | **Nihon no ginkoo de mo Amerika no ginkoo de mo kamaimasen.**

e) **Genkin to kogitte to dochira ga ii desu ka.** | **Genkin de mo kogitte de mo kamaimasen.**

2 Transformation Practice

Example: Teacher: **Terebi o mimasu. Asa-gohan o tabemasu.**
                      "I watch television. I eat breakfast."

              Student: **Terebi o minagara, asa-gohan o tabemasu.**
                      "While watching television, I eat breakfast."

a) **Rajio o kikimasu.**
   Tegami o kaite imasu. | **Rajio o kikinagara, tegami o kaite imasu.**

b) **Shiryoo o yomimasu.**
   Torihiki-jooken o kangaemasu. | **Shiryoo o yominagara, torihiki-jooken o kangaemasu.**

c) **Honsha to renraku o torimasu.**
   Shoodan o susumemasu. | **Honsha to renraku o torinagara, shoodan o susumemasu.**

d) **Katarogu o misemasu.**
   Robotto no setsumee o shimashita. | **Katarogu o misenagara, robotto no setsumee o shimashita.**

e) **Sake o nomimasu.**
   Hanashiaimashoo. | **Sake o nominagara, hanashiaimashoo.**

3 Response Practice

Example: Teacher: **Keeyaku wa doru-date de shimasu ka.**
                      "Is the contract going to be based on dollars
                      [lit. Are you going to make a contract in dollar terms]?"

              Student: **Ee, doru-date de suru koto ni natte imasu.**
                      "Yes, it is our policy to base (it) on dollars
                      [lit. It has been decided that we make (it) in dollar terms]."

a) **Raishuu shutchoo-shimasu ka.** | **Ee, shutchoo-suru koto ni natte imasu.**

b) **Ano koosaku-kikai o kaimasu ka.** | **Ee, kau koto ni natte imasu.**

c) **Robotto no seesan o hajimemasu ka.** | **Ee, (seesan o) hajimeru koto ni natte imasu.**

d) **Kumitate-sagyoo o jidooka-shimasu ka.** | **Ee, jidooka-suru koto ni natte imasu.**

e) **Juugyooin no reiohu wa shimasen ka.** | **Ee, (reiohu wa) shinai koto ni natte imasu.**

25/Payment and Delivery

4 Transformation Practice

Example: Teacher: **Keeyaku-shimasu. Sugu noohin-shimasu.**
"We finalize the contract. I'll deliver (the goods) immediately."

Student: **Keeyaku-shitara, sugu noohin-shimasu.**
"If we finalize the contract, I'll deliver (the goods) immediately."

a)   **En-date de keeyaku-shimasu. Nebiki-dekimasu ka.**
En-date de keeyaku-shitara, nebiki-dekimasu ka.

b)   **Kyoo terekkusu o okurimasu. Ashita henji ga kuru deshoo.**
Kyoo terekkusu o okuttara, ashita henji ga kuru deshoo.

c)   **Roodoo-jooken ga yoku narimasu. Kumiai mo yorokobu hazu desu.**
Roodoo-jooken ga yoku nattara, kumiai mo yorokobu hazu desu.

d)   **Kakaku ga yasui desu. Motto takusan chuumon-shimasu.**
Kakaku ga yasukattara, motto takusan chuumon-shimasu.

e)   **Shachoo ga byooki desu. Rainichi-shinai deshoo.**
Shachoo ga byooki dattara, rainichi-shinai deshoo.

f)   **Rainen zooshi-shimasu. Shihonkin wa go-oku-en ni narimasu.**
Rainen zooshi-shitara, shihonkin wa go-oku-en ni narimasu.

g)   **Doru-date de mo kamaimasen. Kyoo keeyaku-shimashoo.**
Doru-date de mo kamawanakattara, kyoo keeyaku-shimashoo.

h)   **Ashita wa ii tenki desu. Kyooto kenbutsu ga dekimasu.**
Ashita ii tenki dattara, Kyooto kenbutsu ga dekimasu.

i)   **Huzokuhin o iremasen. Kakaku wa yon-man-doru desu.**
Huzokuhin o irenakattara, kakaku wa yon-man-doru desu.

j)   **Wagasha ga soodairiten ni narimasu. Uriage wa huemasu.**
Wagasha ga soodairiten ni nattara, uriage wa huemasu.

5 Comprehension Practice

Directions: The teacher reads aloud the following passage and then asks the student questions about it.

Kyoo Ooyama-buchoo wa Buraun-san o yonde, torihiki-jooken ni tsuite iroiro kaku-nin-shimashita. Pii-ando-shii wa tatene to shite doru-date o kiboo-shite imasu. Shikiri-jooken wa ehu-oo-bii Nyuuyooku de, shiharai-jooken wa hyaku-paasento eru-shii ichi-ran barai da soo desu. Buraun-san wa, keeyaku ni tsuite Yuu-esu-emu to soodan-suru koto ni shimashita.

Questions:

1   **Kyoo Ooyama-buchoo wa dare o yobimashita ka.**
2   **Buraun-san o yonda no wa doo shite desu ka.**
3   **Pii-ando-shii wa tatene to shite doru-date de mo en-date de mo ii desu ka.**
4   **Shiharai-jooken wa nani o kiboo-shite imasu ka.**
5   **Keeyaku ni tsuite wa dare to soodan-shimasu ka.**
6   **Doo shite keeyaku ni tsuite wa Yuu-esu-emu to soodan-suru n desu ka.**

EXERCISES

a)   Using the following conditional clauses, complete the sentences in Japanese:

1   Ashita ame ga huttara (If it rains tomorrow), ...
2   Wagasha no uriage ga huetara (If our company's sales increase),...
3   Wagasha no robotto o doonyuu-shitara (If you introduce our robots), ...
4   Wagasha no katarogu ga hitsuyoo deshitara (If you need our catalogue), ...
5   Keeyaku ga en-date dattara (If the contract is in yen-terms), ...

b)   Inform the teacher in Japanese that:

1   While consulting with Mr. Brown, Mr. Jones is preparing a catalogue for Japanese companies.
2   It has been decided that P & C, Ltd. will become the general agent of USM, Ltd. sometime next month.
3   American companies usually prefer FOB rather than CIF as the delivery terms.
4   It is not necessary to consult with the head office about a discount for the new products.
5   The floating exchange rate [lit. the system of a floating exchange rate] will probably become disadvantageous for Mr. Tanaka's company.
6   It had been arranged that Ms. Yamada would telephone Mr. Brown by three o'clock, but she did not call him.

Model Answers:

b)   **1   Buraun-san to soodan-shinagara, Joonzu-san wa Nihon no kaisha no tame no katarogu o tsukutte imasu.**
2   Pii-ando-shii wa raigetsu-chuu ni Yuu-esu-emu no soodairiten ni naru koto ni natte imasu.
3   Shikiri-jooken to shite, Amerika no kaisha wa taitee shii-ai-ehu yori ehu-oo-bii o kiboo-shimasu.
4   Shin-seehin no nebiki ni tsuite, honsha to soodan-suru hitsuyoo wa arimasen.
5   Hendoo-sooba-see wa Tanaka-san no kaisha ni huri ni naru deshoo.
6   Yamada-san wa san-ji made ni Buraun-san ni denwa-suru koto ni natte imashita ga, (denwa-)shimasen deshita.

BUSINESS INFORMATION

Giving Gifts

Timely payment and delivery are among the most important obligations for business people everywhere. However, since home and office are far more closely intertwined in Japan than in the West, one's professional obligations when stationed in the country also include another, more *personal* kind of payment and delivery, i.e. presenting cash or gifts to clients and staff for weddings, childbirth, illnesses, promotions, anniversaries of company foundings, new office openings, retirement, funerals and other milestone events.

The points outlined below may help you fulfill some of your gift-giving obligations in Japan's "paternalistic" business society.

1 What To Give: The preferred gift for most occasions is money. Unlike many Westerners, Japanese have no qualms about giving or receiving cash. Indeed, when one considers that it costs an average of ¥6.8 million to get married (or cremated) in Japan today, one can well appreciate why money is the most welcome and useful gift of all. Cash presents carry different names in Japan depending on the event they help to commemorate or commiserate with. Whatever the occasion, though, money gifts should consist of unused bank notes (新札, **shinsatsu**). Ten thousand yen, the largest denomination bill, is generally considered average for gifts, but the amount should of course also depend on your wallet and your relationship with the recipient. You should note too that in Japan, the higher you are in the company hierarchy, the more you are expected to contribute to general office causes. Consequently, you should ask the **kanji-san** (幹事さん, organizer/manager) collecting contributions for the event how much your staff and colleagues are giving so you can adjust your donation accordingly. For events concerning people outside the company, it would be best to seek the advice of a knowledgeable Japanese colleague or acquaintance.

2 How To Give: Cash gifts are normally presented in special gift envelopes (祝儀袋, **shuugibukuro**) which can be purchased at stationery stores. **Shuugibukuro** come with different printed messages and decorative ties to suit the various occasions, and in different degrees of elaboration to correspond to the enclosed gifts (See Diagrams). Plain white envelopes are also acceptable in most cases. If you do elect to use a **shuugibukuro**, however, you should make absolutely certain that it matches the occasion. The wrong envelope–like the wrong kind of wrapping on a gift–is a serious breach of etiquette and may sometimes even be interpreted as an ill omen. Better no gift at all, therefore, than one which is improperly presented.

3 How To Reciprocate: For most occasions in Japan, people who receive presents also give return-gifts (お返し, **okaeshi**). Like the initial gifts themselves, return-gifts are assigned different names for different occasions, but they are usually articles, not money. To complicate things further, Japanese etiquette sets certain rules for the *value* of return gifts. Return (or take-home) gifts for weddings, for instance, are about half the value of the gift received to symbolize the couple's sharing of their new-found happiness. On the other hand, the value of **okaeshi** for funeral contributions is usually less than that because, according to ancient tradition, the original gift was accepted in sorrow and giving too much in return is thought to spread similar misfortune to the recipient.

No doubt your mind is spinning now from all this endless giving and taking. If it is any consolation, you should know that the intricacies of gift-giving are just as difficult for the etiquette-conscious Japanese themselves, if not more so. Consequently, you should not feel intimidated when the gift season rolls around. Instead, just give what you feel most comfortable giving and when in doubt, do as the Japanese do: consult, consult, consult.

The following table summarizes appropriate gifts, return-gifts and protocol for the occasions you will most likely be asked to attend or contribute to during your stay in Japan.

Occasion / Gift, etc.	WEDDING 結婚式 kekkonshiki	ILLNESS/ DISASTER 病気/災害 byooki/saigai	FUNERAL お葬式 oshooshiki
Name/Type of Gift	oiwai (お祝い) Cash: ¥10,000 – ¥20,000 if you attend.	omimai (お見舞い) Mostly articles	kooden (香典) Cash: ¥3,000; ¥5,000 if you are a manager.
Type of Envelope/ Message	Red & white or gold & silver cord/ "Kotobuki" (寿, "Happiness")	Red & white or white cord/ "Omimai" (御見舞, "Inquiry")	Black & white cord/ "Goreezen" (御霊前, "To the spirit of the departed")
Timing of Gift	Actual day, reception	As soon as possible	Actual day, reception
Name/Type of Return-Gift	hikidemono (引出物)/Article	uchiiwai/kaikiiwai (内祝/快気祝)* Article	koodengaeshi (香典返し)/Article
Ritual & Protocol	Give a speech (in person, or have prepared text read by someone while you stand beside him/her).	Visit at home, call, write.	Depends on religion. (Observe and follow the leaders ...)
Greetings	**Omedetoo gozaimasu** (Congratulations), **Sue nagaku oshiawase ni** (Wishing you eternal happiness).	[For illness] **Hayaku yoku natte kudasai** (Get well soon), **Ichinichi mo hayai gokaihuku o oinorimooshiage-masu** (Wishing you a speedy recovery).	**Kono tabi wa goshuushoosama desu** (This must be a sorrowful time for you ...), **Nan to ittara ii ka wakari-masen ...** (I don't know what to say ...).

25/Payment and Delivery

* Only for illness and injuries. Return gifts are not necessary for contributions given in sympathy for natural catastrophes.

DIAGRAM 1

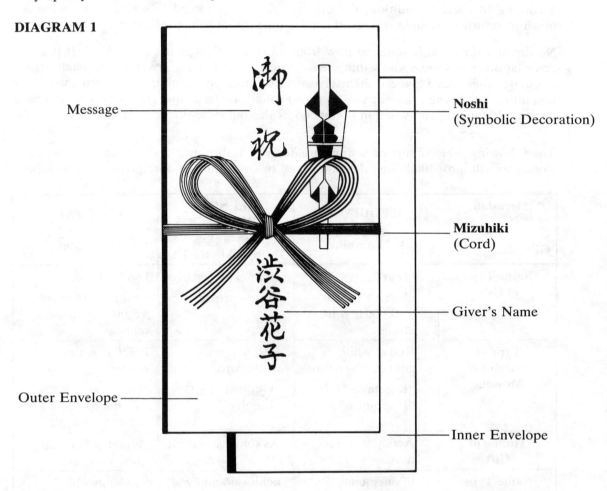

Message

Noshi
(Symbolic Decoration)

Mizuhiki
(Cord)

Giver's Name

Outer Envelope

Inner Envelope

DIAGRAM 2

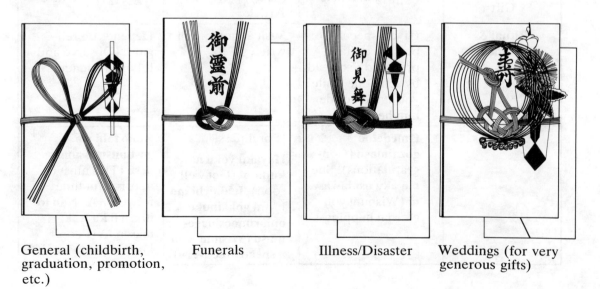

General (childbirth, graduation, promotion, etc.)

Funerals

Illness/Disaster

Weddings (for very generous gifts)

Lesson 26

OBJECTIVES

1   to use bank terminology.

2   to discuss opening an account with a bank clerk.

3   to ask and tell about one's experiences.

4   to practice answering a 'negative' question.

TARGET EXPRESSIONS AND PATTERNS

1	Have you ever done…?	…(shita) koto ga arimasu ka.
2	I have done…	…(shita) koto ga arimasu.
3	(Someone) is accustomed to doing…	…(shi) narete imasu.

SITUATION

As P&C, Ltd. is beginning to enjoy an increase in business, Mr. Brown decides to open up an account with a Japanese bank.

26/At the Bank

DIALOGUE

	bank clerk	**ginkooin**, 銀行員 (ぎんこういん)
Clerk	business	**yooken, goyooken** (polite), 用件, ご用件 (ようけん, ようけん)

> **1** May I help you? What can I do for you today [lit. What is your business today]?
>
> **Irasshaimase. Kyoo wa donna goyooken deshoo ka.**

Brown	to open	**hiraku**, 開く (ひら)

> **2** Well [lit. In reality], (I)'d like to open an account.
>
> **Jitsu wa, kooza o hirakitai to omotte...**

Clerk	individual	**kojin**, 個人 (こじん)

> **3** Would it be a personal account, sir?
>
> **Okyakusama kojin no kooza deshoo ka.**

	for the company	**shayoo**, 社用 (しゃよう)
	ordinary deposit	**hutsuu-yokin**, 普通預金 (ふつうよきん)
Brown	checking account	**kogitte no kooza**, 小切手の口座 (こぎって, こうざ)

> **4** No, it's for the company. (I) would like to open an ordinary deposit and a checking account.
>
> **Iie, shayoo no desu. Hutsuu-yokin to kogitte no kooza o onegai-shimasu.**

Clerk	current, checking account	**tooza (-yokin)**, 当座(預金) (とうざ よきん)

> **5** We can open an ordinary account immediately, but for the current deposit, it is our policy to open it only after having discussed various matters (first) [lit. after having asked various questions].
>
> **Hutsuu-yokin no kooza wa sugu otsu-kuri-shimasu ga, tooza no hoo wa iroiro ohanashi o ukagaimashite kara, otsu-kuri-suru koto ni natte orimasu.**

Brown	troublesome	**mendoo/na/**, 面倒(な) (めんどう)

> **6** Is that so? It's troublesome, isn't it?
>
> **Soo desu ka. Mendoo desu ne.**

Clerk	to have ever (done)	... (shita) koto ga aru, …(した)ことがある

7	Have (you) dealt with a Japanese bank up till now?	**Ima made, Nihon no ginkoo to torihiki-shita koto wa oari deshoo ka.**

	Bank of America	**Banku-obu-Amerika,** バンク・オブ・アメリカ
Brown		

8	No, (this) is my first time. In Japan, (we) have an account at the Bank of America, but it's a little far (from my office), so...	**Iie, hajimete desu. Nihon de wa Banku-obu-Amerika to torihiki ga arimasu ga, chotto tooi no de...**

Clerk

9	Is that so? For what purposes will (you) be using checks?	**Soo desu ka. Kogitte wa nani ni otsukai ni narimasu ka.**

	business partner	**torihikisaki,** 取引先
Brown	and others	**nado,** など

10	(We) plan to use them for such things as employees' wages and remittances to our business partners.	**Shain no kyuuryoo ya torihikisaki e no shiharai nado ni tsukau tsumori desu ga...**

Clerk	bank transfer	**ginkoo-hurikomi,** 銀行振込

11	In such cases, (I) think payment through bank transfer would be more convenient, but...	**Sonna baai, ginkoo-hurikomi no hoo ga benri da to omoimasu ga...**

	we	**wareware,** 我々
	American(s)	**Amerikajin,** アメリカ人
	check	**chekku, kogitte,** チェック,小切手
Brown	to be accustomed to using	**tsukainareru,** 使い慣れる

12	No, well, somehow we Americans are more accustomed to using checks, so...	**Iya, doo mo wareware Amerikajin wa chekku no hoo ga tsukainarete iru no de...**

| | conditions | jootai, 状態 <ruby>状態<rt>じょうたい</rt></ruby> |
| Clerk | to let us see | misete itadaku (humble), 見せていただく <ruby>見<rt>み</rt></ruby>せていただく |

| **13** | Is that right? Then are there any documents you could show us to help us understand the company's financial status? | Soo desu ka. De wa, nani ka kaisha no kee'ee-jootai ga wakaru yoo na shorui o misete itadakemasen ka. |

	statement of accounts	kessan-hookokusho, 決算報告書 <ruby>決算報告書<rt>けっさんほうこくしょ</rt></ruby>
	corporation	hoojin, 法人 <ruby>法人<rt>ほうじん</rt></ruby>
	corporate tax	hoojinzee, 法人税 <ruby>法人税<rt>ほうじんぜい</rt></ruby>
Brown	receipt	uketori, 受取 <ruby>受取<rt>うけとり</rt></ruby>

| **14** | Let me see. Would something like a statement of accounts or corporate tax receipt be all right? | Soo desu nee. Kessan-hookokusho to ka hoojinzee no uketori de mo ii desu ka. |

| Clerk | time deposit | teeki-yokin, 定期預金 <ruby>定期預金<rt>ていきよきん</rt></ruby> |

| **15** | Yes, that's fine. In addition, we would also like to request a time deposit. | Ee, kekkoo desu. Sore ni, teeki-yokin mo onegai-shitai n desu ga. |

| Brown | | |

| **16** | (I) understand. Then, (I)'ll come a-gain, soon. | Wakarimashita. Jaa, chikai uchi ni mata kimasu. |

| Clerk | | |

| **17** | Thank you very much. (We) look forward to seeing you again. | Arigatoo gozaimashita. Omachi-shite orimasu. |

JAPANESE WRITING

1 <ruby>銀行員<rt>ぎんこういん</rt></ruby>： いらっしゃいませ。<ruby>今日<rt>きょう</rt></ruby>はどんな ご<ruby>用件<rt>ようけん</rt></ruby>でしょうか。

2 ブラウン： <ruby>実<rt>じつ</rt></ruby>は、<ruby>口座<rt>こうざ</rt></ruby>を<ruby>開<rt>ひら</rt></ruby>きたいと<ruby>思<rt>おも</rt></ruby>って…

3 <ruby>銀行員<rt>ぎんこういん</rt></ruby>： お<ruby>客様個人<rt>きゃくさまこじん</rt></ruby>の<ruby>口座<rt>こうざ</rt></ruby>でしょうか。

4 ブラウン： いいえ、<ruby>社用<rt>しゃよう</rt></ruby>のです。<ruby>普通預金<rt>ふつうよきん</rt></ruby>と<ruby>小切手<rt>こぎって</rt></ruby>の<ruby>口座<rt>こうざ</rt></ruby>をお<ruby>願<rt>ねが</rt></ruby>いします。

5 <ruby>銀行員<rt>ぎんこういん</rt></ruby>： <ruby>普通預金<rt>ふつうよきん</rt></ruby>の<ruby>口座<rt>こうざ</rt></ruby>は すぐお<ruby>作<rt>つく</rt></ruby>りしますが、<ruby>当座<rt>とうざ</rt></ruby>の<ruby>方<rt>ほう</rt></ruby>はいろいろお<ruby>話<rt>はなし</rt></ruby>を<ruby>伺<rt>うかが</rt></ruby>いましてから、お<ruby>作<rt>つく</rt></ruby>りすることになっております。

6	ブラウン：	そうですか。面倒ですね。
7	銀 行 員：	今まで、日本の銀行と取引したことはおありでしょうか。
8	ブラウン：	いいえ、初めてです。日本ではバンク・オブ・アメリカと取引がありますが、ちょっと 遠いので…
9	銀 行 員：	そうですか。 小切手は 何にお使いになりますか。
10	ブラウン：	社員の給料や取引先への支払などに 使うつもりですが…
11	銀 行 員：	そんな場合、銀行振込の方が 便利だと思いますが…
12	ブラウン：	いや、どうも我々アメリカ人は チェックの方が使い慣れているので…
13	銀 行 員：	そうですか。では、何か会社の経営状態が分かるような書類を見せていただけませんか。
14	ブラウン：	そうですねえ。決算報告書とか法人税の受取でもいいですか。
15	銀 行 員：	ええ、結構です。それに、定期預金もお願いしたいんですが。
16	ブラウン：	わかりました。じゃあ、近いうちにまた来ます。
17	銀 行 員：	ありがとうございました。お待ちしております。

ADDITIONAL USEFUL EXPRESSIONS

1 At the bank

	to deposit	**azukeru,** 預ける

Customer:	I'd like to deposit 500 thousand yen, but...	**Gojuu-man-en azuketai n desu ga …**

Clerk:	Will this be an ordinary deposit?	**Hutsuu-yokin desu ka.**

Customer:	No. It's a one-year time deposit. Around how much is the interest?	**Iie, ichi-nen no teeki(-yokin) desu. Rishi wa dono kurai desu ka.**

	interest (rate)	**kinri,** 金利

Clerk:	The interest rate is 5.5%.	**Kinri wa goo-ten-go-paasento desu.**

Customer:	Is that right? That's fine.	**Soo desu k Kekkoo desu.**

26/At the Bank

form	**yooshi,**	用紙
to fill out	**kakikomu,**	書き込む
seal	**inkan,**	印鑑
to push	**osu,**	押す

Clerk:	Then, please fill out this form and put your seal on it.	**Sore de wa, kono yooshi ni kakikonde, inkan o oshite kudasai.**

Customer:	Is this alright?	**Kore de ii desu ka.**

certificate	**shoosho,**	証書

Clerk:	That's fine. Please wait a second. This is your certificate. Please come again.	**Kekkoo desu. Shooshoo omachi kudasai. Kochira ga shoosho desu. Maido arigatoo gozaimashita.**

2 At the bank

to remit (money)	**sookin-suru,**	送金する

Customer:	I'd like to remit money to Osaka, but...	**Oosaka e sookin-shitai n desu ga...**

Clerk:	To which bank?	**Dochira no ginkoo desu ka.**

branch	**shiten,**	支店

Customer:	Your bank's Osaka branch.	**Kochira no ginkoo no Oosaka-shiten desu.**

remittee	**uketorinin,**	受取人
account number	**kooza-bangoo,**	口座番号

Clerk:	Then, please write here the remittee's address and name, and also the account number.	**De wa koko ni, uketorinin no juusho to onamae, sore ni kooza-bangoo o okaki kudasai.**

Customer:	When will it get there?	**Itsu tsuku deshoo ka.**

telegraph	**denshin,** 電信

Clerk:	If it's a telegraphic (transfer), it will get there sometime tomorrow.	**Denshin deshitara, ashita-juu ni tsukimasu.**

Customer:	Then, please send it that way.	**Jaa, sore de onegai-shimasu.**

3 At the office

to withdraw	**hikidasu,** 引き出す

A:	Please go to the bank and withdraw 150 thousand yen.	**Ginkoo e itte, juugo-man-en hikidashite kite kudasai.**

ten thousand yen note	**ichi-man-en-satsu,** 一万円札

B:	Would everything in ten thousand yen notes be alright?	**Zenbu ichi-man-en-satsu de ii desu ka.**

one thousand yen note	**sen-en-satsu,** 千円札
100 yen coin	**hyaku-en-kooka,** 百円硬貨
100 yen coin	**hyaku-en-dama,** 百円玉

A:	Please have 100 thousand yen in 10 thousand yen notes, 40 thousand yen in one thousand yen notes, and 10 thousand yen in 100 yen coins.	**Juu-man-en wa ichi-man-en-satsu de, yon-man-en wa sen-en-satsu de, ichi-man-en wa hyaku-en-kooka de onegai-shimasu.**

bankbook	**tsuuchoo,** 通帳

B:	Where is the bankbook?	**Tsuuchoo wa doko ni arimasu ka.**

A:	It's right here.	**Koko ni arimasu.**

B:	Then, I'll be going.	**Jaa, itte kimasu.**

26/At the Bank

REFERENCE

kokuzee	国税	national tax
chihoozee	地方税	local tax
chokusetsuzee	直接税	direct tax
kansetsuzee	間接税	indirect tax
shotokuzee	所得税	income tax
hoojinzee	法人税	corporate tax
buppinzee	物品税	commodity tax
kanzee	関税	custom duty
hukakachizee	付加価値税	value added tax

NOTES

1 koto ga aru

A phrase ended with a past verb +**koto ga aru** is used to describe one's past experience and means '(someone) has done such-and-such before' or '(something) has happened before.'

The negative ... **koto wa** (or **ga**) **nai** means '(someone) has never done such-and-such.' Thus,

> **Amerika e itta** *koto ga arimasu.*
> "I've been to America."

> **Amerika e itta** *koto wa arimasen.*
> "I've never been to America."

This combination is often used in asking about others' past experience.

> **Amerika e itta** *koto ga arimasu* **ka.**
> "Have you ever been to America?"

Examples:
  a) **Nihongo o benkyoo-shita** *koto ga arimasu* **ka.**
     "Have you ever studied Japanese?"

  b) **En-date no torihiki o shita** *koto wa arimasen.*
     "We have never done transactions based on yen."

  c) **Kumitate-sagyoo no jidooka o kenkyuu-shita** *koto ga arimasu.*
     "We have studied the automation of assembling operations."

When this combination is preceded by a past negative verb, it may be translated as '(someone) has occasionally NOT done such-and-such.' The implied meaning in such sentences is that (someone) usually does such-and-such. Thus,

> **Shigoto ga isogashikute, hiru-gohan o tabe***nakatta koto ga arimasu.*
> "Being busy with my work, I have occasionally skipped [lit. not eaten] lunch."

When **koto wa nai** is preceded by a past negative verb, the combination may be translated as '(someone) has **never not** done so-and-so', that is, '(someone) always has done such-and-such,' Thus,

> **Hiru-gohan o tabe*nakatta koto wa arimasen*.**
> "I have always eaten lunch [lit. I have never not eaten lunch]."

2 Answering negative questions: Use of **hai/ee/iie**

As mentioned in *BUSINESS JAPANESE*, Lesson 9 (Note **4**), use of **hai/ee** 'yes' and **iie** 'no' differs from the English 'yes' and 'no.' When one answers affirmative questions in Japanese, one can use **hai/ee/iie** in the same way one uses the English 'yes/no.' However, in answer to negative questions, if one wishes to confirm the negative, one uses **hai/ee**, "you are right." If one wishes to deny the negative, one uses **iie**, "you are wrong." Thus,

> **Kinoo jimusho e ikimasen deshita ka.**
> "Didn't you go to the office yesterday?"
>
> *Ee*, **ikimasen deshita.**
> "You're right. I didn't go [lit. Yes, I didn't go]."
>
> *Iie*, **ikimashita.**
> "You're wrong. I did go [lit. No, I did go]."

In other word, **hai/ee** confirms a statement, whether affirmative or negative, and **iie** denies a statement, whether affirmative or negative. In contrast, the English 'yes' is used only in the affirmative, and the English 'no' is used only in the negative.

3 Verb stem + **nareru**

A compound verb consisting of a verb stem +**nareru** means 'to be used to doing such-and-such.' Thus,

> **Waapuro wa Yamada-san ga atsukai*narete* imasu.**
> "Ms. Yamada is skilled in handling the word processor
> [lit. As for the word processor, Ms. Yamada is used to operating it]."
>
> **Yomi*nareta* shinbun ga ichi-ban ii desu.**
> "The newspaper that I am used to reading is the best (for me)."
>
> **Are wa kiki*narenai* ongaku desu nee.**
> "That's unfamiliar music, isn't it?"

PRACTICE

1 Communication Practice

Directions: Using the following patterns, inform your teacher about your bank(s).

Patterns: a) **Watakushi no kaisha wa** (bank) **no** (branch) **to torihiki ga arimasu.**

b) **Sono ginkoo ni wa** (types of accounts) **no kooza ga arimasu.**

c) **Watakushi no kaisha wa kogitte o** (purpose) **nado ni tsukaimasu.**

d) **Watakushi kojin no kooza wa** (bank) **no** (branch) **ni arimasu.**

26/At the Bank

Examples:
    a) **Watakushi no kaisha wa (Huji-ginkoo) no (Shinbashi-shiten) to torihiki ga arimasu.**

    b) **Sono ginkoo ni wa (hutsuu-yokin to tooza-yokin) no kooza ga arimasu.**

    c) **Watakushi no kaisha wa kogitte o (torihikisaki e no shiharai) nado ni tsukaimasu.**

    d) **Watakushi kojin no kooza wa (Mitsubishi-ginkoo) no (Shibuya-shiten) ni arimasu.**

2 Response Practice

Directions: Answer the questions following cues provided by the teacher.

Example: Teacher: **Kyoo kaisha e ikimasen ka.** /ee/
"Aren't you going to the company today?"/you're right/

Student: **Ee, ikimasen.**
"You're right, I'm not going." or "No, I'm not going."

a)	**Tanaka-san wa Jetoro no shokuin dewa arimasen ka.** /iie/	**Iie, Jetoro no shokuin desu.**
b)	**Joonzu-san wa rainichi-shimasen ka.** /iie/	**Iie, rainichi-shimasu.**
c)	**Ano ginkoo to torihiki wa arimasen ka.** /ee/	**Ee, torihiki wa arimasen.**
d)	**Shain no kyuuryoo wa ginkoo-hurikomi ja arimasen ka.** /iie/	**Iie, ginkoo-hurikomi desu.**
e)	**Mada Nihon no ginkoo ni kooza o hira-kimasen ka.** /ee/	**Ee, mada hirakimasen.**

3 Response Practice

Example: Teacher: **Mada Nihon no ginkoo to torihiki-shimasen ka.**
"Don't you have an account yet with a Japanese bank?"

Student: **Iie, torihiki-shita koto ga arimasu.**
"You're wrong. I have made deposits before."

a)	**Mada shingata no robotto o mimasen ka.**	**Iie, mitakoto ga arimasu.**
b)	**Mada Keedanren no Kawamoto-san ni aimasen ka.**	**Iie, atta koto ga arimasu.**
c)	**Mada Nihon no ongaku o kiiteimasen ka.**	**Iie, kiita koto ga arimasu.**
d)	**Mada Ooyama-san ni shiryoo o misete-imasen ka.**	**Iie, miseta koto ga arimasu.**

4 Transformation Practice

Example: Teacher: **Kyooto e ikimashita ka.**
              "Did you go to Kyoto?"

              Student: **Kyooto e itta koto ga arimasu ka.**
              "Have you ever been to Kyoto?"

a)   **Kenkyuu-shimashita ka.**   **Kenkyuu-shita koto ga arimasu ka.**

b)   **Shachoo to soodan-shimashita ka.**   **Shachoo to soodan-shita koto ga arimasu ka.**

c)   **Juugyooin o rei-ohu-shimashita ka.**   **Juugyooin o rei-ohu-shita koto ga arimasu ka.**

d)   **Nihon no ginkoo ni okane o azukemashita ka.**   **Nihon no ginkoo ni okane o azuketa koto ga arimasu ka.**

e)   **Ano koosaku-kikai o tsukaimashita ka.**   **Ano koosaku-kikai o tsukatta koto ga arimasuka.**

5 Transformation Practice

Example: Teacher: **Kogitte wa yoku tsukaimasu.**
              "I often use checks."

              Student: **Kogitte wa tsukainarete imasu.**
              "I am accustomed to using checks."

a)   **Osushi wa yoku tabemasu.**   **Osushi wa tabenarete imasu.**

b)   **Konna tegami wa yoku kakimasu.**   **Konna tegami wa kakinarete imasu.**

c)   **Kono kikai wa yoku atsukaimasu.**   **Kono kikai wa atsukainarete imasu.**

d)   **Sono shinbun wa yoku yomimasu.**   **Sono shinbun wa yominarete imasu.**

e)   **Robotto ni tsuite yoku setsumee-shimasu.**   **Robotto ni tsuite setsumee-shinarete imasu.**

6 Comprehension Practice

Directions: The teacher reads aloud the following passage and then asks the student questions about it.

Pii-ando-shii wa ima made Banku-obu-Amerika to shika torihiki ga arimasen deshita ga, Banku-obu-Amerika wa Marunouchi ni aru no de, jimusho kara tooku, huben deshita. Desu kara, Buraun-san wa kyoo jimusho no chikaku ni aru Nihon no ginkoo e itte, kooza no koto o iroiro soodan-shimashita. Buraun-san wa hutsuu-yokin no kooza to tooza-yokin no kooza o hiraku tsumori deshita. Shikashi, hutsuu-yokin no kooza wa sugu hirakemasu ga, tooza no hoo wa iroiro na shorui ga iru soo desu. Buraun-san wa chikai uchi ni moo ichi-do kessan-hookokusho ya hoojinzee no uketori o motte, sono ginkoo e iku koto ni shimashita.

26/At the Bank

Questions:

1 Buraun-san wa doo shite Nihon no ginkoo e ikimashita ka.
2 Pii-ando-shii wa ima made ginkoo to torihiki ga arimasen deshita ka.
3 Buraun-san wa doo shite Nihon no ginkoo ni kooza o hirakitai n desu ka.
4 Donna kooza o hiraku tsumori desu ka.
5 Kooza wa sugu tsukutte kuremashita ka.
6 Tooza-yokin no kooza o hiraku tame ni, nani ga irimasu ka.
7 Buraun-san wa itsu moo ichi-do sono ginkoo e ikimasu ka.

EXERCISES

Inform the teacher in Japanese that:

1 Mr. Tanaka's company has deposits in Fuji Bank's Shinjuku Branch and Mitsui Bank's Ginza Branch.
2 General Manager Ohyama wants to examine the financial status of P & C, Ltd.
3 Mr. Brown told the clerk at the bank that he cannot show him P & C's statement of accounts.
4 Mr. Jones has never explained the economical efficiency of his company's new NC machine tool to Japanese businessmen.
5 For payment of employees' salaries, the bank transfer system is more convenient than checks.
6 In Japan the interest (rate) on time deposits is less than 5.5%.
7 When you send money, you need to write the recipient's name, address and account number.
8 Mr. Brown said that the Japanese corporate tax is not so expensive.

Model Answers:

1 Tanaka-san no kaisha wa Huji-ginkoo Shinjuku-shiten to Mitsui-ginkoo Ginza shiten ni yokin ga arimasu. (or to torihiki ga arimasu.)
2 Ooyama-buchoo wa Pii-ando-shii no kee'ee-jootai o kentoo-shitai n desu.
3 Buraun-san wa ginkooin ni Pii-ando-shii no kessan-hookokusho wa miserarenai to iimashita.
4 Joonzu-san wa shingata no enu-shii koosakuki no nooritsu ni tsuite Nihonjin no bijinesuman ni setsumee-shita koto wa arimasen.
5 Juugyooin no kyuuryoo no shiharai to shite, ginkoo-hurikomi wa kogitte yori benri desu.
6 Nihon de wa, teeki-yokin no rishi wa goo-ten-go paasento ika desu.
7 Sookin-suru toki, uketorinin no namae to juusho to kooza-bangoo o kaku hitsuyoo ga arimasu.
8 Buraun-san wa Nihon no hoojinzee wa amari takaku nai to iimashita.

BUSINESS INFORMATION

Checks and Savings

The retail services provided by banks in Japan are much like those offered elsewhere around the world, e.g. savings and current accounts, electronic cash transfer, automatic remittances to utilities and other companies, foreign exchange, etc. There are several important differences, however, which are outlined below for your reference.

1 Checking Accounts: Checks are not all that common in Japan. Opening a current checking account for your firm, therefore, can be a nuisance both for yourself and the bank. You will normally be requested to submit your company's Japanese registration (商業登記簿謄本, **shoogyoo-tookibo-toohon**) and verification of your company seal (印鑑証明 , **inkan-shoomee**) as identification. You will also need to leave a deposit in a fixed account. At times you may be asked to provide detailed information about financial standing, as Mr. Brown is in the DIALOGUE, just to give the bank a more rounded picture of your company. Armed with all this supplementary material, the bank then takes anywhere from two weeks to a month to reach its decision as to whether or not to open your current checking account.

Personal checking accounts are equally complicated. Not only do you have to submit verification of your seal and open a fixed account, but the bank occasionally requires a certificate of employment (在職証明 , **zaishoku-shoomee**), proof of residential address (住民票, **juuminhyoo**), as well as your personal income tax statement (確定申告書 , **kakutee-shinkoku-sho**) as back-up information. Occasionally, you will also be asked for a reference from an established customer of the bank, even though such an introduction does not guarantee establishment of your account. Note too that a check made out to you by a friend or associate abroad can take several days to process since the domestic bank usually confirms the issuer's financial status with the bank on which the check is drawn. Moreover, by the time the check has been approved and all the various handling charges taken care of, you may find the original payment whittled down to a pocketful of small change.

These thorough and time-consuming investigations are intended to protect not only the public but the bank's reputation because checks left unhonored in Japan are thought to reflect as poorly on the institutions that processed them as on the issuers themselves. All in all, it is probably best to avoid using checks in your daily personal transactions. Japan is still very much a cash-based society, after all, and you may find that, assuming you do set up your account, it is even more difficult to get your hard-won checks accepted than it was to open that account in the first place.

2 Banking "Through The Mail": In Japan, the humble neighborhood post-office is often favored over sophisticated financial institutions for savings and other routine banking services. This postal savings system, or **yuubin chokin** (郵便貯金), was established in 1875 to encourage nation-wide thriftiness and savings, and was an important step in the Meiji Administration's campaign to catch up with the West. The post-office was the only institution in Japan at the time with a network extensive enough to serve the purpose; and it is perhaps precisely because of these many, far-flung "branches" that the Post has retained its popularity as a retail banking outlet to this day. Travellers in more remote areas in Japan especially welcome the **yuubin chokin** system as it is of course far more convenient to deposit or retrieve cash from the local post-office than to trek from one town to the next in search of a branch of their own bank.

Services offered by post-offices include ordinary savings, installment savings, fixed amount savings, fixed-term savings, utilities payments, etc. Occasionally, postal savings accounts offer higher interest rates and tax benefits. Indeed, since you can also take care of cash deliveries (現金書留 , **genkin kakitome**) at the post-office, it really functions as an ultra-convenient one-stop banking center. Moreover, post-offices require practically no "background information" from their depositors. Anyone can stroll up to his post-office counter and open a **yuubin chokin** account as long as he has a **hanko** (判こ , personal seal) or can sign his own name although, as of January 1, 1986, he will be required for his own protection to submit one other form of personal identification. Perhaps the only draw-backs to banking at the Post are that the harried clerks may not provide the same smiling service you receive at big city banks and may not be accustomed to serving foreigners. And for those of us who regularly replenish our household provisions by going to the bank, it may be useful to know that they also are not as generous with their complimentary tissue paper, aluminum foil and towels.

Lesson 27

A Price Reduction

OBJECTIVES

1   to discuss a discount in the price.

2   to pass on information learned from another source.

3   to express one's intention.

TARGET EXPRESSIONS AND PATTERNS

1	When (Whenever, If) ...	**... (suru) to**
2	According to ...	**... ni yoru to**
3	I'm thinking of doing ...	**... (shiyoo) to omou.**

SITUATION

Mr. Brown receives a phone call from Mr. Ohyama saying that there are some details to be discussed, and visits Nissan shortly thereafter.

27/A Price Reduction

DIALOGUE

	suddenly	**kyuu ni,** 急に
Ohyama	thank you very much	**kyooshuku (-suru),** 恐縮（する）

1 Thank you for taking the trouble to come today [lit. We apologize for calling you suddenly when you were busy]. — **Kyoo wa oisogashii tokoro o kyuu ni oyobi-shite, kyooshuku desu.**

	before long	**kinkin,** 近々
Brown	to call on	**otazune-suru** (polite), お尋ねする

2 Not at all. I was thinking of calling on you one of these days too. — **Doo itashimashite. Watakushi mo kin-kin ichi-do otazune-shiyoo to omotte orimashita.**

Ohyama

3 To tell the truth, (I) thought (I) would discuss once again the estimate (we) got the other day, and ... — **Jitsu wa senjitsu no mitsumori ni tsuite moo ichi-do soodan-shitai to omoimashite ...**

Brown	what (is it)?	**doo iu koto,** どういうこと

4 (Yes,) what is it? — **Doo iu koto deshoo ka.**

	according to ...	**... ni yoru to,** によると
	5.5% discount	**goo-ten-go-paasento-biki,** 5.5パーセント引き
	to increase	**huyasu,** 増やす
	rate	**ritsu,** 率
Ohyama	discount rate	**nebiki-ritsu,** 値引き率

5 According to the estimate, for 10 units, there would be a 5.5 percent discount, but if the order were to increase to 20 units, what would the discount rate be? — **Mitsumori ni yoru to, juu-dai de wa goo-ten-go-paasento-biki da soo desu ga, chuumon o nijuu-dai ni huyasu to, nebiki-ritsu wa doo narimasu ka.**

Brown

6 Does that mean (you) will be ordering 20 units at the same time? — **Nijuu-dai ichi-do ni gochuumon-nasaru wake desu ka.**

| | number of units | **daisuu,** 台数 |
| **Ohyama** | to be decided | **kimaru,** 決まる |

| **7** | The size of the order is not yet decided, but (we) would like to know the estimate for 20 units too, so … | **Chuumon daisuu wa mada kimatte imasen ga, nijuu-dai-bun no mitsumori mo shitte okitai no de …** |

| **Brown** | when, if | **to,** と |

| **8** | If it is for 20 units, (we) can give you up to a six percent discount, but … | **Nijuu-dai desu to, roku-paasento made nebiki-dekimasu ga …** |

	can do something	**doo ni ka naru,** どうにかなる
	for …	**… to shite mo,** としても
	facilities	**shisetsu,** 施設
	remodeling	**kaizoo (-suru),** 改造(する)
Ohyama	to expand	**kasamu,** かさむ

| **9** | Can't you do a little better? For our company, if (we) install these, (we) would run up various expenses such as for remodeling our facilities. | **Moo sukoshi doo ni ka narimasen ka. Wagasha to shite mo, kore o doonyuu-suru to, shisetsu no kaizoo nado iroiro hiyoo ga kasamimasu kara …** |

| | at most | **girigiri,** ぎりぎり |
| **Brown** | line, limit (in this case) | **sen,** 線 |

| **10** | Then, how would 6.2 percent be? This is our (utmost) limit, but … | **De wa roku-ten-ni-paasento de wa ikaga deshoo ka. Kore ga girigiri no sen desu ga …** |

| **Ohyama** | to expect | **kitai-suru,** 期待する |

| **11** | We are expecting about 7 percent, but … | **Watakushidomo wa nana-paasento gurai o kitai-shite imasu ga …** |

| **Brown** | to check, inquire | **toiawaseru,** 問い合わせる |

| **12** | For a discount larger than this, I cannot answer without checking with the head office, so … | **Kore ijoo no nebiki wa honsha ni toiawasemasen to, okotae-dekimasen no de …** |

27/A Price Reduction

Ohyama

13	Then, please do so. After (we) receive that reply, we will examine this further.	De wa onegai-shimasu. Sono ohenji o itadaite kara, mata kentoo-itashimasu.

Brown   with this, now   **kore de,** これで

14	Is that so? Then if you would excuse me... [impl. (for today) I'm going to leave now.]	Soo desu ka. De wa kyoo wa kore de shitsuree-shimasu.

Ohyama

15	Then, (I) hope to hear from you soon.	Jaa, yoroshiku onegai-shimasu.

JAPANESE WRITING

1　大　山：今日は お忙しいところを 急にお呼びして、恐縮です。
2　ブラウン：どういたしまして。 私も 近々一度お訪ねしようと 思っておりました。
3　大　山：実は 先日の見積りについて もう一度相談したいと 思いまして…
4　ブラウン：どういうことでしょうか。
5　大　山：見積りによると、10台では 5.5パーセント引きだそうですが、注文を20台に増やすと、値引き率は どうなりますか。
6　ブラウン：20台一度に ご注文なさるわけですか。
7　大　山：注文台数は まだ決まっていませんが、20台分の見積りも 知っておきたいので…
8　ブラウン：20台ですと、6パーセントまで値引きできますが…
9　大　山：もう少しどうにかなりませんか。 我社としても、これを導入すると、施設の改造など いろいろ費用がかさみますから…
10　ブラウン：では 6.2パーセントでは いかがでしょうか。これが ぎりぎりの線ですが…
11　大　山：私共は 7パーセントぐらいを 期待していますが…
12　ブラウン：これ以上の値引きは 本社に問い合わせませんと、お答えできませんので…
13　大　山：では お願いします。 そのお返事をいただいてから、また検討いたします。
14　ブラウン：そうですか。 では 今日は これで失礼します。
15　大　山：じゃあ、 よろしくお願いします。

ADDITIONAL USEFUL EXPRESSIONS

1 At the office

| | sale | hanbai (-suru), 販売(する) |

| A: | Are the sales for that product going well? | Ano seihin no hanbai wa umaku itte i-masu ka. |

| | very much | zuibun, ずいぶん |

| B: | To tell the truth, there was a little problem, and I don't know what to do [lit. I'm troubled]. On our side, we're putting in a lot of effort, but ... | Jitsu wa chotto mondai ga atte, komatte iru n desu. Wagasha to shite wa zuibun chikara o irete iru n desu ga ... |

| | does that mean? | to iu to, と言うと |
| | to decrease | heru, 減る |

| A: | Does that mean your sales are de-creasing? | To iu to, uriage ga hette iru n desu ka. |

	returns	henpin (-suru), 返品(する)
	purchase	koonyuu (-suru), 購入(する)
	cancellation	torikeshi, 取消

| B: | No, sales are increasing, but recent-ly, there are lots of returns and order cancellations. | Iie, uriage wa huete imasu ga, saikin henpin ya koonyuu no torikeshi ga ooi n desu. |

| | cause | gen'in, 原因 |

| A: | That is a problem. And have you figured out the cause? | Sore wa mondai desu ne. Gen'in ga wakarimashita ka. |

| B: | No, right now, we are investigating, but we don't know yet. | Iie, ima, choosa-chuu desu ga, mada wakarimasen. |

2 At the office

| A: | How did those negotiations go? | Ano shoodan wa doo narimashita ka. |

	to decide	kimeru, 決める

B:	We're still discussing [lit. not deciding] the discount rate.	**Mada nebikiritsu o kimete imasen.**

	firm stand, tough	tsuyoki/na/, 強気（な）

A:	Is that so? That company is tough, so those talks must be very difficult.	**Soo desu ka. Ano kaisha wa tsuyoki da kara, kooshoo mo taihen deshoo.**

B:	Yes, they say they want a 35 percent discount.	**San-wari-go-bu no nebiki o shite moraitai to itte imasu.**

	profit	mooke, もうけ
	to vanish	nakunaru, なくなる

A:	That is outrageous. That means our company will have no profit.	**Sore wa hidoi desu nee. Sore jaa, wagasha no mooke wa nakunarimasu yo.**

B:	Therefore, it will take much time.	**Desu kara, mada jikan ga kakarimasu.**

NOTES

1 To clause

The particle **to** following phrases that end with non-past verb, adjective or copula is used to mean 'when', 'whenever' or 'if'.

Examples:
a) **Kesa shinbun o miru *to*, anata no koto ga kaite arimashita.**
"When I read the newspaper this morning, there was something written about you."

b) **Huyu ni naru *to*, kono hen wa mainichi yuki ga hurimasu.**
"When winter comes, it snows in this area everyday."

c) **Joonzu-san ga rainichi-suru *to*, Buraun-san ga paatii o shimasu.**
"Whenever Mr. Jones comes to Japan, Mr. Brown gives a party (for him)."

d) **Robotto o doonyuu-suru koto ni suru *to*, kumiai ga hantai-suru deshoo.**
"If we decide to introduce robots, the labor union will probably oppose (it)."

e) **Buchoo ga sansee-shinai *to*, chuumon wa dekimasen.**
"Unless the General Manager agrees, we cannot order (it)."

Note: When this **to** clause is used in the conditional mood, as in Examples **d)** and **e)** above, the following sentence or phrase is always in the 'non-past' tense.

2 Informal Tentative Verb + **to omou**

A tentative verb is translated as 'let's do such-and-such' or 'I guess I'll do such-and-such' [Compare: the formal tentative consisting of a verb stem + **mashoo**, *BUSINESS JAPANESE*, Lesson 7].
To form the informal tentative:

A)   Class 1 verb (or **-ru** verb): Substitute **-yoo** for final **-ru**.

Example: **taberu** 'to eat' — **tabe*yoo*** 'let's eat, I guess I'll eat'

B)   Class 2 verb (or **-u** verb): Substitute **-oo** for final **-u**.

Example: **hanasu** 'to speak' — **hanas*oo*** 'let's speak, I guess I'll speak'

C)   Irregular verbs:

Examples: **kuru** 'to come' — ***koyoo*** 'let's come, I guess I'll come'
suru 'to do' — ***shiyoo*** 'let's do, I guess I'll do'

An informal verb tentative + **to omou** is used to express the speaker's intention and means 'to think I'll (do such-and-such), to think of (doing such-and-such).'

Examples: **a)** **Kono kikai o ka*oo* to omoimasu.**
"I think I'll buy this machine."

b) **Kogitte no kooza o tsukur*oo* to omoimashita ga ...**
"I was thinking of opening a checking account, but ..."

c) **Nebiki-shi*yoo* to wa omoimasen.**
"I don't think I'll offer any discount."

On the other hand, the **tai** form of a verb + **to omou** indicates the speaker's desire and means '(I think) I would like to do such-and-such, I hope I'll do such-and-such.'

Uriage o motto huyashi*tai* to omoimasu.
"I hope we will increase the sales."

Note: **-tai** + **to omou** is a more polite and indirect expression than **-tai n desu.**

3 ...ni yoru to

In order to indicate a source of information, the name of the source plus **ni yoru to** may be used. Its English equivalent is 'according to ...' This combination often occurs with **soo da** 'it is said ..., they say ...' [Refer to *BUSINESS JAPANESE*, Lesson 19, Note **6**].

Examples: **a)** **Takada-san *ni yoru to*, Joonzu-san wa raishuu kikoku-suru *soo desu*.**
"According to Mr. Takada, Mr. Jones will be going home next week."

    b) **Shachoo no hanashi *ni yoru to*, wagasha no keeki wa yoku nai *soo desu*.**
       "According to what the president said, our company's situation is not good [lit. According to the president's story …]."

    c) **Kesa no shinbun *ni yoru to*, Tanaka-san no kaisha wa zooshi-suru *soo desu*.**
       "According to this morning's newspaper, Mr. Tanaka's company will increase its capital."

This combination **… ni yoru to** sometimes occurs with **… koto ni natte iru** 'it has been decided that ….' Thus,

    Keeyaku *ni yoru to*, konshuu-chuu ni noohin-suru *koto ni natte imasu*.
    "According to the contract, it has been decided (the goods) will be delivered sometime this week."

4 Tokoro

Tokoro literally means 'place', but it can sometimes also mean 'occasion' or 'time.' Thus,

    Oisogashii *tokoro* o oyobi-shimashite, shitsuree-shimashita.
    "I'm sorry. I called you at such a busy time."
    Tanaka-san ga tegami o kaite iru *tokoro* o mimashita.
    "I saw Mr. Tanaka just as he was writing a letter [lit. … at the time he was writing a letter]."

PRACTICE

1 Communication Practice

Directions: Give the teacher the following information, using the pattern, **… ni yoru to, … soo da** "According to so-and-so/such-and-such, it is said…"

Example: Teacher: **Yamada-san wa wain ga ichi-ban suki da to iimashita.**
             "Ms. Yamada said she likes wine best."

           Student: **Yamada-san ni yoru to, wain ga ichi-ban suki da soo desu.**
             "According to Ms. Yamada, she likes wine best."

a) **Buraun-san wa Joonzu-san wa seerusu-enjinia da to iimashita.**
b) **Ooyama-san wa shisetsu no kaizoo ni wa hiyoo ga kasamu to iimashita.**
c) **Kesa no rajio wa keeki wa yoku naranai to iimashita.**
d) **Shachoo wa kotoshi wa robotto o doonyuu-shinai to iimashita.**
e) **Kawamoto-san wa Pii-ando-shii wa ii kaisha da to iimashita.**

2 Transformation Practice

Example: Teacher: **Ame ga hurimasu. Sono sagyoo wa dekimasen.**
             "It's going to rain. We can't conduct those operations."

           Student: **Ame ga huru to, sono sagyoo wa dekimasen.**
             "If it rains, we can't conduct those operations."

a) Robotto o doonyuu-shimasu.
   Rei-ohu o okonau deshoo.

   Robotto o doonyuu-suru to, rei-ohu o okonau deshoo.

b) Chuumon o huyashimasu.
   Nebiki-ritsu ga yoku narimasu.

   Chuumon o huyasu to, nebiki-ritsu ga yoku narimasu.

c) Seesan-shisetsu o kaizoo-shimasu.
   Hiyoo ga kasamimasu.

   Seesan-shisetsu o kaizoo-suru to, hiyoo ga kasamimasu.

d) Kono hon o yomimasu.
   Nihon no kaisha no koto ga yoku waka-rimasu.

   Kono hon o yomu to, Nihon no kaisha no koto ga yoku wakarimasu.

3 Transformation Practice

Example: Teacher: **Joonzu-san ga Nihon e kimasu. Issho ni Kyooto e ikimasu.**
"Mr. Jones comes to Japan. We go to Kyoto together."

Student: **Joonzu-san ga Nihon e kuru to, issho ni Kyooto e ikimasu.**
"When(ever) Mr. Jones comes to Japan, we go to Kyoto together."

a) Kyuuryoo o moraimasu.
   Ginkoo ni azukemasu.

   Kyuuryoo o morau to, ginkoo ni azukemasu.

b) Aki ni narimasu.
   Suzushiku narimasu.

   Aki ni naru to, suzushiku narimasu.

c) Shachoo ga rainichi-shimasu.
   Narita e mukae ni ikimasu.

   Shachoo ga rainichi-suru to, Narita e mukae ni ikimasu.

d) Kore ijoo uriage ga huemasu.
   Kee'ee-jootai ga yoku narimasu.

   Kore ijoo uriage ga hueru to, kee'ee-jootai ga yoku narimasu.

e) Kaisha no mono o kaimasu.
   Uketori o moraimasu.

   Kaisha no mono o kau to, uketori o moraimasu.

4 Transformation Practice

Example: Teacher: **Honsha ni toiawasemasen. Nebiki-dekimasen.**
"We don't check with the main office. We can't discount."

Student: **Honsha ni toiawasenai to, nebiki-dekimasen.**
"If we don't check with the main office, we can't discount."

a) Shachoo ga kimasen.
   Kaigi wa hajimeraremasen.

   Shachoo ga konai to, kaigi wa hajime-raremasen.

b) Tenki ga yoku narimasen.
   Kyooto-kenbutsu wa dekimasen.

   Tenki ga yoku naranai to, Kyooto-kenbutsu wa dekimasen.

c) Buchoo ga sansee-shimasen.
   Keeyaku wa muzukashii desu.

   Buchoo ga sansee-shinai to, keeyaku wa muzukashii desu.

d) Uriage ga huemasen.
   Boonasu mo huemasen.

   Uriage ga huenai to, boonasu mo huemasen.

e) Noohin ga maniaimasen.
   Tsugi no keeyaku wa shimasen.

   Noohin ga maniawanai to, tsugi no keeyaku wa shimasen.

27/A Price Reduction

5 Response Practice:

Example: Teacher: **Kyoo ginkoo e ikimasu ka.**
      "Will you go to the bank today?"

     Student: **Ee, ikoo to omotte imasu.**
      "Yes, I'm thinking of going."

a)	Honsha ni toiawasemasu ka.	Ee, toiawaseyoo to omotte imasu.
b)	Chuumon o huyashimasu ka.	Ee, huyasoo to omotte imasu.
c)	Kono mitsumori o kentoo-shimasu ka.	Ee, kentoo-shiyoo to omotte imasu.
d)	Kotoshi zooshi-shimasu ka.	Ee, zooshi-shiyoo to omotte imasu.
e)	Doru de shiharaimasu ka.	Ee, doru de shiharaoo to omotte imasu.
f)	Kono shiryoo o yomimasu ka.	Ee, yomoo to omotte imasu.
g)	Ano hito o yatoimasu ka.	Ee, yatooo to omotte imasu.
h)	Tanaka-san ni denwa o kakemasu ka.	Ee, kakeyoo to omotte imasu.

6 Comprehension Practice

Directions: The teacher reads aloud the following passage and then asks the student questions about it.

Nissan no Ooyama-buchoo wa senjitsu no mitsumori ni tsuite moo ichi-do soodan-shitai no de, Buraun-san ni denwa o kakete, yobimashita. Senjitsu no mitsumori ni yoru to, robotto o 10-dai chuumon-suru to, nebiki wa 5.5 paasento ni naru soo desu ga, Ooyama-san wa motto nebiki-shite moraitai to omotte imasu. Buraun-san ni yoru to, 20-dai chuumon-shite mo, nebiki-ritsu wa 6.2 paasento da soo desu ga, Ooyama-san wa 7 paasento gurai o kitai-shite imasu. Shikashi, sonna ookii nebiki wa Buraun-san ga kimeru koto wa dekimasen kara, honsha ni toiawaseru koto ni shimashita. Ooyama-buchoo wa sono henji o kiite kara, mata kentoo-suru to iimashita.

Questions:

1 Ooyama-buchoo wa dare ni denwa o kakemashita ka.
2 Doo shite, sono hito o yobimashita ka.
3 Robotto 10-dai no baai, nebiki-ritsu wa nan-paasento desu ka.
4 20-dai no baai, nebiki-ritsu wa doo narimasu ka.
5 Ooyama-buchoo wa nan-paasento gurai o kitai-shite imasu ka.
6 Buraun-san wa doo kotaemashita ka.
7 Buraun-san wa nan ni tsuite honsha ni toiawasemasu ka.

27/A Price Reduction

EXERCISES

a) Complete the sentences, using the following patterns:

1 Kyoo watakushi wa (place) **e ikoo to omotte imasu.**
2 (Name of bank) **ni kooza o hirakoo to omotte imasu.**
3 Konshuu-chuu ni (article) **o kaoo to omotte imasu.**
4 Konban (food) **o tabeyoo to omotte imasu.**
5 Ashita (name of person) **ni aoo to omotte imasu.**
6 Wagasha mo (machine) **o doonyuu-shiyoo to omotte imasu.**

b) Inform the teacher in Japanese that:

1 President Smith is thinking of visiting Nissan soon.
2 Unless P&C, Ltd. gives a larger discount, Mr. Ohyama will probably not make a contract (with P&C, Ltd.).
3 According to Mr. Brown, a 6.2% discount is the utmost limit.
4 If the delivery of goods is late, our policy is that we will not buy them [lit. It has been decided not to buy them].
5 In the case of this transaction, P & C's profit was very small.
6 According to today's newspaper, sales of cars will increase this year.

Model Answers:

b)
1 Sumisu-shachoo wa chikaku Nissan ni/e ikoo to omotte imasu.
2 Pii-ando-shii ga motto nebiki-shinai to, Ooyama-san wa keeyaku-shinai deshoo.
3 Buraun-san ni yoru to, 6.2 paasento no nebiki wa girigiri no sen da soo desu.
4 Noohin ga okureru to, koonyuu-shinai (or kawanai) koto ni natte imasu.
5 Kono torihiki no baai, Pii-ando-shii no mooke wa totemo sukunakatta.
6 Kyoo no shinbun ni yoru to, kotoshi wa kuruma no uriage ga hueru soo desu.

BUSINESS INFORMATION

Advanced Negotiations

For those unfamiliar with Japanese culture, negotiations with Japanese businessmen can be one very long exercise in frustration. A glimpse at what goes on behind the scenes can help explain why decisions require so much time, and perhaps also make the wait for those decisions a little less aggravating.

1 Group Decisions, or "All in Favor...": The Western businessman often chooses to go it alone in negotiations. He arrives solo at the negotiating table and moreover has full authority to make decisions there by himself on behalf of his company. As mentioned before, however, Japanese negotiators usually work in teams (*BUSINESS JAPANESE Business Information 18*). Not only do they attend meetings and collect information about the proposed business together, but they go to great lengths to ensure that the final decision for or against the proposed business is likewise taken en masse. First, the negotiating team members will hold lengthy discussions among themselves to review the various courses of action. When a tentative position emerges, the members of the team will then scatter throughout the company to find support for that position. Further in-house discussions will take place, as many different views as possible–even from "unrelated" personnel–will be pooled and the various pros and cons weighed carefully . Only when a company-wide consensus has been reached and the consensus form, or **ringisho** (稟議書), has been circulated, will the negotiating team return to the table to present this painstakingly formulated group decision to the "other side."

For all the complexity, consensus-based decision-making does have its advantages. Because everyone has been invited to participate in the decision, everyone feels personally responsible for it. Everyone will therefore also work much more enthusiastically when the time comes for its inplementation than if that decision had simply been passed down to them by their superiors as *fait accompli*. And as one foreign businessman put it, once the ball starts rolling, it rolls very, very quickly because the path before it has already been made straight and all conceivable obstacles removed long in advance.

2 The Schedule, or "As Time Goes By": Obviously, it requires much more time to arrive at a group consensus than it does to make up one mind. Experienced consultants estimate that it takes at least 5-6 times longer for business negotiations to yield a decision in Japan than in the West, and you should plan your business schedules accordingly. Of course, no businessman is expected to sit around idly while their Japanese counterparts go about their protracted consensus-gathering. If you do have to return home in the interim, you should at least keep in touch with your prospective business partners by phone or telex or mail, even if the responses to such contacts are not quick in coming, or very encouraging. You should also try not to switch players in mid-stream in spite of other pressing assignments that crop up as you wait and wait for the decision in Japan to materialize. This is because Japanese businessmen often feel that a change of face in their counterpart's negotiation team signifies a new and different direction. At the very least, they may think that the new representative could provide fresh insights or hitherto undisclosed information and that they had thus better get to know you all over again–which, of course, could send the whole negotiation right back to square one.

By now it will be obvious that, in Japan, time is of no consequence when it comes to business negotiations. The Japanese feel rather that if one truly values a relationship, one would be pleased to invest time and effort in making it as sound as possible and to thus ensure its long-term success. Consequently, it is best not to chafe at the seemingly endless delays. Simply remind yourself of how the Japanese decision-making machine operates, keep your business goals in sight and remember: "All things come round to him who will but wait." (Longfellow)

3 The Contract, or "When a deal is not a deal": Few businesses in the West are concluded without a lengthy contract spelling out the terms of the transaction in black and white. All parties are moreover expected to abide by these terms even though, of course, provisions have already been carefully inserted to protect everybody from everybody else just in case they don't. In Japan, though, contracts are not iron-clad. Most written agreements function rather as a confirmation or symbol of an existing relationship–not as a definition of the terms of that relationship. Many Japanese businessmen in fact feel that contracts can be redundant. If two parties are sincere about doing business together, there is no need to refer constantly to the written agreement since each will automatically do whatever is necessary for mutual benefit. Moreover, once the initial foundation of trust has been laid, one should not be overly concerned about minor violations such as delayed deliveries, but instead grant as much leeway to the other party as possible. You will probably find, therefore, that your Japanese associates do not always follow agreements to the letter; sometimes they even alter things substantively after the deal was supposed to have been "finalized." It is best not to point to the fine print when this happens or to threaten legal action, since this will suggest either that you lack confidence in the partnership or that you place greater emphasis on printed matter than on flesh and blood cooperation. Instead, just keep your long-range objectives in mind and remember: in Japan, a lasting relationship is worth a thousand words.

4 A Pocket Check-List for Negotiations: Do's and Don'ts
(1) **Dont't** push your negotiating counterparts for answers–they may not be able to give any on the spot. They are not always the decision-makers and may not have any idea of what the answers are or will be.
(2) **Don't** complain about decisions handed to you by the negotiating team or argue with them–the verdict isn't theirs alone. Most decisions reflect the majority view.
(3) **Don't** expect major concessions from the Japanese at the negotiating table–they do not necessarily have the authority to give them. They don't come to bargain, but to *present* a set, preordained position.
(4) **Don't** be in a hurry–things take time.
(5) **Do** leave your attorney at home.

27/A Price Reduction

Below is a sample of a **ringisho** commonly circulated for decisions about equipment purchase. Persons concerned place their seal of approval in the appropriate boxes at the bottom.

	申 請 **Shinsee**, Request No.	許 可 **Kyoka**, Approval No.
りん ぎ しょ # 稟 議 書 **RINGISHO** Consensus Form	年 月 日 **Nen Gatsu Nichi** Year Month Day	年 月 日 **Nen Gatsu Nichi** Year Month Day

下記の件ご稟議の上許可をお願いします。
Kaki no ken goringi no ue kyoka o onegai shimasu.
Your approval is kindly requested for the following matter.

件 名 (**Kenmee**, Subject) _____

_____

1. 購入物品名
   Koonyuu buppin-mee, Item for Purchase _____
2. 形式（規格）及び数量
   Keeshiki (kikaku) oyobi suuryoo, Description (Item Category); Number of Units _____
3. 料金
   Ryookin, Cost _____
4. 支払予定日
   Shiharai yotee-bi, Schedule for Payment _____
5. 支払先
   Shiharai saki, Payee _____
6. 予算措置
   Yosan sochi, Budget Plan _____
7. 経費負担部課名
   Keehi-hutan bukamee, Department to Undertake Expenses _____
8. 資料添付
   Shiryoo tenpu, Documents Attached

本社通達事項 **Honsha tsuutatsu jikoo** Additional Notes or Remarks.

所属上長 **Shozoku joochoo** Project Supervisors	場所長 **Basho-choo** Project Manager	合議先 **Googi saki** Persons to be Consulted	監理部長 **Kanri-bucho** Budget Administrator	社長 **Shachoo** President	会長 **Kaichoo** Chairman
大 60.10.22 平	鈴 60.10.21 木	福 60.10.22 田	田 60.10.23 中	三 60.10.23 木	佐 60.10.24 藤

Lesson 28

OBJECTIVES

1   to discuss the progress of business talks.

2   to discuss employment conditions.

3   to give advice.

4   to use Copula + "n desu."

TARGET EXPRESSIONS AND PATTERNS

1   You had better (do) ...   ... (shita) hoo ga ii.
2   to say something about ...   ... to ka iu
3   <X> is <Y>.   <X> wa <Y> na n desu.
4   not anything   nani mo (+ nai)

SITUATION

Mr. Brown returns to his office and tells his secretary, Ms. Yamada, about the negotiation with Nissan. After Mr. Brown's explanation, Ms. Yamada tells him that Mr. Imai wants to see him to confirm the terms of employment.

28/At the Office II

DIALOGUE

	manager of a branch	**shishachoo,** 支社長
Yamada	welcome back	**okaerinasai,** お帰りなさい

> **1** Oh, welcome back, sir [lit. Branch Office Manager].
>
> **Aa, shishachoo, okaerinasai.**

	I'm back.	**tadaima,** ただいま
Brown	not anything	**nani mo … nai,** 何も…ない

> **2** I'm back. Didn't anything happen while I was gone?
>
> **Tadaima. Rusu-chuu nani mo arimasen deshita ka.**

	to come, appear	**mieru** (polite), 見える
	to come, appear	**omie ni naru** (respectful), お見えになる
Yamada	to say something about …	**… to ka iu,** …とか言う

> **3** Mr. Takada of JETRO came and left this for you. (He) mentioned something about an invitation.
>
> **Jetoro no Takada-san ga omie ni natte, kore o shishachoo ni to osshatte imashita. Shootaijoo da to ka osshatte imashita.**

Brown	commemoration	**kinen (-suru),** 記念(する)

> **4** Thank you. (They)'re inviting me to a party to celebrate JETRO's founding [lit. foundation anniversary party].
>
> **Aa, arigatoo. Jetoro no sooritsu-kinen paatii ni shootai-shite kureta n desu yo.**

Yamada

> **5** By the way, as for Nissan, how did the talks go?
>
> **Tokoro de, Nissan no hoo wa donna ohanashi deshita ka.**

Brown	that [impl. which you know well]	**ree no,** 例の

> **6** Well, the discussion was about the discount for that robot, and they are asking if (there) could be a 7 percent discount for a 20-unit order.
>
> **Sore ga ree no robotto no nebiki no soodan datta n desu ga, nijuu-dai datta-ra, nana-paasento-biki ni naranai ka to iu hanashi deshita.**

Yamada

| 7 | Seven percent is difficult. What are you going to do? | Nana-paasento wa kibishii desu ne. Doo nasaimasu ka. |

Brown

| 8 | First of all, (I)'m thinking of consulting with the head office and having them talk it over with USM. | Mazu, honsha ni soodan-shite, Yuu-esu-emu to hanashiatte moraoo to omoimasu. |

| | to inform, notify | shiraseru, 知らせる |
| **Yamada** | (you) had better do | ... (shita) hoo ga ii, …(した)ほうがいい |

| 9 | (I) think we had better inform Mr. Jones right away also, but ... | Joonzu-san ni mo sugu shiraseta hoo ga ii to omoimasu ga ... |

| | certain | tashika/na/, 確か（な） |
| **Brown** | but | keredo, けれど |

| 10 | (I) intend to do so. The discount is certainly difficult, but it is a good opportunity to enter the Japanese market, isn't it? | Soo suru tsumori desu. Nebiki wa tashika ni kibishii keredo, Nihon no shijoo ni hairu ii kikai desu kara ne. |

Yamada

| 11 | Yes, it is. (We) certainly want to get this contract. Oh, and Mr. Imai says he'd like to speak with you, but ... | Soo desu ne. Kono keeyaku wa zehi toritai desu ne. Aa, sore kara, Imai-san ga ohanashi-shitai to itte imasu ga ... |

	employment	koyoo (-suru), 雇用(する)
	employment terms	koyoo-jooken, 雇用条件
	next month	raigetsu, 来月
Brown	official employment	honsaiyoo, 本採用

| 12 | (I) think it's about the employment terms. Mr. Imai will also be officially employed from next month, won't he? | Aa, koyoo-jooken no koto deshoo. Imai-san mo raigetsu kara honsaiyoo desu ne. |

28/At the Office II

	salary raises	**shookyuu (-suru),** 昇給（する）
Yamada	to ask, hear	**okiki-suru** (polite), お聞きする

13 Yes, therefore, (he) says (he) wants to ask (you) about such things as salary raises, overtime pay and social insurance.

Ee, desu kara, shookyuu ya zangyoo-teate, shakai-hoken nado doo naru ka okiki-shitai soo desu.

	in/after 30 minutes	**sanjup-pun shitara,** 三十分したら
	report	**hookoku (-suru),** 報告（する）
	written report	**hookoku-sho,** 報告書
	report for the head office	**honsha e no hookoku-sho,** 本社への報告書
Brown	to finish writing	**kaite shimau,** 書いてしまう

14 Then, please call (him) in 30 minutes. By then, (I)'ll have finished writing the report for the head office, so ...

Jaa, sanjuppun shitara, yonde kudasai. Sore made ni, honsha e no hookokusho o kaite shimaimasu kara ...

Yamada

15 Certainly [lit. I understand].

Kashikomarimashita.

JAPANESE WRITING

1 山　田：ああ、支社長、お帰りなさい。

2 ブラウン：ただいま。留守中 何もありませんでしたか。

3 山　田：ジェトロの高田さんが お見えになって、これを支社長にと おっしゃっていました。招待状だとか おっしゃっていました。

4 ブラウン：ああ、ありがとう。ジェトロの創立記念パーティに 招待してくれたんですよ。

5 山　田：ところで、日産の方は どんなお話でしたか。

6 ブラウン：それが例のロボットの値引きの相談だったんですが、20台だったら、7パーセント引きに ならないかという話でした。

7 山　田：7パーセントは きびしいですね。 どうなさいますか。

8 ブラウン：まず、本社に相談して、ユー・エス・エムと 話し合ってもらおうと思います。

9 山　田：ジョーンズさんにも すぐ知らせた方がいいと思いますが…

10 ブラウン：そうするつもりです。値引きは確かにきびしいけれど、日本の市場に入る いい機会ですからね。

11 山田： そうですね。この契約は ぜひ取りたいですね。ああ、それから、今井さんが お話したいと言っていますが…

12 ブラウン： ああ、雇用条件のことでしょう。今井さんも 来月から本採用ですね。

13 山田： ええ、ですから、昇給や残業手当、社会保険など どうなるか お聞きしたいそうです。

14 ブラウン： じゃあ、30分したら、呼んでください。それまでに、本社への報告書を書いてしまいますから。

15 山田： かしこまりました。

ADDITIONAL USEFUL EXPRESSIONS

1 At the office

A:	I heard you've become officially employed this time. Congratulations!	**Kondo honsaiyoo ni natta soo desu ne. Omedetoo gozaimasu.**

temporary employment	**rinji-yatoi,** 臨時雇い
unstable	**huantee/na/,** 不安定（な）

B:	Yes, because temporary employment is unstable, so …	**Ee, rinji-yatoi wa huantee desu kara …**

part-time job, side job	**arubaito,** アルバイト
vacations	**kyuuka,** 休暇
paid vacations	**yuukyuu-kyuuka,** 有給休暇

A:	That's right. There are no paid vacations or bounuses with a part-time job, so …	**Soo desu ne. Arubaito de wa, yuukyuu-kyuuka ya boonasu mo arimasen kara ne.**

such things as	**nanka,** なんか
such things as allowances	**teate nanka,** 手当なんか
duty	**gimu,** 義務

B:	Moreover, there are no such things as pension or (other) various allowances… But now (my) responsibilities [lit. duty] have increased, so the job is very difficult.	**Sore ni nenkin ya iron na teate nanka mo nai desu kara… Demo, ima wa gimu ga huete, shigoto ga taihen desu.**

28/At the Office II

| A: | That may be true, but please keep up the good work for the company and for (your) family. | Soo deshoo ga, kore kara mo kaisha ya kazoku no tame ni ganbatte kudasai. |

2 At the office

| | to take a holiday(s) | yasumi o toru, 休みを取る |

| A: | Are you going to take a holiday this summer? | Kotoshi no natsu wa yasumi o torimasu ka. |

| | to rest, to go on holiday | yasumu, 休む |

| B: | I would like to [lit. take], but I think I cannot [lit. go on holiday]. | Toritai n desu ga, yasumenai to omoimasu. |

| | to take along with | tsureru, 連れる |
| | hot spring | onsen, 温泉 |

| A: | I can take two days off, so I'll take (my) family to a hot spring. | Boku wa hutsuka yasumi ga toreta no de, kazoku o tsurete, onsen e itte kimasu. |

	(is) envious	urayamashii, うらやましい
	sea, beach	umi, 海
	mountain(s)	yama, 山

| B: | How I envy you! I also want to go with my children to the beach or mountains, but ... | Urayamashii desu ne. Boku mo kodomo to umi ka yama e ikitai n desu ga ... |

| A: | Is that right? That's too bad. | Soo desu ka. Taihen desu nee. |

REFERENCE

honkyuu	本給	regular pay
kazoku-teate	家族手当	family allowance
tsuukin-teate	通勤手当	commuting allowance
chooka-kinmu-teate	超過勤務手当	overtime [lit. extra service] allowance

kinmuchi-teate	勤務地手当	service-area allowance
kiken-teate	危険手当	occupational risk [lit. danger] allowance
gensen-chooshuu	源泉徴収	withholding [lit. at source]
shuukyuu	週給	weekly pay
nikkyuu	日給	daily pay
jikankyuu	時間給	hourly pay

NOTES

1 Informal past verb + **hoo ga ii**

The combination of an informal past verb + **hoo ga ii** is often used to give advice. Its English equivalents are 'you (or so-and-so) had better do (such-and-such)', 'it would be better/best if so-and-so did (such-and-such).'

Examples: a)   **Honsha ni toiawaseta** *hoo ga ii* **desu yo.**
"You had better check with the head office."

b)   **Shachoo ga narubeku hayaku rainichi-shita** *hoo ga ii* **to omoimasu.**
"I think the President had better come to Japan as soon as he can."

This combination may be used in a question to ask advice. Thus,

Kyoo mitsumori o todoketa *hoo ga ii* **desu ka.**
"Would it be better if I delivered the written estimate today?"

When advising against something, **hoo ga ii** is preceded by an informal non-past negative verb. Thus,

Kono koto wa Joonzu-san ni shirasenai *hoo ga ii* **desu yo.**
"It would be better not to inform Mr. Jones of this matter."

An informal non-past affirmative verb may also precede **hoo ga ii**, but this combination usually indicates a *general* principle or recommendation.

Compare: **Wakaranai toki wa sensee ni kiku** *hoo ga ii* **desu yo.**
"When you don't understand, it's best to ask the teacher."

and

Sore wa ima sugu sensee ni kiita *hoo ga ii* **desu yo.**
"You had better ask the teacher about it right now."

2 ... **to ka iu**

... **to ka iu** at the end of a sentence or clause means 'to say something to the effect that ...,' 'to say something about ...' It is used when the speaker is not confident that he/she can exactly quote what someone else has said. **To ka** may also be used with other verbs, such as **kiku** 'to hear', **kaku** 'to write', etc.

28/At the Office II

Examples: **a)** **Takada-san wa raishuu Oosaka e iku *to ka* iimashita.**
"Mr. Takada said something about going to Osaka next week."

b) **Ano kaisha wa kee'ee-jootai ga waruku natta *to ka* kikimashita.**
"I heard something to the effect that that company's financial situation has gone down [lit. became bad]."

c) **Tanaka-san no tegami ni shoodan wa umaku itte iru *to ka kaite* arimasu.**
"Mr. Tanaka's letter says [lit. In Mr. Tanaka's letter it is written] something to the effect that the business talks are going well."

The **to ka** pattern may also occur in a modifying clause.

Compare: **Yuu-esu-emu to iu kaisha**
'A company called USM (Ltd.)'

and

Yuu-esu-emu to ka iu kaisha
'A company called something like USM, (Ltd).'

3 Gerund + **shimau**

When a verb gerund is followed by the verb **shimau** 'to finish', the combination means 'to finish doing such-and-such,' 'to do such-and-such completely' or 'to end up doing such-and-such.'

Examples: **a)** **Moo ano shiryoo wa yonde *shimaimashita*.**
"I've already finished reading those materials."

b) **Mitsumori wa kinoo kaite *shimaimashita* ka.**
"Did you finish writing the estimate yesterday?"

c) **Kono shigoto o shite *shimatte* kara, hiru-gohan o tabemashoo.**
"After finishing this work completely, let's have lunch."

4 Interrogative + **mo** + /negative/

An interrogative + **mo** followed by the negative particle **nai** or a negative verb may mean, 'nothing/nobody/nowhere/none', etc. Thus,

Interrogative	mo + /negative/	Meaning
nani 'what?'	**nani** *mo* + /**nai**/	nothing, not anything
dare 'who?'	**dare** *mo* + /**nai**/	nobody, not anyone
doko 'where?'	**doko** *mo* + /**nai**/	nowhere, not any place
dore 'which?'	**dore** *mo* + /**nai**/	none (of three or more)
dochira 'which?'	**dochira** *mo* + /**nai**/	neither one

Note: **Itsu** 'when?' + **mo** may be used either with a negative, in which case it means 'never', or with an affirmative, in which case it means 'always.' Thus,

> **Ano hito wa** *itsu mo* **yoku benkyoo-shimasu.**
> "He always studies very well."

> **Nichiyoobi wa** *itsu mo* **uchi ni imasen.**
> "I never stay at home on Sundays."

Examples: a) **Kyoo wa mada** *nani mo* **tabeteimasen.**
"I haven't eaten anything yet today."

b) **Kinoo Tanaka-san no otaku e ikimashita ga,** *dare mo* **imasen deshita.**
"I went to Mr. Tanaka's house, but nobody was there."

c) **Ashita wa** *doko (e)*mo* **ikanaide, uchi ni imasu.**
"I'm not going anywhere tomorrow, and will stay at home."

d) **Koko ni aru mono wa** *dore mo* **suki ja arimasen.**
"I don't like any of the things here."

* Some particles may occur between the interrogative and **mo**.

5 Copula + **n desu**

Like a verb or an adjective + **n desu** (see *BUSINESS JAPANESE*, Lesson 18, Note **4**), a copula may occur before **n desu**. However, in the case of the non-past copula **da/desu**, the copula is always replaced by **na**.

Compare: **Yuu-esu-emu wa yuumee na kaisha** *desu*.
"USM, Ltd. is a famous company."

and

Yuu-esu-emu wa yuumee na kaisha *na n desu*.
"USM, Ltd. is a famous company."

PRACTICE

1 Response Practice

Example: Teacher: **Nani o kaimasu ka.**
"What are you going to buy?"

Student: **Nani mo kaimasen.**
"I won't buy anything."

a)   **Dare o reiohu-shimasu ka.**   **Dare mo reiohu-shimasen.**

b)   **Kono keeyaku wa doko ga dame desu ka.**   **Doko mo dame ja arimasen.**

c)   **Dore ga Amerika-see desu ka.**   **Dore mo Amerika-see ja arimasen.**

d)   **Uisukii to biiru to dochira ga suki desu ka.**   **Dochira mo suki ja arimasen.**

e)   **Joonzu-san ni nani o agemashita ka.**   **Nani mo agemasen deshita.**

28/At the Office II

2 Response Practice

Example: Teacher: **Joonzu-san ni shirasemashoo ka.**
"Shall I inform Mr. Jones?"

Student: **Ee, shiraseta hoo ga ii deshoo.**
"Yes, you had better inform (him)."

a) Kyoo keeyaku-shimashoo ka. Ee, keeyaku-shita hoo ga ii deshoo.

b) Kogitte no kooza o tsukurimashoo ka. Ee, tsukutta hoo ga ii deshoo.

c) Ima mitsumori o todokemashoo ka. Ee, todoketa hoo ga ii deshoo.

d) Kono kikai o kenkyuu-shimashoo ka. Ee, kenkyuu-shita hoo ga ii deshoo.

e) Roodoo-jooken o yoku shimashoo ka. Ee, yoku shita hoo ga ii deshoo.

3 Transformation Practice

Example: Teacher: **Ashita mata kuru to iimashita.**
"(He) said he'll come again tomorrow."

Student: **Ashita mata kuru to ka iimashita.**
"(He) said something to the effect that he'll come again tomorrow."

a) Sumisu-san wa konban paatii e iku to iimashita. Sumisu-san wa konban paatii e iku to ka iimashita.

b) Ano kaisha wa koyoo-jooken ga warui to kikimashita. Ano kaisha wa koyoo-jooken ga warui to ka kikimashita.

c) Buraun-san wa Nihon no shijoo ni hairu no wa muzukashii to iimashita. Buraun-san wa Nihon no shijoo ni hairu no wa muzukashii to ka iimashita.

d) Yuu-esu-emu wa doru-date o kiboo-suru to iimashita. Yuu-esu-emu wa doru-date o kiboo-suru to ka iimashita.

e) Kono robotto wa jidoosha-koojoo ni muite iru to kikimashita. Kono robotto wa jidoosha-koojoo ni muite iru to ka kikimashita.

4 Response Practice

Example: Teacher: **Hookokusho o kakimashita ka.**
"Did you write the report?"

Student: **Ee, moo kaite shimaimashita.**
"Yes, I already finished writing (it)."

a) Shiryoo o shirabemashita ka. Ee, moo shirabete shimaimashita.

b) Hookokusho o okurimashita ka. Ee, moo okutte shimaimashita.

c) Robotto o chuumon-shimashita ka. Ee, moo chuumon-shite shimaimashita.

d) Joonzu-san wa kaerimashita ka. Ee, moo kaette shimaimashita.

e) Shachoo ni hanashimashita ka. Ee, hanashite shimaimashita.

5 Comprehension Practice

Directions: The teacher reads aloud the following passage and then asks the student questions about it.

Buraun-san wa Ooyama-buchoo to nebiki ni tsuite soodan-shite kara, jimusho ni kaette kimashita. Rusu-chuu ni Jetoro no Takada-san ga shootaijoo o todokete kure-mashita. Sore wa Jetoro no sooritsu-kinen-paatii no shootaijoo deshita. Yamada-san ga Nissan no hanashi ni tsuite kikimashita kara, Buraun-san wa kuwashiku setsumee-shimashita. Atarashii shain no Imai-san ga Buraun-san ni aitai to ka itte iru soo desu kara, Buraun-san wa honsha e no hookokusho o kaite shimatte kara, au koto ni shimashita.

Questions:

1 Buraun-san wa dare to nan ni tsuite soodan-shimashita ka.
2 Sono ato de, doko e ikimashita ka.
3 Rusu-chuu dare ka kimashita ka.
4 Takada-san wa nan no tame ni kimashita ka.
5 Buraun-san wa nan ni tsuite Yamada-san ni setsumee-shimashita ka.
6 Dare ga Buraun-san ni aitai n desu ka.
7 Buraun-san wa Imai-san ni itsu aimasu ka.

EXERCISES

Inform the teacher in Japanese that:

1 It has been arranged that Mr. Imai will be officially employed tomorrow.
2 Mr. Brown will attend the party to celebrate the anniversary of Nissan's founding.
3 Mr. Ohyama said something to the effect that he expects a 7% discount.
4 Mr. Jones thinks that this business talk is a good opportunity to enter the Japanese market.
5 P & C, Ltd.'s employment terms are very good, but there is no pension (system).
6 If foreign businessmen want to enter the Japanese market, I think they had better study Japanese.
7 Mr. Brown is thinking of explaining to new employees such things as salary raises, overtime pay, social insurance, bonuses and paid holidays.
8 Mr. Jones has already finished writing a report concerning the business negotiations with Nissan.

Model Answers:

1 Imai-san wa ashita honsaiyoo ni naru koto ni natte imasu.
2 Buraun-san wa Nissan no sooritsu-kinen paatii ni shusseki-shimasu.
3 Ooyama-san wa nana-paasento no nebiki o kitai-shite iru to ka iimashita.
4 Joonzu-san wa kono shoodan wa Nihon no shijoo ni hairu ii kikai da to omotte imasu.
5 Pii-ando-shii no koyoo-jooken wa totemo ii n desu ga, nenkin wa arimasen.
6 Gaikokujin bijinesuman ga Nihon no shijoo ni hairitakattara, Nihongo o benkyoo-shita hoo ga ii to omoimasu.
7 Buraun-san wa atarashii shain ni shookyuu ya zangyoo-teate, shakai-hoken, boonasu, yuukyuu-kyuuka nado o setsumee-shiyoo to omotte imasu.
8 Joonzu-san wa moo Nissan to no shoodan ni tsuite hookokusho o kaite shimaimashita.

BUSINESS INFORMATION

Hiring And Training Staff

Recruitment season in Japan can be a time of fierce, and sometimes rather peculiar, competition for candidates and corporations alike. An understanding of the general principles of hiring and training Japanese employees may help you compete more effectively for capable staff for your office.

1 Recruitment: Unlike the Western firm which recruits people of different ages as it needs them, Japanese corporations generally hire right out of school. This is because the Japanese company selects employees not on the basis of specific talents or experience as its Western counterparts do, but rather on the basis of their attitude, character and overall potential (See *BUSINESS JAPANESE Business Information 16*). It is as important for the employee to fit well into the company environment and become a reliable team-player as it is to develop skills in sales or marketing or whatever. And, usually, the younger the employee, the more receptive he is to company ideals–and the higher the chances of a long, productive and loyal term of service. Employers seldom have a specific post in mind when they interview an applicant, therefore; nor does the applicant ask for a specific assignment to suit his own interests and aptitude. Instead, if the company feels the chemistry is right, the job is his.

Japanese corporations take great pains every year to secure a good freshman crop. Millions are spent on advertisements and corporate image campaigns, for example, and staff are regularly dispatched to their respective alma maters to canvass recruits (*BUSINESS JAPANESE Business Information 15*). These working alumni ("old boys" or "OB" 's in Japan) will even stake out nearby coffee shops and restaurants to sell their company to student-customers. Once the companies determine who the choice candidates are, they do their utmost to hold on to them. This could mean scheduling interviews at the same time as their rivals, thus forcing the would-be employee to choose between them, or arranging outings in the country and other gala events to sweep the candidates off their feet. To go or not to go on these seemingly casual, company-sponsored excursions is not a decision to be taken lightly. Accepting the invitation often signifies acceptance of the company's offer of employment while declining, naturally, will drop you out of the running altogether.

2 Training Freshmen: Japanese corporations also invest a great deal of time and energy in training their freshman staff. Training sessions for new employees (新入社員教育, **shinnyuu shain kyooiku**) come in all shapes and sizes, from simple in-house meetings to intensive 1-2 week seminars at special locations. In contrast to the West, however, class-time does not focus on specific job training alone, but also includes detailed instruction in the basic patterns of business conduct and etiquette. Men may be taught how to receive and exchange meishi and take effective memos, for example, while women learn in addition the proper way to receive visitors and serve tea. All usually receive some form of instruction in the intricacies of **keego** or polite speech (See *BUSINESS JAPANESE Business Information 6*), as well as English lessons. At the end of basic training, each employee will have brushed up on all the social graces he or she needs to be accepted, and to perform with polish, in the Japanese business community.

3 Hiring Non-Freshmen: Foreign firms in Japan are obviously disadvantaged in the race for qualified freshman. Few overseas companies can afford the protracted recruitment or provide the comprehensive "community" training that their Japanese competitors do. Many older Japanese workers are also wary of joining foreign companies who they feel may be here today and gone tomorrow with no thought for the employees they leave in their wake. And, finally, even when there *are* people willing to join a foreign firm, they are not always as specialized in their respective fields as in other countries. Because of Japan's unique recruitment and training process, most of the candidates you interview will be business "generalists." They will have been rotated from position to position in their last company to develop a well-rounded perspective (See *BUSINESS JAPANESE Business Information 16*), and may thus be jacks of all trades–but not necessarily masters of the specific areas you have been looking for.

All is not lost, however. There are in fact two new breeds of Japanese professionals who are fast becoming the most sought-after employees for foreign firms in Japan: the MBA holder and the business woman. For a number of years now, large international Japanese firms have been sending promising employees to get MBA's from prestigious universities in the U.S. and other countries, and subsequently grooming these employees for management positions upon their return. Sometimes, however, the returning MBA's find themselves assigned to jobs that do not let them utilize their education creatively because Japanese companies tend to promote on the basis of seniority and ability, and not academic credentials. Occasionally, it is the MBA's themselves who do not readjust to the "generalist" Japanese organization after their stint in the highly specialized corporate environment of the West. These disenchanted MBA's may be less reluctant than most to forego the security of traditional life-employment and to jump ship for more challenging –and usually also more lucrative–positions in foreign companies.

Japanese business women are also being actively recruited by foreign companies–and, increasingly, also by their Japanese counterparts. Since women are generally under less pressure than men to get an early start in established blue-chip companies in Japan, more women study abroad upon graduation from college and are consequently more accustomed to Western ways by the time they start serious job-hunting. Having been exposed to the Western working environment, many returnees are also less hesitant about carving out specialized niches for themselves in business. If you are having trouble inviting qualified staff in Japan, therefore, you may find a growing pool of valuable resources in frustrated MBA's and business women who together can help to compensate for some of your disadvantages in the annual forays for freshmen.

4 Examples of Japanese Freshman Training: The following are instructions for greeting visitors and seating order in vehicles, excerpted from a manual for new recruits.

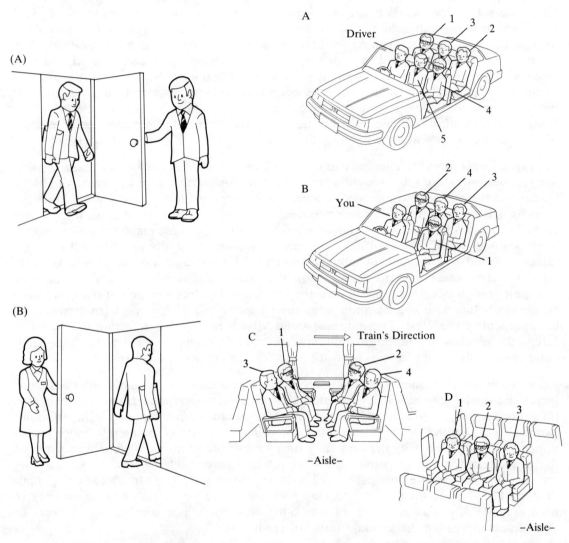

1. Always stand and move with the guest's convenience in mind.
2. In corridors, precede the guest by about 2-3 paces, keeping to his left.
3. Adjust your own pace to that of your guest.
4. Announce corners when turning, announce floors when riding elevators.
5. When doors open into the room, enter first and hold the door open for the guest (A).
6. When doors open out of the room, stand outside and let the guest enter first (B).

A. In taxis and hired cars, the most important person sits in the innermost corner of the back seat, directly behind the driver.
B. In your own car, the most important person sits next to you in the front seat.
C. In trains, the most important person sits by the window, facing the direction the train is moving.
D. In airplanes, the most important person sits by the window; the most junior person sits in the middle.

Lesson 29

At a Business Gathering

OBJECTIVES

1 to describe one's business activities.

2 to discuss business conditions.

3 to describe one's personality.

4 to use Japanese proverbs.

TARGET EXPRESSIONS AND PATTERNS

1	\<clause A> and \<clause B>.	\<clause **A**> **shi,** \<clause **B**>
2	in order to (do)...	**... (suru) no ni**
3	many people	**nan-nin mo**
4	just as...	**... toori**

SITUATION

Mr. Brown meets Mr. Takada at JETRO's party, and they discuss Mr. Brown's negotiations with Nissan and Japanese business practices.

115

29/At a Business Gathering

DIALOGUE

Takada

| 1 | How is business these days? | **Kono goro, keeki wa doo desu ka.** |

	so-so	**maamaa,** まあ まあ
	a certain	**aru,** ある
	a certain automobile company	**aru jidoosha-gaisha,** ある自動車会社
	to sell, make a sale	**urikomu,** 売り込む
	in order to sell	**urikomu no ni,** 売り込むのに
Brown	to have a hard time	**kuroo-suru,** 苦労する

| 2 | So-so, but now (I)'m having a hard time selling American robots to a certain automobile company. | **Maamaa desu ga, ima wa aru jidoosha-gaisha ni Amerika-see no robotto o urikomu no ni kuroo-shite imasu.** |

	to develop, open	**kaitaku-suru,** 開拓する
	opening (a market)	**kaitaku-suru no,** 開拓するの
Takada	easy	**raku/na/,** 楽(な)

| 3 | It can't be easy to get a new customer, can it? | **Atarashii torihikisaki o kaitaku-suru no wa raku ja nai deshoo ne.** |

	high-tech product	**hai-teku-seehin,** ハイテク製品
	handling	**atsukau no,** 扱うの
	first time	**hajimete,** 初めて
	customs	**shuukan,** 習慣
Brown	business practices	**shooshuukan,** 商習慣

| 4 | It is also the first time we're handling high-tech products, and business practices are also different from those in America, so... | **Hai-teku-seehin o atsukau no mo hajimete desu shi, shooshuukan mo Beekoku to wa chigaimasu kara...** |

| | specialized | **senmonteki/na/,** 専門的(な) |
| **Takada** | knowledge | **chishiki,** 知識 |

| 5 | (You) need specialized knowledge when it comes to robot transactions, don't you? | **Robotto no torihiki de wa senmonteki na chishiki ga hitsuyoo na n deshoo.** |

| | manufacturer | seezoomoto, | せいぞうもと
製造元 |
| Brown | to send | haken-suru, | はけん
派遣する |

6 | That's not a problem, because the manufacturer sent us a specialist, so… | Sore wa mondai arimasen. Seezoomoto ga senmonka o haken-shite kuremashita kara…

Takada

7 | Then [lit. If you say that], what is the problem? | To iu to, nani ga mondai na n desu ka.

| | for several months | nan-kagetsu mo, | なん か げつ
何ケ月も |
| Brown | as (one) says | iu toori, | い とお
言う通り |

8 | Well, it's the negotiations. (We)'ve been talking it over for several months, and (we)'ve also agreed to their prices [lit. made the price as they said], but… | Shoodan no hoo na n desu ga. Moo nan-kagetsu mo hanashiatte iru shi, kakaku mo aite no iu toori ni shita n desu ga…

| | not at all | zenzen … nai, | ぜんぜん
全然…ない |
| Takada | to progress | susumu, | すす
進む |

9 | Do you mean the talks aren't progressing at all? | Hanashi ga zenzen susumanai to iu wake desu ka.

	that's it	sono toori da,	とお その通りだ
	person in charge	tantoosha,	たんとうしゃ 担当者
	in-house proposal,	ringisho,	りん ぎ しょ 稟議書
Brown	the *ringi* memorandum		

10 | That's it. According to the person in charge, (they)'re about to write the ringi memorandum, but … | Sono toori na n desu. Tantoosha no hanashi de wa kinkin ringisho o kaku soo desu ga …

	not yet, still more	madamada,	まだ まだ
	for the time being	toobun,	とうぶん 当分
Takada	patient	kinaga/na/,	き なが 気長(な)

11 | Then, there's still a long way (to go). For the time being, you'll have to wait patiently. | Jaa, madamada desu yo. Toobun wa kinaga ni matsu koto desu ne.

29/At a Business Gathering

	impatient	**kimijika/na/**, 気短(な)
	waiting	**matsu no**, 待つの
Brown	weak, weak point	**nigate/na/**, 苦手(な)

12 Well, I'm an impatient (man) and waiting is my weak point.

Doo mo boku wa kimijika de, matsu no wa nigate na n desu.

	(is) not good	**ikenai**, いけない
	village	**goo**, 郷
	if one enters	**iraba** (archaic), 入らば
Takada	to obey	**shitagau**, 従う

13 That's not very good, you know. "Do in Rome as the Romans do!"

Sore wa ikemasen ne. "Goo ni iraba goo ni shitagae" desu yo.

	advice	**chuukoku (-suru)/gochuukoku** (polite),
Brown		忠告/ご忠告

14 You're right. Thanks (for your) advice.

Soo desu ne. Gochuukoku, arigatoo.

JAPANESE WRITING

1 高田： この頃、景気は どうですか。

2 ブラウン： まあまあですが、今は ある自動車会社に アメリカ製のロボットを売り込むのに 苦労しています。

3 高田： 新しい取引先を 開拓するのは 楽じゃないでしょうね。

4 ブラウン： ハイテク製品を 扱うのも初めてですし、商習慣も 米国とは違いますから…

5 高田： ロボットの取引では 専門的な知識が 必要なんでしょう。

6 ブラウン： それは問題ありません。製造元が 専門家を 派遣してくれましたから…

7 高田： と言うと、 何が問題なんですか。

8 ブラウン： 商談の方なんですが。 もう何か月も 話し合っているし、価格も 相手の言う通りにしたんですが…

9 高田： 話がぜんぜん進まない というわけですか。

10 ブラウン： その通りなんです。担当者の話では 近々稟議書を書くそうですが…

11 高田： じゃあ、まだまだですよ。 当分は 気長に待つことですね。

12 ブラウン： どうも僕は気短で、 待つのは苦手なんです。

13 高田： それはいけませんね。「郷に入らば 郷に従え」ですよ。

14 ブラウン： そうですね。御忠告、有り難う。

ADDITIONAL USEFUL EXPRESSIONS

1 At the party

A:	My, it's been a long time (since we met). How's business?	**Yaa, shibaraku. Keeki wa doo desu ka.**

bad business conditions	**hukeeki/na/,** 不景気(な)

B:	Well, times are bad and we're having trouble.	**Sore ga hukeeki de, komatte imasu.**

very much, quite	**daibu,** 大分

A:	But, last year business was going quite well, wasn't it?	**De mo, kyonen wa daibu keeki ga yokatta yoo deshita ga...**

boom, period of prosperity	**kookyoo,** 好況

B:	Yes, America was a brisk market until the autumn, so ...	**Ee, aki made wa Amerika ga kookyoo deshita kara...**

A:	Are your company's business partners mostly American?	**Otaku no kaisha no torihikisaki wa Amerika ga ooi n desu ka.**

influential	**yuuryoku/na/,** 有力(な)
customer	**otokui,** お得意
almost	**hotondo,** ほとんど

B:	Yes, the influential customers are mostly American firms.	**Ee, yuuryoku na otokui wa hotondo Amerika no kigyoo desu.**

business depression	**hukyoo,** 不況

A:	In that case, it'll be a big problem if America falls into a depression.	**Sore de wa Amerika ga hukyoo ni naru to, taihen desu ne.**

29/At a Business Gathering

2

easy-going	**nonki/na/,**	呑気(な)
impatient, hasty	**sekkachi/na/,**	せっかち(な)
kind	**shinsetsu/na/,**	親切(な)
unkind	**hushinsetsu/na/,**	不親切(な)
highly qualified	**yuushuu/na/,**	優秀(な)
(is) gentle	**yasashii,**	優しい
(is) cold-hearted	**tsumetai,**	冷い
(is) cunning, dishonest	**zurui,**	ずるい
a hasty person	**awatemono,**	あわて者

That person is easy-going.	**Ano hito wa nonki desu nee.**

NOTES

1 Particle **shi**

The particle **shi** following a verb, adjective or copula at the end of a clause is used to connect clauses, and may be translated as 'and also', 'and what is more', 'moreover.'

Examples:
    a) **Yamada-san wa yoku hataraku *shi*, eego mo totemo joozu desu.**
        "Ms. Yamada works hard and also speaks very good English."

    b) **Ano kikai wa yasui *shi*, benri desu.**
        "That machine is cheap and, what's more, useful."

    c) **Kinoo wa honsha ni tegami o kaita *shi*, robotto no mitsumori mo tsuku-rimashita.**
        "Yesterday I wrote a letter to the head office and also prepared a written estimate of the robot."

    d) **Joonzu-san wa Nihongo no uta o utaimasu *shi*, sake mo yoku nomimasu.**
        "Mr. Jones sings Japanese songs and also drinks a lot of *sake*."

As you can see in the above examples, **shi** follows both formal and informal forms and non-past and past tenses.

The gerund is also used to connect clauses, especially when there is a time sequence implied in the clauses. However, if there is no time difference implied, the particle **shi** should be used.

Compare: **Ongaku o kiite, hon o yomimashita.**
        "I listened to the music and (then) read the book."

    and

    Ongaku o kiita *shi*, hon mo yomimashita.
        "I listened to the music and, what's more, read the book."

2 ... **no ni**

An informal non-past verb + **no ni** may be translated as 'in order to do such-and-such', 'in the process of doing such-and-such.'

Examples: a)   **Kogitte no kooza o hiraku *no ni* wa, jikan ga kakaru n desu.**
"It takes time to open a checking account."

                 b)   **Nihon no shooshuukan o kenkyuu-suru *no ni* kuroo-shite imasu.**
"I'm having a hard time studying Japanese business practices."

Note that when the combination is used to mean 'in order to do', the particle **wa** often follows, as in **Example a)**.

3   Interrogative + counter + **mo**

Interrogative words consisting of **nan** 'what?' + counter (e.g. **ka-getsu** 'month') + the particle **mo** means 'many', 'a large number of ...'

Interrogative + counter		+ mo	Meaning
nan-nin	'how many people?'	**nan-nin** *mo*	many people
nan-jikan	'how many hours?'	**nan-jikan** *mo*	many hours
nan-nichi	'how many days?'	**nan-nichi** *mo*	many days
nan-nen	'how many years?	**nan-nen** *mo*	many years
nan-do	'how many times?'	**nan-do** *mo*	many times
nan-dai	'how many units?'	**nan-dai** *mo*	many units
nan-doru	'how many dollars?'	**nan-doru** *mo*	a lot of money [lit. dollars]

Examples: a)   **Kono kaisha de wa robotto o kenkyuu-shite iru hito wa *nan-nin mo* imasu.**
"In this company there are many people who are studying robots."
[lit. In this company, the people studying robots are many people.]

                 b)   ***Nan-jikan mo* matte imashita ga...**
"I was waiting for hours [lit. many hours]."

4   Verb + **toori**

Toori preceded by a verb means '(just) as ...'

Examples: a)   **Watakushi no iu *toori* (ni)* shite kudasai.**
"Please do as I say."

                 b)   **Shinbun ni kaite aru *toori* wagasha no jigyoo-naiyoo wa totemo ii desu.**
"As was mentioned [lit. written] in the newspaper, our company's financial position [lit. business contents] is very good."

c) **Anata ga osshatta** *toori* **Nihon to Amerika wa shooshuukan ga chi-gaimasu.**
"Business practices are different between Japan and America, just as you told me."

* The particle **ni** may occur after **toori**.

5 Zenzen + /negative/

Zenzen usually occurs with a negative verb, adjective or copula and means '/not/ at all', 'never.'

Examples:
a) **Suzuki-san wa osake o** *zenzen* **nomimasen.**
"Mr. Suzuki never drinks *sake*."

b) **Kono hon wa** *zenzen* **omoshiroku arimasen.**
"This book is not interesting at all."

c) **Juu-nen mae wa ano kaisha mo** *zenzen* **yuumee ja arimasen deshita.**
"Ten years ago, that company wasn't famous at all either."

PRACTICE

1 Transformation Practice

Example: Teacher: **Robotto o urikomimasu. Kuroo-shite imasu.**
"I sell robots. I'm having a hard time."

Student: **Robotto o urikomu no ni kuroo-shite imasu.**
"I'm having a hard time selling robots."

a) **Gijutsuteki na setsumee o shimasu. Sen-monteki na chishiki ga irimasu.**
   Gijutsuteki na setsumee o suru no ni senmonteki na chishiki ga irimasu.

b) **Ootemachi e ikimasu. Chikatetsu ga ichiban benri desu.**
   Ootemachi e iku no ni chikatetsu ga ichiban benri desu.

c) **Atarashii torihikisaki o kaitakushimasu. Kuroo-shite imasu.**
   Atarashii torihikisaki o kaitakusuru no ni kuroo-shite imasu.

d) **Honsha ni renraku-shimasu. Terekkusu o tsukaimasu.**
   Honsha ni renraku-suru no ni terekkusu o tsukaimasu.

e) **Robotto o doonyuu-shimasu. Kumiai no sansee ga irimasu.**
   Robotto o doonyuu-suru no ni kumiai no sansee ga irimasu.

2 Transformation Practice

Example: Teacher: **Hisho o yatoimashita. Waapuro mo kaimashita.**
"I employed a secretary. I bought a word processor."

Student: **Hisho o yatotta shi, waapuro mo kaimashita.**
"I employed a secretary and also bought a word processor."

a) **Hito o yatoimasu. Kooza mo hiraki-masu.**   **Hito o yatou shi, kooza mo hirakimasu.**

b) **Nara e ikimashita. Kyooto mo kenbutsu-shimashita.**   **Nara e itta shi, Kyooto mo kenbutsu-shimashita.**

c) **Ringisho wa kakimashita. Nemawashi mo shimashita.**   **Ringisho wa kaita shi, nemawashi mo shimashita.**

d) **Kumiai ga hantai-shimasu. Kakaku mo takai desu.**   **Kumiai ga hantai-suru shi, kakaku mo takai desu.**

e) **Rekishi no aru kaisha desu. Jigyoo-naiyoo mo ii desu.**   **Rekishi no aru kaisha da shi, jigyoo-naiyoo mo ii desu.**

3 Response Practice

Example: Teacher: **Senmonteki na chishiki ga hitsuyoo desu ka.**
                "Do we need specialized knowledge?"

           Student: **Iie, zenzen hitsuyoo ja arimasen.**
                "No, you don't need it at all."

a) **Shoodan wa susunde imasu ka.**   **Iie, zenzen susunde imasen.**

b) **Omoshiroi desu ka.**   **Iie, zenzen omoshiroku arimasen.**

c) **Ano hito wa shinsetsu desu ka.**   **Iie, zenzen shinsetsu ja arimasen.**

d) **Nihon ni torihikisaki ga arimasu ka.** **Iie, zenzen arimasen.**

e) **Juutaku-teate o moratte imasu ka.**   **Iie, zenzen moratte imasen.**

4 Response Practice

Example: Teacher: **Nan-kagetsu gurai hanashiatte imasu ka.**
                "How many months have you been talking with (him)?"

           Student: **Nan-kagetsu mo hanashiatte imasu.**
                "We have been talking for many months."

a) **Nan-jikan gurai machimashita ka.**   **Nan-jikan mo machimashita.**

b) **Nan-nin gurai reiohu-shimashita ka.**   **Nan-nin mo reiohu-shimashita.**

c) **Nan-dai gurai kuruma o urimashita ka.**   **Nan-dai mo urimashita.**

d) **Nan-bai gurai biiru o nomimashita ka.**   **Nan-bai mo nomimashita.**

e) **Nan-do gurai Kyooto e ikimashita ka.**   **Nan-do mo ikimashita.**

5 Comprehension Practice

Directions: The teacher reads aloud the following passage and then asks the student questions about it.

29/At a Business Gathering

Buraun-san wa Jetoro no paatii de Takada-san ni aimashita. Buraun-san wa saikin Yuu-esu-emu no robotto o urikomu no ni kuroo-shite iru to iimashita. Buraun-san no hanashi de wa hai-teku-seehin o atsukau no wa hajimete desu shi, senmonteki na chishiki mo nai shi, Beekoku to shooshuukan mo chigau no de, kuroo-shite iru soo desu. Moo nan-kagetsu mo hanashiatte iru shi, nebiki mo aite no iu toori ni shimashita ga, shoodan wa zenzen susumanai soo desu. Nissan no Ooyama-buchoo ni yoru to, ringisho o kaite iru soo desu kara, Buraun-san wa kinaga ni matsu koto ni suru to iimashita.

Questions:

1   Buraun-san wa doko de Takada-san ni aimashita ka.
2   Buraun-san wa ima nani o shite iru to iimashita ka.
3   Buraun-san wa ima doo shite kuroo-shite imasu ka.
4   Buraun-san wa dono gurai Nissan to hanashiatte imasu ka.
5   Buraun-san wa nebiki-shimashita ka. Dono gurai nebiki-shimashita ka.
6   Ooyama-buchoo ni yoru to, Nissan wa ima nani o shite imasu ka.

EXERCISES

Inform the teacher in Japanese that:

1   Mr. Brown has a hard time selling American-made robots to Nissan.
2   Mr. Brown has no specialized knowledge about robots, but USM, Ltd. will send a specialist soon.
3   Because Mr. Tanaka did not reduce the price, the business talks are not progressing at all.
4   When in Rome, do as the Romans do.
5   Mr. Ohyama is very kind and is also an excellent businessman.
6   Foreign businessmen are waiting patiently until Japanese people begin to buy foreign products.
7   Explaining Japanese business practices is my weak point.
8   The company President employed a person to be in charge of the negotiations with Nissan.

Model Answers:

1   Buraun-san wa Nissan e Amerika-see no robotto o urikomu no ni kuroo-shite imasu.
2   Buraun-san wa robotto ni tsuite senmonteki na chishiki wa arimasen ga, Yuu-esu-emu wa sugu senmonka o haken-shimasu.
3   Tanaka-san ga nebiki-shinakatta kara, shoodan wa zenzen susunde imasen.
4   Goo ni iraba, goo ni shitagae.
5   Ooyama-san wa shinsetsu desu shi, yuushuu na bijinesuman desu.
6   Gaikokujin bijinesuman wa Nihonjin ga gaikoku-seehin o kaihajimeru made, kinaga ni matte imasu.
7   Nihon no shooshuukan o setsumee-suru no wa nigate desu.
8   Shachoo wa Nissan to no kooshoo o tantoo-suru hito o yatoimashita.

BUSINESS INFORMATION

Finding an Office

Few business organizations are as conveniently located near the heart of Tokyo as the Japan External Trade Organization (JETRO) mentioned in the DIALOGUE. Offices are hard to find, extremely costly and often hopelessly cramped by Western standards. The following information is provided for your guidance should you wish to set up operations in Japan.

1 The Location: The first step in scouting office space is to call a reputable real estate agent, or **hudoosanya** (不動産屋), preferably one specialized in serving foreigners. Japanese landlords are rarely willing to deal directly with prospective tenants, especially if they are from overseas. Occasionally, the landlord or agent will even request that you produce a **hoshoonin** (保証人, guarantor)–usually a **buchoo, shachoo** or other titled Japanese–who will vouch for your good conduct and assume all legal and financial responsibility should you default on your obligations. When casting around for office space, you should aim for key, central areas in the big cities though these are naturally also the most congested and expensive. Outlying areas may offer lower rates and more spacious accomodations, but the added inconvenience and lost prestige may not be worth the savings. Most businessmen feel that even narrow quarters in a good commercial district are preferable to spacious premises far from the business center, and most enterprises tend to cluster together in select metropolitan areas as a result. In Tokyo, for example, practically all government offices are located in Kasumigaseki; banks and insurance firms are in Marunouchi, securities firms in Nihonbashi, and so forth. Consequently, you should check around to see where the most prominent representatives of your industry are located and hang your shingle in the vicinity so as not to miss out on the action.

2 The Expense: Even more difficult than finding good office space is convincing one's head office that the space actually costs as much as it does. As of September, 1985, rents in Tokyo ranged from about ¥23,000 per **tsubo** (坪, 3.3 sq. m.) per month to over ¥35,000 per **tsubo** in prime locations; and a 75 sq. m. office accomodating three staff members required as much as ¥40-60 million a year in annual rent and operating expenses. In addition, landlords also ask for a sizeable deposit, or **shikikin** (敷金), which can be determined by the number of **tsubo** or paid in advance in a lump sum equivalent to 3-6 months–or even a year's–rent. This deposit is usually returned in total when the tenant vacates the premises, but in some cases, a certain percentage of the **shikikin**, e.g. 20%, is retained by the landlord as a fee. In other arrangements, a fee or **reekin** (礼金) amounting to about 1 month's rent is paid directly to the landlord *in lieu* of a deposit.

Heating and cooling, electricity, **kanrihi** (管理費, maintenance) and other expenses borne by the tenant usually run about 5-8% of rent, which may not sound like much until one recalls that monthly rental can run upwards of ¥2,000,000 in central locations. If your building provides parking, you may be able to negotiate a single car space for about ¥30,000; non-tenants, though, should be prepared to cough up ¥50-60,000. Also, most leasing or rental agreements stipulate that the premises be returned to their original condition, or **genjoo-hukki** (原状復帰), when they are vacated. This means removing any partitions you may have put up, plugging up holes in walls where you had hung prints and bulletin boards, etc.–all of which, again, entail additional expense. Frequently, the tenant and landlord will determine together what should remain and what should be taken down; some of the changes you introduced may have actually enhanced the property, enabling the landlord to charge his next tenant more for the use of your "left-overs". Finally, Japan being the service-oriented society that it is, it is customary to give gifts to the maintenance staff or the landlord on all appropriate occasions (See *BUSINESS JAPANESE II Business Information 32*). Remembering the **kanri** staff is not only a thoughtful gesture but, more important, will ensure prompt action and cooperation during emergencies, e.g. when large equipment has to be installed on short notice or when the cooler breaks down.

3 Other: If you are short-staffed, you may be relieved to know that near-by coffee shops usually offer catering service so you can provide refreshments to your guests without having to tinker around in the kitchen yourself. Numerous other services can be negotiated with outside firms. For a pittance, you can have the mouthpieces of your phones changed once a month in the interest of general hygiene (電話掃除 , **denwa-sooji**); if you don't have a green thumb, you can arrange to have plants and greenery rotated on a monthly basis (貸し植木 , **kashi-ueki**); doormats can be regularly cleaned and replaced (マット・チェンジ, **matto-chenji**) and so forth.

4 Alternatives: If you cannot afford the time and expense of setting up your own quarters in Japan, or if you are waiting for office space to open up, there are numerous "executive centers" sprouting up in major cities that can accomodate your needs in the interim. "Executive centers" come equipped with all essential office gadgetry, including telexes, facsimile machines and personal computers; they are staffed with receptionists and secretaries and usually also offer very low overhead. The staff will moreover provide answering service and a private telex and phone number if you wish to create an impression of being permanently established. If even these executive centers are not to your liking, you can always share office facilities with another business until you have become successful enough to set up shop on your own.

Lesson 30

At the Factory

OBJECTIVES

1   to converse about working conditions.

2   to use basic terms concerning Quality Control.

3   to use the Provisional form.

TARGET EXPRESSIONS AND PATTERNS

1   Provided (such-and-such) happens...   **... reba,**

2   (It) has become ...   **... te kuru.**

3   Adverbial Use of Verb Gerund

4   Gerund of Adjectives

SITUATION

In order to further discuss technical matters, Nissan invites Mr. Jones to its factory. After touring the factory, Mr. Jones returns to the factory manager's office and converses with Mr. Kawai, the Factory Manager, and Mr. Machida, the General Manager of the Engineering Department.

30/At the Factory

DIALOGUE

	to be tired	**tsukareru,** 疲れる
	thanks for your efforts	**otsukare-sama,** お疲れさま
Kawai	impression	**kansoo, gokansoo** (polite), 感想, ご感想

1	Thank you for being with us [lit. you've been tired out]. What are your impressions?	**Doo mo otsukare sama deshita. Gokansoo wa ikaga desu ka.**

	(is) well-lit	**akarui,** 明るい
Jones	to be impressed	**kanshin-suru,** 感心する

2	(It)'s a well-lit and clean factory, isn't it? (I) was impressed.	**Akarukute, kiree na koojoo desu ne. Kanshin-shimashita.**

	efficiency	**nooritsu,** 能率
Kawai	to rise	**agaru,** 上がる

3	Yes. In a dirty factory, (you) don't get good results [lit. efficiency wouldn't rise].	**Ee, kitanai koojoo de wa nooritsu ga agarimasen kara...**

	environment	**kankyoo,** 環境
	if (it) is not good	**yokunakereba,** 良くなければ
Machida	quality	**hinshitsu,** 品質

4	Unless the working environment is good, (we) cannot produce good quality cars.	**Sagyoo-kankyoo ga yokunakereba, hinshitsu no ii kuruma wa tsukuremasen.**

Jones

5	(I) agree 100 percent [lit. Exactly as you say].	**Mattaku ossharu toori desu.**

Kawai	what do you think?	**doo okangae desu ka,** どうお考えですか

6	What do you think of Japanese robots?	**Nihon-see no robotto wa doo okangae desu ka.**

	accurate	**seekaku/na/,** 正確(な)
Jones	(is) fast	**hayai,** 速い

7	(I) think (they) are truly wonderful. (Their) operations are accurate and fast.	**Totemo subarashii to omoimasu. Sagyoo mo seekaku de, hayai desu ne.**

	thanks to	**okage,** お陰
	thanks to robots	**robotto no okage de,** ロボットのお陰で
	productivity	**seesansee,** 生産性
	significantly	**medatte,** 目立って
	to improve, advance	**koojoo-suru,** 向上する
Kawai	to have improved	**koojoo-shite kuru,** 向上してくる

8	Thanks to those robots, productivity here has increased significantly.	**Ano robotto no okage de, koko no seesansee mo medatte koojoo-shite kimashita.**

	to join	**kuwawaru,** 加わる
	demon	**oni,** 鬼
Jones	iron bar	**kanaboo,** 金棒

9	Then, if ours were to be added, it would be like giving a club to Hercules [lit. an iron bar to the demon].	**Jaa, sore ni wagasha no ga kuwawareba, "Oni ni kanaboo" desu yo.**

Kawai	enthusiastic	**nesshin/na/,** 熱心(な)
	enthusiastic about business	**shoobai-nesshin/na/,** 商売熱心(な)

10	Oh, Mr. Jones, you're very enthusiastic about business, aren't you?	**Iya, Joonzu-san mo nakanaka shoobai-nesshin desu ne.**

Jones

11	Thank you.	**Osoreirimasu.**

	research department	kenkyuushitsu, 研究室
	now, soon	sorosoro, そろそろ
Machida	laboratory	kenkyuujo, 研究所

12 (Well) then, the research staff are probably waiting for us, so shall we head for the laboratory now?

De wa, kenkyuushitsu no sutahhu mo matte iru deshoo kara, sorosoro kenkyuujo no hoo e ikimashoo ka.

| **Jones** | factory manager | koojoochoo, 工場長 |

13 Yes, that's right. Well, Mr. Kawai [lit. Mr. Kawai Factory Manager], thank you for everything today. I hope to see you again some day.

Soo desu ne. De wa, Kawai-koojoochoo, honjitsu wa iroiro arigatoo gozaimashita. Mata izure ome ni kakarimasu.

| **Kawai** | please come | odekake kudasai, お出掛けください |

14 Yes. Please do come out again by all means.

Soo desu ne. Mata, zehi odekake kudasai.

JAPANESE WRITING

1 川井： どうも お疲れさまでした。ご感想は いかがですか。

2 ジョーンズ： 明るくて、きれいな工場 ですね。 感心しました。

3 川井： ええ、きたない工場 では 能率が 上がりませんから…

4 町田： 作業環境が 良くなければ、 品質のいい車は 作れません。

5 ジョーンズ： まったく おっしゃる通りです。

6 川井： 日本製のロボットは どうお考えですか。

7 ジョーンズ： とても すばらしいと思います。 作業も正確で、速いですね。

8 川井： あのロボットのお陰で、ここの生産性も 目立って向上してきました。

9 ジョーンズ： じゃあ、 それに我社のが加われば、「鬼に金棒」ですよ。

10 川井： いや、ジョーンズさんも なかなか商売熱心ですね。

11 ジョーンズ： 恐れ入ります。

12 町田： では、 研究室のスタッフも 待っているでしょうから、そろそろ研究所の方へ 行きましょうか。

13 ジョーンズ： そうですね。 では、川井工場長、本日は いろいろ有り難うございました。 また いずれお目にかかります。

14 川井： そうですね。 また、是非お出掛けください。

ADDITIONAL USEFUL EXPRESSIONS

1 At a trade gathering

reputation	**hyooban,**	評判
to have a good reputation	**hyooban ga ii,**	評判がいい

A:	Your company's products have a good reputation.
	Onsha no seehin wa hyooban ga ii desu ne.

management	**kanri(-suru),**	管理(する)
quality control	**hinshitsu-kanri,**	品質管理

B:	We are really emphasizing quality control, so...
	Hinshitsu-kanri ni chikara o irete imasu kara...

QC (quality control) circles	**Kyuu-shii-saakuru,**	ＱＣサークル
flourishing	**sakan/na/,**	盛ん(な)

A:	QC circles also seem to be very active [lit. flourishing], don't they?
	Kyuu-shii-saakuru mo sakan na yoo desu ne.

to do, perform	**yaru,**	やる
actual place	**genba,**	現場
not only...	**...dake de naku,**	だけでなく
throughout the company	**zenshateki/na/,**	全社的(な)
TQC (total quality control)	**Tii-kyuu-shii,**	ＴＱＣ

B:	We have been using QC circles since about 10 years ago. But now, we have TQC, not only on the production site, but throughout the company.
	Kyuu-shii-saakuru wa juu-nen gurai mae kara yatte imasu. Demo, ima wa seesangenba dake de naku, zenshateki na Tii-kyuu-shii o okonatte imasu.

therefore	**dakara,**	だから
profit	**shuueki,**	収益

A:	That is why both productivity and profit are high at your company, isn't it?
	Dakara, onsha wa seesansee mo shuueki mo takai n desu ne.

30/At the Factory

2 At the factory

	facilities	**setsubi,** 設備

A:	The facilities here are old, aren't they?	**Koko no setsubi wa hurui desu ne.**

	(is) dark	**kurai,** 暗い

B:	Furthermore, it is dark, and the working environment is also not good.	**Sore ni, kurakute, sagyoo-kankyoo mo yoku arimasen.**

	to go down	**sagaru,** 下る

A:	At this rate, efficiency will also decrease.	**Kore de wa, nooritsu mo sagarimasu.**

	improvement	**kaizen (-suru),** 改善(する)

B:	It's necessary to improve the factory facilities, isn't it?	**Koojoo-shisetsu no kaizen ga hitsuyoo desu ne.**

	to agree	**dookan da,** 同感だ

A:	I agree 100 percent.	**Mattaku, dookan desu.**

3 At the office

	raw materials	**genryoo,** 原料

A:	The import of the raw materials seems to be late, doesn't it?	**Genryoo no yunyuu ga okurete iru yoo desu ne.**

	shipping strike	**kaiun-suto,** 海運スト
	due to...	**...(no) see de,** …(の)せいで
	to dispatch, send	**shukka-suru,** 出荷する

B:	Yes, they say (they) cannot dispatch (the materials) due to the shipping strike.	**Ee, kaiun-suto no see de, shukka-dekinai soo desu.**

132

country	**kuni,**	国
strike	**sutoraiki, suto,**	ストライキ, スト

A:	That's a problem. There are many strikes in that country.	**Komarimasu ne. Ano kuni wa sutoraiki ga ooi desu ne.**

NOTES

1 The Provisional Form

All verbs, adjectives and copula in Japanese have provisional forms which may be translated as 'if such-and-such (happens),' 'provided such-and such (happens),' 'if (it) is such-and-such.'

To form the provisional:

Verb: Drop the final **-u** of the informal non-past and add **-eba**.

Adjective: Drop the final **-i** of the non-past and add **-kereba**.

Copula: The provisional of **da** is **nara** or **naraba**.

	Informal non-past		Provisional	
Verb	**iku**	'to go'	**ikeba**	'provided so-and-so goes'
Adjective	**ookii**	'(is) big'	**ookikereba**	'provided it is big'
Copula	**da**	'to be'	**nara/naraba**	'if it is …'

Examples:
a) **Kono robotto o doonyuu-sureba, sagyoo no nooritsu ga agarimasu.**
   "If you introduce this robot, the efficiency of the operations will be raised [lit. will rise]."

b) **Nedan ga yasukereba, motto ureru deshoo.**
   "If the price is cheap, you can probably sell more."

c) **Kuruma nara, koojoo made sanjup-pun gurai shika kakarimasen.**
   "If you go by car [lit. if it's a car], it takes only about 30 minutes to go to the factory."

d) **Hinshitsu ga yoku nakereba, seehin wa uremasen.**
   "If the quality is not good, you cannot sell the products."

The provisional copula form **nara** sometimes occurs after other inflected verbs and adjectives and the combination may be translated as 'if it is a matter of (doing).' Thus,

Oosaka e iku (no)* nara, Shinkansen ga ichiban benri desu.
"If you go to Osaka [lit. if it's a matter of going to Osaka], the Shinkansen line is the most convenient."

Kaitai (no)* nara, katte agemasu.
"If you want to buy it [lit. if it's the case that you want to buy it], I'll buy it for you."

Watakushi *nara*, sonna torihiki wa shimasen.
"If it were me, I would never do such business."

* Note that the particle **no** may also occur before **nara** in this combination without affecting the meaning of the sentence.

The English equivalent for both the provisional and the conditional forms (see *BUSINESS JAPANESE II*, Lesson 25, Note **1**) is 'if ...', but there is a slight difference in meaning between the two forms.
The conditional is usually used in a specific situation, while the provisional commonly describes a general situation.

Compare: **Ame ga *hureba*, kaisha e kuruma de ikimasu.**
"If it rains, I go to the company by car." (provisional)

and

Ashita ame ga *huttara*, kaisha e kuruma de ikimasu.
"If it rains tomorrow, I'll go to the company by car." (conditional)

2 Gerund of Adjectives

The gerund of adjectives is formed by dropping the final **-i** and adding **-kute**. Thus,

ooi	'(is) many'	**oo*kute***	'(being) many'
atarashii	'(is) new'	**atarashi*kute***	'(being) new'
ii	'(is) good'	**yo*kute***	'(being) good'

Like verb and copula gerunds, an adjective gerund is used to combine two clauses or sentences. Thus,

Kono kikai wa atarashi*kute*, ano kikai wa hurui desu.
"This machine is new and that machine over there is old."

An adjective gerund may also combine two (or more) adjectives modifying a noun. Thus,

Yasu*kute* ii waapuro wa arimasen ka.
"Don't you have a cheap and good word processor?"

Koko wa akaru*kute* kiree na jimusho desu nee.
"This [lit. Here] is a well-lit and clean office, isn't it?"

3 Adverbial Use of the Verb Gerund

A verb gerund is sometimes used as a kind of adverb to modify another verb, adjective, or noun + **da**.

Examples: a) **Seesansee ga *medatte** koojoo-shimashita.**
"Productivity has increased significantly."

* **medatte** is the gerund of the verb **medatsu** 'to be prominent.'

b) **Anata no paatii ni *yorokonde** ukagaimasu.**
"I'll be glad to come to your party
[lit. I'll go to your party, being glad]."

* **yorokonde** is the gerund of the verb **yorokobu** 'to be glad.'

4 Verb Gerund + **kuru**

A verb gerund + **kuru** 'to come' indicates an action which started in the past and which has continued for a while, usually up till the present.

Examples:
  a) **Jidoo-koosakuki ga *huete kimashita*.**
     "Automatic machine tools have increased."

  b) **Keeki wa dandan waruku *natte kite* imasu.**
     "Business conditions have been worsening steadily."

  c) **Kyonen no juu-gatsu made kuruma no uriage wa *hette kite* imashita ga, juuichi-gatsu kara yoku *natte kite* imasu.**
     "Sales of cars had been decreasing until last October, but since November (they) have improved."

PRACTICE

1 Response Practice

Example: Teacher: **Seesansee ga koojoo-shite kimashita ka./robotto/**
                   "Has productivity increased?"/robots/

              Student: **Ee, robotto no okage de koojoo-shite kimashita.**
                   "Yes, it has increased thanks to the robots."

a) **Ooyama-san ni aemashita ka. /Takada-san/**

   Ee, Takada-san no okage de aemashita.

b) **Shoodan wa susunde imasu ka. /anata no chuukoku/**

   Ee, anata no chuukoku no okage de susunde imasu.

c) **Nihon no shooshuukan ni narete kimashita ka. /minasan/**

   Ee, minasan no okage de narete kimashita.

d) **Kono kikai wa Nihon de urete imasu ka. /dairiten/**

   Ee, dairiten no okage de urete imasu.

e) **Sagyoo-kankyoo ga yoku narimashita ka. /shisetsu no kaizoo/**

   Ee, shisetsu no kaizoo no okage de yoku narimashita.

2 Transformation Practice

Example: Teacher: **Koojoo wa akarui desu. Kiree desu.**
                   "The factory is well-lit. It is clean."

              Student: **Koojoo wa akarukute kiree desu.**
                   "The factory is well-lit and clean."

a) **Robotto no sagyoo wa hayai desu. Seekaku desu.**

   Robotto no sagyoo wa hayakute, seekaku desu.

b) **Kono shigoto wa muzukashii desu. Abunai desu.**

   Kono shigoto wa muzukashikute, abunai desu.

c)   Ano resutoran wa yasui desu.   Ano resutoran wa yasukute oishii desu.
     Oishii desu.

d)   Kono jisho wa chiisai desu.   Kono jisho wa chiisakute benri desu.
     Benri desu.

e)   Wagasha no koojoo wa atarashii desu.   Wagasha no koojoo wa atarashikute
     Subarashii desu.   subarashii desu.

3 Transformation Practice

Example: Teacher: **Sagyoo-kankyoo ga yoku narimasu. Nooritsu ga agarimasu.**
                        "The working environment becomes better. Efficiency will im-
                        prove."

              Student: **Sagyoo-kankyoo ga yoku nareba, nooritsu ga agarimasu.**
                        "If the working environment becomes better, efficiency will im-
                        prove."

a)   Ima honsha ni denwa-shimasu.   Ima honsha ni denwa-sureba, shachoo
     Shachoo ga iru hazu desu.   ga iru hazu desu.

b)   Moo sukoshi nebiki-dekimasu.   Moo sukoshi nebiki-dekireba, motto
     Motto chuumon ga kimasu.   chuumon ga kimasu.

c)   Ashita ame ga hurimasu.   Ashita ame ga hureba, Kyooto e ikanai
     Kyooto e ikanai tsumori desu.   tsumori desu.

d)   Honsha ni toiawasemasen.   Honsha ni toiawasenakereba, keeyaku
     Keeyaku wa dekimasen.   wa dekimasen.

e)   Senmonteki na setsumee ga hitsuyoo   Senmonteki na setsumee ga hitsuyoo
     desu.   nara, honsha kara senmonka ga kimasu.
     Honsha kara senmonka ga kimasu.

f)   Takada-san ni aitai desu.   Takada-san ni aitakereba, shookaijoo o
     Shookaijoo o kaite agemasu.   kaite agemasu.

g)   Robotto o doonyuu-shimasen.   Robotto o doonyuu-shinakereba, seesan-
     Seesansee wa koojoo-shinai deshoo. see wa koojoo-shinai deshoo.

4 Transformation Practice

Example: Teacher: **Oosaka e ikimasu. Shinkansen ga benri desu.**
                        "You go to Osaka. The Shinkansen line is convenient."

              Student: **Oosaka e iku (no) nara, Shinkansen ga benri desu.**
                        "If you go to Osaka, the Shinkansen line is convenient
                        [lit. If it's a matter of you going to Osaka, ...]."

a)   Honsha ni denwa-shimasu.   Honsha ni denwa-suru (no) nara, yoru
     Yoru juu-ji goro ga ii desu.   juu-ji goro ga ii desu.

b) Kawamoto-san ni aimasu.
Kono shootaijoo o todokete kudasai.

Kawamoto-san ni au (no) nara, kono shootaijoo o todokete kudasai.

c) Torihikisaki o kaitaku-shitai desu.
Takada-san ni soodan-shita hoo ga ii desu.

Torihikisaki o kaitaku-shitai (no) nara, Takada-san ni soodan-shita hoo ga ii desu.

d) En-date de keeyaku-shimasu.
Kawase no mondai mo soodan-shimasu.

En-date de keeyaku-suru (no) nara, kawase no mondai mo soodan-shimasu.

e) Sagyoo-kankyoo ga yoku arimasen.
Nooritsu wa agarimasen.

Sagyoo-kankyoo ga yoku nai (no) nara, nooritsu wa agarimasen.

5 Response Practice

Example: Teacher: **Seesansee ga koojoo-shite imasu ka.**
"Is productivity increasing?"

Student: **Ee, koojoo-shite kite imasu.**
"Yes, it has been increasing."

a) Robotto no uriage wa huete imasu ka.   Ee, huete kite imasu.

b) Keeki wa yoku natte imasu ka.   Ee, yoku natte kite imasu.

c) Mooke wa hette imasu ka.   Ee, hette kite imasu.

d) Koojoo no nooritsu wa agatte imasu ka.   Ee, agatte kite imasu.

e) Kyuu-shii-saakuru no kazu wa huete imasu ka.   Ee, huete kite imasu.

6 Comprehension Practice

Directions: The teacher reads aloud the following passage and then asks the student questions about it.

Joonzu-san wa kyoo Nissan no koojoo e ikimashita. Akarukute kiree na koojoo desu kara, sagyoo-kankyoo wa totemo ii yoo desu. Koojoo de wa takusan no Nihon-see no robotto ga sagyoo o shite imasu. Gijutsu-buchoo no Machida-san no hanashi de wa, kono robotto o doonyuu-shite kara, koojoo no seesansee ga koojoo-shita soo desu. Dono robotto mo sagyoo ga hayai shi, seekaku da soo desu. Joonzu-san wa nooritsu o motto ageru no ni wa Yuu-esu-emu no robotto mo hitsuyoo da to setsumee-shimashita. Shikashi, Machida-san wa sore ni tsuite nani mo iimasen deshita.

Questions:

1 Joonzu-san wa kyoo doko e ikimashita ka.
2 Sono koojoo no sagyoo-kankyoo wa doo desu ka.
3 Doo shite sono koojoo no seesansee ga koojoo-shite kimashita ka.
4 Nihon-see no robotto no sagyoo wa doo desu ka.
5 Joonzu-san ni yoru to nooritsu o motto ageru no ni nani ga irimasu ka.
6 Sore ni tsuite, Machida-san wa doo iimashita ka.

30/At the Factory

EXERCISES

Inform the teacher in Japanese that:

1   In this factory (they) are producing the best quality cars in Japan.
2   A good working environment is necessary to produce good quality products.
3   Thanks to Mr. Takada of JETRO, Mr. Jones was able to meet Mr. Machida, the General Manager of the Engineering Department of Nissan.
4   Mr. Jones was impressed because the factory is well-lit and clean.
5   That company has been emphasizing quality control for fifteen years [lit. since 15 years ago].
6   Efficiency in this factory has decreased due to (its) old facilities.

Model Answers:

1   **Kono koojoo de wa Nihon de ichiban hinshitsu no ii kuruma o seesan-shite imasu.**
2   **Hinshitsu no ii seehin o tsukuru no ni wa ii sagyoo-kankyoo ga hitsuyoo desu.**
3   **Jetoro no Takada-san no okage de, Joonzu-san wa Nissan no gijutsu-buchoo no Machida-san ni aemashita.**
4   **Koojoo ga akarukute kiree na no de, Joonzu-san wa kanshin-shimashita.**
5   **Ano kaisha wa juugo-nen mae kara hinshitsu-kanri ni chikara o irete kimashita.**
6   **Hurui setsubi no see de, kono koojoo no nooritsu wa sagatte kimashita.**

BUSINESS INFORMATION

Business Proverbs

The Japanese generally do not use proverbs in daily conversation to the same extent that foreigners do. All the same, nobody wants to run around speaking just text-book Japanese. If you ever want to spice up your conversation with colloquial Japanese expressions and proverbs, as Mr. Jones does in the DIALOGUE, you may find the following examples useful.

suffering	**ku** (苦)
seed	**tane** (種)

1 Responding to Compliments: Ku wa raku no tane (苦は楽の種).
Anyone who tries to speak Japanese will at some time or another be praised for his efforts even if these are clumsy or downright laughable. To the standard compliment, "**Maa, Nihongo ojoozu desu nee**" or "My, your Japanese is good," you could reply "**Zuibun benkyoo wa taihen deshita ga, ku wa raku no tane desu** (Studying was quite a problem, but suffering is the seed of comfort)." In other words, no pain, no gain.

one-time, temporary	**ichi-ji** (一時)
shame, embarrassment	**haji** (恥)
life-time	**isshoo** (一生)
words, vocabulary	**tango** (単語)
meaning	**imi** (意味)

2 Asking for Explanations: Kiku wa ichi-ji no haji, kikanu wa isshoo no haji (聞くは一時の恥、聞かぬは一生の恥).
Everyone in Japan will also occasionally come across words and expressions he isn't familiar with. You can of course feign understanding for the moment and then consult your dictionary later. However, you may not be able to recall the words in their proper context afterwards and, more important, you could miss valuable information in the meantime. Consequently, you should screw up your courage and ask for an explanation, as follows: "**Kiku wa ichiji no haji, kikanu wa isshoo no haji to iimasu kara, nan demo wakaranai tango wa imi o kiku koto ni shiteiru no desu** (As they say, asking is a temporary embarrassment but not asking is a lifelong embarrassment, so I'm making a point of asking about the meaning of words I don't know)." In other words, better safe than sorry.

stomach, belly	**hara** (slang) (腹)
to reduce, go flat	**heru** (slang) (減る)
war, battle	**ikusa** (戦)
service, use	**choo** (長)
medicine	**yaku** (薬)

30/At the Factory

3 Entertaining: Hara ga hette wa ikusa ga dekinu (腹が減っては 戦 ができぬ); **Sake wa hyaku-yaku no choo** (酒は 百 薬の 長).

During after-hours socializing, some of your guests or colleagues will occasionally refrain from eating and drinking. To encourage them to help themselves, you may want to say: "**Hara ga hette wa ikusa ga dekinu to iimasu kara ne** (They say you can't do battle on an empty stomach)!" On the other hand, if everyone drinks to excess, you should not feel obligated to restrain them; alcohol is not such a vice in Japanese society and even immoderate drinking is commonly tolerated. Instead of being alarmed, therefore, you could say: "**Iya, sake wa hyaku-yaku no choo desu yo** (Sake is the medicine for a hundred cures/the best of all medicines)." Or simply, a glass a day keeps the doctor away.

| long belt around waist of kimono | **obi** (帯) |
| short sash to tie up sleeve of kimono | **tasuki** (襷) |

4 Recruiting: Obi ni mijikashi, tasuki ni nagashi (帯に 短 し、 襷 に長し).

It is not easy to find the staff you need in Japan (See *BUSINESS JAPANESE Business Information 15, BUSINESS JAPANESE II Business Information 28*). Either the candidates speak English, but no Japanese, or vice versa, or they do not have the specialized background and qualifications. When your recruitment efforts don't meet with success, you may want to express your frustration by saying: "**Tekitoo na hito ga kimasen nee. Minna obi ni mijikashi, tasuki ni nagashi desu** (Suitable people don't come, do they. They're all too long for the belt and too short for the sleeve)." In other words, no one quite fits the bill.

| throat | **nodo** (喉) |
| to the extent (of/that) | **hodo** (程) |

5 Eyeing New Business: Nodo kara te ga deru (喉から手が出る).

Every so often, there will be business prospects the very thought of which can make your fingers twitch with eagerness. To describe your enthusiasm, you could say, "**Nodo kara te ga deru hodo ano keeyaku ga hoshii desu** (I want that business so badly, a hand is about to come out of my throat [to grab it])." Unfortunately, nothing quite so graphic exists in the English repertory of proverbs; suffice it to say that you are waiting to secure this contract with bated breath and outstretched neck.

| demon, devil | **oni** (鬼) |
| laugh | **warau** (笑う) |

7 Future Prospects: Rainen no koto o ieba oni ga warau (来年の事を言えば鬼が笑う).

And finally, upon achieving the desired contract, you may be congratulated by a Japanese associate and perhaps asked what your expectations for the future are. Rather than exude confidence, which could be interpreted as boasting, you might simply sidestep the question altogether with: "**Rainen no koto o ieba oni ga warau** (If you talk about next year, the devil will laugh)." That is, it's best not to tempt fate by counting chickens before they're hatched. "Que sera, sera."

Lesson 31

More Technical Discussions

OBJECTIVES

1   to explain industrial robots.

2   to use terms relating to factories.

3   to indicate what someone must do.

TARGET EXPRESSIONS AND PATTERNS

1   (Someone) must do...   **...shinakereba naranai.**

2   (Someone) is just about to do...   **...suru tokoro da.**

3   may   **...ka mo shirenai.**

4   the more..., the more...   **...sureba, suru hodo ...**

SITUATION

In Nissan's research laboratory, Mr. Jones explains to Mr. Machida how the new USM robots could be useful to Nissan in automobile production.

31/More Technical Discussions

DIALOGUE

to use, make good use of	**riyoo-suru,** 利用する
about …	**… ni tsuite,** について
about how to use (them)	**doo riyoo-suru ka ni tsuite,**
Machida	どう利用するかについて

1 (I)'ll come right to the point, but (we) would like to consult with (you) about how to use your company's robots.

Sassoku desu ga, kondo wa onsha no robotto o doo riyoo-suru ka ni tsuite soodan-shitai to omoimasu.

Jones

2 That's fine. Please ask (me) anything.

Kekkoo desu. Nan de mo okiki kudasai.

	plan	**keekaku(-suru),** 計画(する)
Machida	just, in the middle of	**tokoro,** ところ

3 Presently, we are in the middle of making plans for the automation of our assembling operations.

Genzai, wagasha wa kumitate-sagyoo no jidooka o keekaku-shite iru tokoro desu.

Jones	ideal	**saiteki/na/,** 最適(な)

4 Is it the assembling operations? That new robot would be ideal for that.

Kumitate-sagyoo desu ka. Sore ni wa ano shingata robotto ga saiteki desu.

	particular	**toku ni,** 特に
	color	**iro,** 色
	shape	**katachi,** 形
	for	**… ni taisuru,** に対する
Machida	installation, mounting	**toritsuke,** 取り付け

5 Yes, in particular, (I) think the color and shape sensors would be useful for mounting (parts).

Soo desu ne. Toku ni iro ya katachi ni taisuru sensaa ga toritsuke ni benri da to omoimasu.

31/More Technical Discussions

| Jones | parts | **buhin,** 部品 |

| **6** | . What sort of mounting [lit. of parts] are you thinking of using (it) for?. | **Donna buhin no toritsuke ni tsukau okangae desu ka.** |

	well, I dare say	**maa,** まあ
	steering wheel	**handoru,** ハンドル
	tire	**taiya,** タイヤ
	battery	**batterii,** バッテリー
Machida	seat	**shiito,** シート

| **7** | (We)'re studying that right now too, but... well, (we)'re examining the mounting of such (parts) as steering wheels, tires, batteries and seats. | **Sore mo ima kenkyuu-shite iru tokoro desu ga, maa, handoru, taiya, batterii, shiito nado no toritsuke o kentoo-shite imasu.** |

| Jones | to carry | **hakobu,** 運ぶ |

| **8** | Then, that means (it) will be moving quite heavy objects, doesn't it? | **De wa, kanari omoi mono mo hakobu wake desu ne.** |

	(is) strong	**tsuyoi,** 強い
	the stronger, the better	**tsuyokereba tsuyoi hodo ii,** 強ければ強い程いい
Machida		

| **9** | Yes, that's why the stronger it is, the better. | **Soo desu. Desu kara, chikara wa tsuyokereba tsuyoi hodo ii n desu.** |

	pound, lb.	**pondo,** ポンド
	kilogram, kg.	**kiro,** キロ
	to be suitable, fit	**tekisuru,** 適する
	must develop	**kaihatsu-shinakereba naranai,** 開発しなければならない
Jones		

| **10** | This robot can easily carry 40 lbs, in other words about 18 kg, but we will have to develop a "hand" suitable for (such) operations. | **Kono robotto wa yonjup-pondo, tsumari juuhachi-kiro gurai no mono wa raku ni hakobimasu ga, sagyoo ni tekishita 'te' o kaihatsu-shinakereba narimasen.** |

to manufacture for trial	**shisaku-suru,**	試作する
already	**sude ni,**	既に
several	**ikutsuka no,**	いくつかの
to borrow	**kariru,**	借りる
to borrow	**okari-suru** (polite),	お借りする
maybe	**... ka mo shirenai,**	かもしれない

Machida

11	We're now also manufacturing various trial products for that. (We) have already obtained several patents and utility models, but (we) may request your assistance [lit. borrow your power] again, too, some day.	Sore wa watakushidomo mo iroiro shisaku-shite iru tokoro desu. Sude ni ikutsu ka no tokkyo ya jitsuyoo-shin'an mo totte aru n desu ga, mata izure sochira no ochikara mo okari-suru ka mo shiremasen.

Jones

12	Yes, (I) would be glad to be of help anytime.	Ee, itsu de mo yorokonde otetsudai-shimasu.

Machida

13	Then, (we) will look forward to your assistance at that time.	De wa, sono toki wa yoroshiku onegai-shimasu.

JAPANESE WRITING

1 町田： さっそくですが、今度は御社のロボットを どう利用するかについて 相談したいと思います。

2 ジョーンズ： 結構です。何でも お聞きください。

3 町田： 現在、わが社は組み立て作業の 自動化を計画しているところです。

4 ジョーンズ： 組み立て作業ですか。 それには あの新型ロボットが最適です。

5 町田： そうですね。 特に色や形に対するセンサーが 取り付けに便利だと思います。

6 ジョーンズ： どんな部品の取り付けに 使うお考えですか。

7 町田： それも 今研究しているところですが、 まあ、ハンドル、タイヤ、バッテリー、シートなどの 取り付けを検討しています。

8 ジョーンズ： では、かなり重いものも運ぶわけですね。

9 町田： そうです。 ですから、力は強ければ強いほどいいんです。

10 ジョーンズ： このロボットは40ポンド、 つまり18キロぐらいのものは 楽に運びますが、作業に適した「手」を 開発しなければなりません。

11 町田： それは 私共も いろいろ試作しているところです。既にいくつかの 特許 や実用新案も とってあるんですが、 又 いずれ そちらの お力も お借り するかも知れません。

12 ジョーンズ： ええ、いつでも よろこんで お手伝いします。

13 町田： では、 その時は よろしくお願いします。

ADDITIONAL USEFUL EXPRESSIONS

1 A conversation between friends

to automate	**ootomeeshonka-suru,** オートメーション化する

A:	Our company has now also decided to automate our factories.	**Uchi no kaisha mo kondo, koojoo o ootomeeshonka-suru koto ni narima-shita.**

B:	That's very good. There are many hazardous operations in your factories.	**Sore wa yokatta. Otaku no koojoo wa kiken na sagyoo ga ooi kara...**

factory worker	**kooin,** 工員
accident	**jiko,** 事故
leg	**ashi,** 足
injury	**kega,** 怪我
serious injury	**ookega,** 大怪我
to be seriously injured	**ookega o suru,** 大怪我をする

A:	Yes. Just the other day, a worker injured his leg seriously in an accident.	**Ee, senjitsu mo kooin no hitori ga jiko de ashi ni ookega o shimashita.**

B:	Is that right? That must have been terrible.	**Soo desu ka. Sore wa taihen deshita ne.**

2 At the office

A:	Is Mr. Tanaka in?	**Tanaka-kun,* iru?**

31/More Technical Discussions

B:	He left just now.	**Ima, dekaketa tokoro desu.**

	destination	**yukisaki/ikisaki,** 行き先き

A:	Where to?	**Ikisaki wa doko.**

B:	The Patent Office.	**Tokkyochoo desu.**

A:	Then, when he gets back, please tell him to come to my office.	**Jaa, kaette kitara, boku no heya ni kuru yoo ni itte kudasai.**

B:	Yes, I'll tell him. [lit. convey (it)].	**Hai, tsutaemasu.**

* **-kun** is friendly equivalent of **-san** 'Mr./Ms.' and is added to family or given names. It is more informal than **-san** and implies familiarity. Often, it is used to address those younger than oneself, and one's subordinates [Refer to *BUSINESS JAPANESE*, Lesson 10. Dialogue **10**].

REFERENCE

zairyoo	材料	materials
katai	堅い	(is) hard
yawarakai	柔らかい	(is) soft
yowai	弱い	(is) weak
joobu/na/	丈夫/な	durable
karada	体	body
atama	頭	head
kao	顔	face
me	目	eye
hana	鼻	nose
mimi	耳	ear
kuchi	口	mouth
ha	歯	tooth/teeth
kubi	首	neck
mune	胸	chest
hara, onaka	腹、お腹	belly
senaka	背中	back

146

koshi	腰	lower back
ude	腕	arm
yubi	指	finger
tsume	つめ	nail

NOTES

 Verb + **tokoro da**

The noun **tokoro**, which is literally 'place', may also refer to a 'time' or 'point' or 'occasion' when it occurs in the combination of verb + **tokoro** + copula **da**. The combination may be translated as '(just) about to do such-and-such', or '(just) doing such-and-such.'

Taberu *tokoro* **desu.**	'I'm just about to eat.'
Taberu *tokoro* **deshita.**	'I was just about to eat.'
Tabeta *tokoro* **desu.**	'I have just (now) eaten.'
Tabeta *tokoro* **deshita.**	'I had just (then) eaten.'
Tabete *iru tokoro* **desu.**	'I'm just (now) eating.'
Tabete *iru tokoro* **deshita.**	'I was just (then) eating.'
Tabete *ita tokoro* **desu.**	'I have just been eating.'
Tabete *ita tokoro* **deshita.**	'I had just been eating.'

Examples:

a) **Ima Ooyama-san ni denwa-suru** *tokoro* **desu.**
"I'm just about to call Mr. Ohyama."

b) **Takada-san ga kita toki, jimusho o deru** *tokoro* **deshita.**
"When Mr. Takada came, I was just about to leave the office."

c) **Yamada-san wa ima kaetta** *tokoro* **desu.**
"Ms. Yamada has just left (the office)."

d) **Sono toki, mitsumori o moratta** *tokoro* **deshita.**
"At that time, I had just received the written estimate."

e) **Ima robotto o kenkyuu-shite** *iru tokoro* **desu.**
"I'm just now studying robots."

f) **Shachoo ni tegami o kaite** *iru tokoro* **deshita.**
"I was just writing a letter to the President."

g) **Hirugohan o tabete** *ita tokoro* **desu.**
"I have just been having lunch."

h) **Boku ga kaetta toki, buchoo wa denwa-shite** *ita tokoro* **deshita.**
"When I came back, the General Manager had just been telephoning."

31/More Technical Discussions

2 **Ka mo shirenai** 'may/maybe'

A clause + **ka mo shirenai** means 'may ...' or 'maybe'. The pattern may be used with a clause ending with an informal non-past or past verb or adjective, or a noun + informal past copula **datta**. However, the informal non-past copula **da** is always omitted before **ka mo shirenai**.

Examples:
a) **Shachoo ga rainichi-suru** *ka mo shiremasen.*
   "Maybe the President will come to Japan."

b) **Moo mitsumori o todoketa** *ka mo shiremasen.*
   "Maybe he has already delivered the written estimate."

c) **Kono sagyoo wa muzukashii** *ka mo shiremasen.*
   "This work may be difficult."

d) **Ano hito wa seerusu-enjinia** *ka mo shiremasen.*
   "Maybe he is a sales engineer."

3 Negative Provisional + **naranai** 'must'

The combination of a negative provisional + **naranai** means 'must do such-and-such.' Thus,

Kyoo-juu ni Tanaka-san ni renraku-shi*nakereba narimasen.*
"You must contact Mr. Tanaka sometime today."

Ima ginkoo e ika*nakereba narimasen* **ka.*
"Must I go to the bank now?"

Konban wa shi*nakereba naranai* **shigoto ga aru no de, paatii e wa ikimasen.**
"There's work I must do this evening, so I won't go to the party."

* Note that in a negative answer to a question with 'must,' a negative gerund + **mo ii** is often used. Thus,

Ikanakereba narimasen ka.   **Iie, ika***nakute mo ii* **desu.**

"Must I go?"   "No, you don't have to go."

4 'The more ..., the more ...'

A provisional form + the citation form of the same verb or adjective + **hodo** is used as the Japanese equivalent of the English expression 'the more ..., the more ...' For example, **tsuyokereba tsuyoi hodo (ii)** 'the stronger, the better.'

Examples:
a) **Ookikereba ookii** *hodo* **takai n desu.**
   "The bigger (it is), the more expensive."

b) **Tsukureba tsukuru** *hodo* **nedan wa yasuku narimasu.**
   "The more we make, the cheaper the price becomes."

c) **Kono hon wa yomeba yomu** *hodo* **omoshiroku narimasu.**
   "The more I read this book, the more interesting it becomes."

d) **Sono mondai wa kenkyuu-sureba (kenkyuu-)suru** *hodo* **muzukashiku narimasu.**
   "The more I study that problem, the more difficult it becomes."

148

5 **Doo** + verb + **ka** 'How to (do)'

The combination, **doo** 'how' + citation form of a verb + particle **ka** means 'how to (do).'
Thus,

> **Kono waapuro o *doo* tsukau *ka* (o) oshiete kudasai**.
> "Please teach me how to use this word processor."

> **Kono ryoori wa *doo* taberu *ka* (ga) wakarimasen**.
> "I don't know how to eat this food."

Note that certain particles which commonly occur in the sentences, depending on their context, are often omitted when using this expression. The combination, **doo** + verb + **ka** is equivalent in meaning to the combination, verb stem + **kata**, e.g. **kakikata** 'way of writing' [Refer to *BUSINESS JAPANESE*, Lesson 12. Note **6**].

PRACTICE

1 Response Practice

Example:	Teacher:	**Robotto o kenkyuu-shite imasu ka.**
		"Are you studying robots?"
	Student:	**Ee, kenkyuu-shite iru tokoro desu.**
		"Yes, we are just studying (them)."

a)	**Ima dekakemasu ka.**	**Ee, dekakeru tokoro desu.**
b)	**Moo tegami o kakimashita ka.**	**Ee, kaita tokoro desu.**
c)	**Mitsumori o kentoo-shite imasu ka.**	**Ee, kentoo-shite iru tokoro desu.**
d)	**Honsha ni denwa-shimashita ka.**	**Ee, (denwa-)shita tokoro desu.**
e)	**Buchoo ni soodan-shimasu ka.**	**Ee, soodan-suru tokoro desu.**
f)	**Sagyoo no jidooka o keekaku-shite imasu ka.**	**Ee, keekaku-shite iru tokoro desu.**
g)	**Atarashii sensaa o kaihatsu-shite imasu ka.**	**Ee, kaihatsu-shite iru tokoro desu.**
h)	**Moo katarogu o todokemashita ka.**	**Ee, todoketa tokoro desu.**
i)	**Jidoo-koosakuki o shisaku-shimasu ka.**	**Ee, shisaku-suru tokoro desu.**
j)	**Tanaka-san wa moo kaerimashita ka.**	**Ee, kaetta tokoro desu.**

2 Response Practice

Example:	Teacher:	**Ashita ame ga huru to omoimasu ka.**
		"Do you think it'll rain tomorrow?"
	Student:	**Ee, huru ka mo shiremasen.**
		"Yes, maybe it'll rain."

a)	**Shachoo wa rainichi-suru to omoimasu ka.**	**Ee, rainichi-suru ka mo shiremasen.**

b) Kono robotto wa omoi mono o hakoberu   Ee, hakoberu ka mo shiremasen.
    to omoimasu ka.

c) Moo tokkyo o totta to omoimasu ka.   Ee, totta ka mo shiremasen.

d) Ano kaisha mo koosaku-kikai o kai-   Ee, kaihatsu-shite iru ka mo
    hatsu-shite iru to omoimasu ka.   shiremasen.

e) Kono buhin no toritsuke ni ano robotto   Ee, benri ka mo shiremasen.
    ga benri da to omoimasu ka.

3 Response Practice

Example: Teacher: **Atarashii robotto o kaihatsu-shinakute mo ii n desu ka.**
             "Is it alright (even) if we don't develop new robots?"

             Student: **Iie, kaihatsu-shinakereba narimasen.**
             "No [lit. you're wrong], we must develop (them)."

a) Kyoo kono shigoto o shinakute mo ii   Iie, shinakereba narimasen.
    desu ka.

b) Buchoo ni soodan-shinakute mo ii desu   Iie, soodan-shinakereba narimasen.
    ka.

c) Konban Takada-san ni awanakute mo ii   Iie, awanakereba narimasen.
    desu ka.

d) Ginkoo e ikanakute mo ii desu ka.   Iie, ikanakereba narimasen.

e) Tanaka-san no chikara o karinakute mo   Iie, karinakereba narimasen.
    ii desu ka.

4 Response Practice

Example: Teacher: **Tsuyoi hoo ga ii desu ka.**
             "Is the stronger one better?"

             Student: **Ee, tsuyokereba tsuyoi hodo ii desu.**
             "Yes, the stronger, the better."

a) Chiisai hoo ga yasui desu ka.   Ee, chiisakereba chiisai hodo yasui desu.

b) Atarashii hoo ga takai desu ka.   Ee, atarashikereba atarashii hodo takai
                                               desu.

c) Hurui hoo ga kachi ga arimasu ka.   Ee, hurukereba hurui hodo kachi ga
                                               arimasu.

d) Karui hoo ga benri desu ka.   Ee, karukereba karui hodo benri desu.

e) Hayai hoo ga ii desu ka.   Ee, hayakereba hayai hodo ii desu.

5 Response Practice

Example: Teacher: **Benkyoo-suru to, omoshiroku narimasu ka.**
"If one studies (it), will it become interesting?"

Student: **Benkyoo-sureba suru hodo omoshiroku narimasu.**
"The more one studies (it), the more interesting it becomes."

a) **Takusan kau to, yasuku narimasu ka.**   **Kaeba kau hodo yasuku narimasu.**

b) **Taberu to, suki ni narimasu ka.**   **Tabereba taberu hodo suki ni narimasu.**

c) **Miru to, tanoshiku narimasu ka.**   **Mireba miru hodo tanoshiku narimasu.**

d) **Chiisaku naru to, benri desu ka.**   **Chiisaku nareba naru hodo benri desu.**

e) **Kenkyuu-suru to, ii buhin ga tsu-kuremasu ka.**   **Kenkyuu-sureba suru hodo ii buhin ga tsukuremasu.**

6 Transformation Practice

Example: Teacher: **Kono kanji no yomikata o oshiete kudasai.**
"Please teach me the way to read this Chinese character."

Student: **Kono kanji o doo yomu ka (o) oshiete kudasai.**
"Please teach me how to read this Chinese character."

a) **Waapuro no tsukaikata o shitte imasu ka.**   **Waapuro o doo tsukau ka (o) shitte imasu ka.**

b) **Robotto no riyoo-no-shikata ni tsuite soodan-shimashoo.**   **Robotto o doo riyoo-suru ka ni tsuite soodan-shimashoo.**

c) **Kono ryoori no tabekata ga wakari-masen.**   **Kono ryoori o doo taberu ka (ga) wakarimasen.**

d) **Tokkyo no torikata o kenkyuu-shite imasu.**   **Tokkyo o doo toru ka (o) kenkyuu-shite imasu.**

e) **Mitsumori no kakikata o oshiete imasu.**   **Mitsumori o doo kaku ka (o) oshiete imasu.**

7 Comprehension Practice

Directions: The teacher reads aloud the following passage and then asks the student questions about it.

Joonzu-san to Machida-buchoo wa kenkyuujo de Yuu-esu-emu no robotto o doo riyoo-suru ka ni tsuite soodan-shite iru tokoro desu. Nissan wa ima kuruma no kumitate-sagyoo no jidooka o keekaku-shite imasu. Yuu-esu-emu no robotto ni wa iro ya katachi ni taisuru subarashii sensaa ga arimasu kara, kumitate sagyoo ni benri desu. Mata, kono robotto wa chikara ga tsuyoi no de, kanari omoi mono o hakobemasu kara, batterii, taiya, shiito nado no toritsuke ni benri desu. Robotto o umaku tsukau no ni wa sagyoo ni tekishita 'te' o kaihatsu-shinakereba narimasen ga, Nissan wa moo mae kara sonna kenkyuu o shiteiru shi, ikutsu ka no tokkyo mo totte aru soo desu.

31/More Technical Discussions

Questions:

1 Joonzu-san to Machida-buchoo wa doko de hanashite imasu ka.
2 Nan ni tsuite soodan-shite imasu ka.
3 Nissan wa ima donna koto o keekaku-shite imasu ka.
4 Yuu-esu-emu no robotto wa doo shite kumitate sagyoo ni benri desu ka.
5 Yuu-esu-emu no robotto wa omoi mono ga hakobemasu ka.
6 De wa sonna mono no toritsuke ni muite imasu ka.
7 Nissan wa nani o kaihatsu-shiteimasu ka.
8 Sono kenkyuu wa zenzen susunde imasen ka.

EXERCISES

Inform the teacher in Japanese that:

1 Mr. Jones is just explaining how to use USM's robots.
2 General Manager Machida thinks the robot must carry heavy objects, so as far as power goes [lit. as for power], the stronger it is, the better.
3 USM, Ltd. is just developing sensors suitable for mounting operations.
4 Mr. Ohyama said that, as for the price, the cheaper the better.
5 Maybe Mr. Brown has already contacted his head office.
6 President Smith has many things to do in America, so maybe he cannot come to Japan.
7 Mr. Takada has just come back to the office.
8 USM, Ltd. has obtained many patents and utility models for machine tools in Japan.

Model Answers:

1 Joonzu-san wa Yuu-esu-emu no robotto o doo tsukau ka ni tsuite setsumee-shite iru tokoro desu.
2 Machida-buchoo wa robotto wa omoi mono o hakobanakereba naranai no de, chikara wa tsuyokereba tsuyoi hodo ii to omotte imasu.
3 Yuu-esu-emu wa toritsuke-sagyoo ni tekishita sensaa o kaihatsu-shite iru tokoro desu.
4 Ooyama-san wa kakaku wa yasukereba yasui hodo ii to iimashita.
5 Buraun-san wa moo honsha ni renraku-shita ka mo shiremasen.
6 Sumisu-shachoo wa Amerika de shinakereba naranai koto ga takusan aru no de, Nihon e korarenai ka mo shiremasen.
7 Takada-san wa jimusho ni kaette kita tokoro desu.
8 Yuu-esu-emu wa Nihon de koosaku-kikai no tokkyo ya jitsuyoo-shin'an o takusan torimashita.

BUSINESS INFORMATION

Negotiating Parlance

Technical jargon about robots can be tricky at first but with a good manual and informed assistance, anyone can quickly master it. Likewise, with a little practice, you will eventually be able to read the various signs in Japanese negotiating parlance and thus break through the thick shell of courtesy to the message at its core.

1 Japanese Officialese: Every language has its own brand of "diplomatese" or "officialese", i.e. special euphemistic vocabulary used to avoid direct confrontation and occasionally even hide one's real intentions. In English, for example, "to take action at the appropriate time" can mean never; "to engage in frank and constructive talks" can mean heated arguments and fist-pounding. Below are some examples of Japanese bureaucratic language.* For your reference, the common interpretation of each "officialese" expression has been provided in parentheses alongside its official translation.

Shohan no jijoo ni yori... (諸般の事情により…)	... for various reasons (that no one can understand ...)
Kakyuu-teki sumiyaka ni... (可及的速やかに…)	... with all urgent speed (... maybe in a couple of years.)
Maemuki ni kentoo (suru). (前向きに検討(する)。)	study (it) with a forward-looking attitude (... but nothing more.)
Eei doryoku shitai. (鋭意努力したい。)	to want to make a sincere effort to do (... but won't.)
Zensho suru. (善処する。)	to deal/cope with as appropriate (... but it's not important, so why bother?)

* Katsuya Mogami, "Administrative Reform on Terminology: Problems Pertaining to Terminology in Documents Issued by Government Agencies." *NHK Monthly Report on Broadcast Research*, July 1985.

Caution: Note that these interpretations do not always hold true; there are of course times when the speaker of such "officialese" means exactly what he says.

2 Postponing The Decision: Japanese negotiating parlance is especially rich in ways of saying "no" without really saying so. Simple procrastination is an all-time favorite. Sometimes, Japanese businessmen will go through all the motions of complying with a request, even though they know they are in no position to do so or the proposed course of action is fruitless. This is not to mislead but rather to avoid the unpleasantness of having to say "no" on the spot. Consequently, you should not always take an expressed *intention* to cooperate at face value but instead keep in mind that, in Japan, there are times when you don't say "no" today when you can say "no" tomorrow.

Following are a few expressions occasionally used as "delay" tactics:

Ichioo yatte mimashoo.
（一応やってみましょう。）

Well, I'll at least give it a try (... but there's a 50% chance of failure.)

Yarudake yatte mimasu.
（やるだけやってみます。）

I'll do all I can (... but don't expect any great results.)

Kentoo shimasu.
（検討します。）

I'll consider it (... but I might have to tell you "no" later.)

Kangaete okimasu.
（考えておきます。）

I'll think about it (... but I can't promise anything.)

3 Changing The Subject: Another ploy to avoid saying "no" directly is to ramble on and on about irrelevant matters or to deviate repeatedly from the subject, as shown in the following example:

A: So, our products meet your conditions 100%. And how soon do you think you can place an order?

Soo suru to, uchi no seehin wa onsha no jooken o subete mitashite iru to iu koto desu ne. De itsu goro gochuumon o itadakemasu ka.

B: Let's see, one of your company's plants is located in San Diego, right?

Soo desu nee. Onsha no koojoo no hitotsu wa San Diego ni arimashita nee.

A: Yes, in San Diego. And... do you think we can expect an answer within the month?

Ee, San diego ni mo arimasu. De, kongetsu-chuu ni gohenji itadakemasu ka.

B: In 1963, I stayed in San Diego for a year, and ...

Sen-kyuu-hyaku-roku-juu-san nen ni ichinen kan San Diego ni imashita ga ...

A: Is that right? And ...

So desu ka. De ...

B: It is such a pleasant place ...

Ii tokoro desu nee.

At this point, the other members of the Japanese negotiating team will no doubt have picked up the hint and will chime in with their own wonderful impressions of San Diego. Having been once derailed, you should not try to force your way back on track. Not only will it *not* do any good, but you may offend your well-meaning partners whose convoluted "ring around the no's" is actually intended only to spare you the unpleasant tidings.

4 Agreeing, or When A Yes Is No Yes: Japanese negotiating parlance also includes numerous expressions for "yes" which don't mean "yes" at all. For example, you may find your audience nodding and repeating "**Ee**" （ええ, yes) or "**Hai, hai**" （はい、はい, yes, yes) throughout your presentation. You may think that the Japanese are a remarkably congenial people or even pat yourself on the back for your own irresistible salesmanship. In fact, however, these sounds of agreement are no more than **aizuchi** （相槌, echoing sounds) widely used to indicate attentiveness, not agreement. Consequently, all the **hai, hai**'s are best interpreted as "I understand, I understand" or "I'm listening, I'm listening" rather than "I agree, I agree." When all is said and done, it may be advisable just to remember the wisdom of author Masaaki Imai: In Japan, one should "never take a smile for a yes [and] never take yes for an answer."

Lesson 32

Service and Maintenance

OBJECTIVES

1 to discuss warranty terms.

2 to learn contract related vocabulary.

3 to use the Causative form.

TARGET EXPRESSIONS AND PATTERNS

1 to make (someone) do …   … saseru.

2 Apparently …   … rashii.

3 There are times when …   … suru koto ga aru.
   happens/does

4 before doing …   … suru mae

5 after doing …   … shita ato

SITUATION

As the negotiations enter their final phase, Mr. Ohyama calls Mr. Brown and Mr. Jones to discuss the trial period for USM's robots, as well as their maintenance.

32/Service and Maintenance

DIALOGUE

	(is) long	**nagai,** 長い
	for a long time	**nagai aida,** 長い間
Ohyama	to keep (you) waiting	**omatase-suru** (polite), お待たせする

1	(We) have kept (you) waiting for a long time, but the technical investigation has been completed at last.	**Nagai aida omatase-shimashita ga, yatto gijutsuteki na kentoo ga owari-mashita.**

Brown

2	Is that right? And what was the conclusion of the Engineering Department?	**Soo desu ka. Sore de, Gijutsu-bu no ketsuron wa ikaga deshita ka.**

	argument	**giron(-suru),** 議論(する)
	(an) argument takes place	**giron ga deru,** 議論がでる
	(it) seems	**rashii,** らしい
Ohyama	after all, finally	**kekkyoku,** 結局

3	(It) seems there were various arguments, but finally it was decided that it would be better to introduce (the robots).	**Iroiro giron mo deta rashii desu ga, kekkyoku doonyuu-shita hoo ga ii to iu koto ni narimashita.**

Brown	to be relieved	**hotto-suru,** ほっとする

4	Thank you (very much). I am relieved (to hear) this.	**Arigatoo gozaimashita. Kore de, watakushi mo hotto-shimashita.**

	before finalizing the contract	**keeyaku-suru mae (ni),** 契約する前(に)
	two or three	**ni, san,** 2、3
Ohyama	to confirm	**tashikameru,** 確かめる

5	There are 2-3 points (I) would like to check before finalizing [lit. doing] the contract, so ...	**Soko de, keeyaku-suru mae ni, ni, san tashikametai koto ga arimasu no de ...**

Brown

6	Yes [lit. What are they]?	**Nan deshoo ka.**

	trial use	**shiyoo(-suru),** 試用(する)
	period	**kikan,** 期間
Ohyama	trial period	**shiyoo-kikan,** 試用期間

7	First of all, about the trial period. How would three months be?	**Mazu, shiyoo-kikan desu ga, san-kage-tsu de doo deshoo ka.**

Brown

8	That is fine.	**Kekkoo desu.**

	engineer	**gishi,** 技師
Ohyama	to send	**yokosu,** 寄越す

9	About how many engineers would USM send (us)?	**Yuu-esu-emu no gishi wa nan-nin gurai yokoshite kuremasu ka.**

stage, step	**dankai,** 段階
each, respectively	**sorezore,** それぞれ
counter for people	**-mee,** 名
10 persons	**juu-mee,** 十名
construction	**kooji(-suru),** 工事(する)
to complete	**kansee-suru,** 完成する
after completing	**kansee-shita ato (de),** 完成した後で
operation	**unten(-suru),** 運転(する)
maintenance	**hoshu(-suru),** 保守(する)
each	**zutsu,** ずつ
Jones to remain	**nokoru,** 残る

10	During the installation stage, about 10 different specialists would be coming, but after the construction has been completed, one engineer for operation and one for maintenance would remain.	**Husetsu no dankai de wa, sorezore no senmonka ga juu-mee gurai kimasu ga, kooji ga kansee-shita ato wa, unten no gishi to hoshu no gishi ga hitori zutsu nokorimasu.**

32/Service and Maintenance

	guarantee	hoshoo(-suru), 保証(する)
Ohyama	warranty period	hoshoo-kikan, 保証期間

11	The warranty period is one year, isn't it?	Hoshoo-kikan wa ichi-nen desu ne.

Brown

12	Yes, one year after the end of the trial period.	Hai, shiyoo-kikan ga owatte kara, ichi-nen desu.

	out of order	koshoo(-suru), 故障(する)
	free of charge	muryoo, 無料
Ohyama	to fix	naosu, 直す

13	So that means (you) will fix all problems during the warranty period free of charge?	Hoshoo-kikan-chuu no koshoo wa subete muryoo de naoshite kureru wake desu ne.

	to have someone fix	naosaseru, 直させる
	charges	yuuryoo, 有料
	may sometimes also (happen)	(suru) koto mo aru, (する)事もある
	concerning ...	... ni kansuru, に関する
Jones	regulations	kitee(-suru), 規定(する)

14	(We) will have USM engineers fix all (mechanical) problems, but there may be charges applicable depending on the cause of the problems. The terms of the warranty [lit. regulations concerning the warranty] are explained in detail in this brochure, so please ...	Koshoo wa subete Yuu-esu-emu no gishi ni naosasemasu ga, koshoo no gen'in ni yotte wa yuuryoo ni naru koto mo arimasu. Hoshoo ni kan-suru kitee wa kono shorui ni kuwashiku kaite arimasu kara, doozo.

Ohyama	to have someone examine	kentoo-saseru, 検討させる

15	Then, (I) will have (my staff) examine this immediately.	Jaa, sassoku kore o kentoo-sasemashoo.

Brown	to start	torikakaru, とりかかる

16	Well then, (I) too shall start preparing the contract.	De wa, watakushi mo keeyakusho no junbi ni torikakarimasu.

JAPANESE WRITING

1 大山： 長い間お待たせしましたが、やっと技術的な検討が終わりました。

2 ブラウン： そうですか。 それで、技術部の結論はいかがでしたか。

3 大山： いろいろ議論も出たらしいですが、結局導入した方がいい ということになりました。

4 ジョーンズ： ありがとうございました。 これで、私もほっとしました。

5 大山： そこで、契約する前に、2、3確かめたいことがありますので…

6 ブラウン： 何でしょうか。

7 大山： まず、試用期間ですが、 3か月でどうでしょうか。

8 ジョーンズ： 結構です。

9 大山： ユー・エス・エムの技師は何人ぐらい寄越してくれますか。

10 ジョーンズ： 付設の段階では、それぞれの専門家が十名ぐらい来ますが、工事が完成した後は、運転の技師と保守の技師が一人ずつ残ります。

11 大山： 保証期間は一年ですね。

12 ブラウン： はい、試用期間が終わってから、一年です。

13 大山： 保証期間中の故障はすべて無料で直してくれるわけですね。

14 ブラウン： 故障はすべてユー・エス・エムの技師に直させますが、故障の原因によっては有料になることもあります。 保証に関する規定はこの書類に詳しく書いてありますから、 どうぞ。

15 大山： じゃあ、さっそく これを検討させましょう。

16 ブラウン： では、私も契約書の準備にとりかかります。

ADDITIONAL USEFUL EXPRESSIONS

1 During business negotiations

inventory **zaiko,** 在庫

A:	Does this product have a large inventory?	**Kono seehin wa zaiko ga ooi desu ka.**

to sell well **yoku ureru,** よく売れる

B:	No. It is selling well, so I think the inventory is small.	**Iie, yoku urete imasu kara, zaiko wa sukunai to omoimasu.**

A:	Then, around when will (it) be delivered?	**De wa, nooki wa itsu goro ni narimasu ka.**

32/Service and Maintenance

B:	It will be about one month after (you) have signed the contract.	**Keeyaku-shite itadaite kara, ik-kagetsu gurai ato ni narimasu.**

goods in stock	**zaikobun,** 在庫分 （ざいこぶん）
to deliver	**noonyuu-suru,** 納入する （のうにゅう）

A:	(That) is quite slow. In any case, I will sign the contract today, so please deliver (all that you have) right away, even if it's just the goods in stock.	**Osoi desu nee. Tonikaku, kyoo kee-yaku-shimasu kara, zaikobun dake de mo, sugu noonyuu-shite kudasai.**

to arrange	**tehai-suru,** 手配する （てはい）

B:	Thank you very much. We will arrange that immediately.	**Arigatoo gozaimasu. Sassoku tehai-shimasu.**

2 During business negotiations

after-sales service	**ahutaa-saabisu,** アフターサービス
sure, safe	**daijoobu/na/,** 大丈夫(な) （だいじょうぶ）

A:	Is the servicing alright?	**Ahutaa-saabisu wa daijoobu deshoo nee.**

every	**goto ni,** 毎に （ごと）
inspection	**tenken(-suru),** 点検(する) （てんけん）

B:	Yes, of course. We will be here for inspection every 6 months.	**Hai, mochiron desu. Rok-kagetsu goto ni tenken ni ukagaimasu.**

A:	And in case there is a problem?	**Koshoo no baai wa.**

repairs	**shuuri(-suru),** 修理(する) （しゅうり）
each place	**kakuchi,** 各地 （かくち）

B:	The local agencies [lit. agencies of each place] will do simple repairs, but for difficult problems we will dispatch engineers from our head office.	**Kantan na shuuri wa kakuchi no dairiten ga shimasu ga, muzukashii koshoo wa honsha no gishi o haken-shimasu.**

	immediately after (doing) ...	... -tara sugu, …たらすぐ

A:	Then, if there is any problem, you would come immediately, right?	**Jaa, nani ka attara, sugu kite kureru n desu ne.**

B:	Yes, we will come as soon as (we) are contacted.	**Hai, renraku ga attara, sugu ukagai-masu.**

	to conclude	**ketsuron o dasu,** 結論を出す

A:	Then, we will reach a conclusion within 2, 3 days, so ...	**Jaa, ni, san-nichi-chuu ni ketsuron o dashimasu kara ...**

B:	Please [imp. if you would be so kind]...	**Yoroshiku onegai-shimasu.**

NOTES

1 The Causative Form

Most Japanese verbs have causative forms meaning 'to make/have (someone) do such-and-such,' 'to cause (someone) to do such-and-such' and 'to let (someone) do such-and-such.' To form the causative:

A) Class 1 verb (or **-ru** verb): Drop the final **-ru** and add **-saseru**.

Example: **taberu** 'to eat' — **tabe*saseru*** 'to make (someone) eat'

B) Class 2 verb (or **-u** verb): Drop the final **-u** and add **-aseru**.

Example: hanasu 'to speak' — **hana*saseru*** 'to make (someone) speak'

Note: In the case of **-u** verbs ending in two vowels (e.g.**tsukau**), drop **-u** and add **-waseru**.

Example: **tsukau** 'to use' — tsuka*waseru* 'to make (someone) use'

C) Class 3 verb (or **-aru** verb): No causative forms.

D) Irregular verbs:

Example: **kuru** 'to come' — *kosaseru* 'to make (someone) come'
                suru 'to do' — *saseru* 'to make (someone) do'

Note: All causatives may themselves be considered Class 1 verbs (or **-ru** verbs).

32/Service and Maintenance

Pattern:

Person(s) acting/ who cause(s)	Person(s) acted upon	Object	Causative Verb
Joonzu-san + wa	**gishi + ni**	**koshoo + o**	**naosasemashita.**
Mr. Jones made the engineer fix the mechanical problem.			

Note: The person acted upon (i.e. **gishi**) is usually followed by the particle **ni**. However, in the case of the causative of intransitive verbs, the person acted upon may also be followed by the particle **o**. Thus,

> Yamada-san *ni* ikasemasu. "I'll have/make Ms. Yamada go."
> or
> Yamada-san *o* ikasemasu. "I'll have/make Ms. Yamada go."

Examples:
a) **Buraun-san wa Yamada-san *ni* chizu o kawasemashita.**
"Mr. Brown had Ms. Yamada buy a map."

b) **Dare *ni* mitsumori o todokesasemashoo ka.**
"Who shall we have deliver the written estimate?"

c) **Ooyama-buchoo wa Suzuki-san *ni* keeyakusho o kakaseru tsumori desu.**
"General Manager Ohyama intends to make Mr. Suzuki write the contract."

d) **Yuu-esu-emu wa Joonzu-san *o* Nihon e kosasemashita.**
"USM, Ltd. made Mr. Jones come to Japan."

The causative gerund is sometimes followed by **kudasai** or **kudasaimasen ka** to politely ask permission. Thus,

> **Anata no waapuro o tsuka*wasete kudasai*.**
> "Please let me use your word processor."

> **Musuko o kono kaisha de hatara*kasete kudasaimasen ka*.**
> "Won't you please let my son work in this company?"

2 Rashii

The adjective **rashii** may occur after verbs, adjectives, past copula **datta**, nouns and some particles, and means 'is apparent (that)', 'apparently.'

Examples:
a) **Kawamoto-san wa raishuu Amerika e iku *rashii* desu.**
"Mr. Kawamoto is apparently going to America next week [lit. (it) is apparent (that) ...]."

b) **Gijutsubu no kentoo wa owatta *rashii* desu.**
"Apparently, the Engineering Department has completed (its) examination [lit. the examination... has been completed]."

c) **Ano ryooriya wa totemo takai *rashii* desu.**
"That Japanese restaurant is apparently expensive."

d) **Ano onna no hito wa Takada-san no okusan *rashii* desu yo.**
"Apparently, that woman is Mr. Takada's wife."

e) **Senshuu Yamada-san wa byooki datta *rashii* desu.**
"Apparently, Ms. Yamada was sick last week."

Note: **rashii** is sometimes used to indicate that something or someone is typical. Thus,

Kare wa Amerikajin *rashii* Amerikajin desu.
"He is a typical American [lit. an apparently-American American]."

3 Non-past Verb + **mae**; Past Verb + **ato**

A) Mae
The noun **mae** 'the front', 'the front (part),' when preceded by a non-past verb, may also mean 'before (doing such-and-such),' e.g. **kuru mae** 'before coming.' When this sequence is used to indicate the timing of a specific action or occurence, it is often followed by the particle **ni**. Thus,

Nihon e *kuru mae ni*, Amerika no daigaku de nihongo o benkyoo-shimashita.
"I studied Japanese at an American university before coming to Japan."

Keeyaku *suru mae ni*, jooken o yoku kentoo shimashoo.
"Let's examine the conditions well before making the contract."

When the non-past verb + **mae** sequence modifies a noun, it is followed by **no**. Thus,

Nihon e *kuru mae no* junbi to shite, kono hon o yomimashita.
"I read this book as a preparation for coming to Japan [lit. before coming to Japan preparation]."

As you can see in the above examples, **mae** always occurs after a non-past verb even when the action of the sentence has occured in the past.

B) Ato
The noun **ato** 'the back', 'the rear' may also occur after a past verb and means 'after (doing such-and-such).' When this sequence is used to indicate the timing of a specific action or occurence, it is often followed by the particle **de**. Thus,

Nihon e *kita ato de*, Nihongo no benkyoo o hajimemashita.
"I started learning Japanese after coming to Japan."

When the past verb + **ato** sequence modifies a noun, it is always followed by the particle **no**.

Kore wa shachoo to *soodan-shita ato no* ketsuron desu.
"This is the conclusion after consulting with the president."

4 Non-past verb + **koto ga aru**

A past verb + **koto ga aru** was previously introduced [Refer to *BUSINESS JAPANESE II*, Lesson 26, Note **1**]. When **koto ga aru** is preceded by a non-past verb, it means 'there are times when (someone does such-and-such),' 'there are times when (such-and-such happens).'

Compare: **Kyooto e itta koto ga arimasu.**
"I have been to Kyoto."

and

Kyooto e iku koto ga arimasu.
"I go to Kyoto occasionally [lit. There are times when I go to Kyoto]."

32/Service and Maintenance

Examples: a)   **Nichiyoobi ni mo hataraku koto ga arimasu.**
"There are times when I work even on Sunday."

                b)   **Nichiyoobi ni hataraku koto wa arimasen.**
"I never work on Sunday
[lit. There is never a time when I work on Sunday]."

                c)   **Nichiyoobi ni hatarakanai koto ga arimasu.**
"There are times when I don't work on Sunday."

                d)   **Nichiyoobi ni hatarakanai koto wa arimasen.**
"I always work on Sundays
[lit. There is never a time when I don't work on Sunday]."

PRACTICE

1 Response Practice

Example: Teacher: **Dare ga koshoo o naoshimasu ka. /gishi/**
                     "Who will fix the mechanical problem?" /engineer/

            Student: **Gishi ni naosasemasu.**
                     "I will have the engineer fix (it)."

a)   **Dare ga mitsumori o kakimasu ka.**   **Imai-san ni kakasemasu.**
     /Imai-san/

b)   **Dare ga shachoo ni denwa-shimasu ka.**   **Yamada-san ni denwa-sasemasu.**
     /Yamada-san/

c)   **Dare ga katarogu o todokemasu ka.**   **Suzuki-san ni todokesasemasu.**
     /Suzuki-san/

d)   **Dare ga torihiki-jooken o kentoo-**   **Bengoshi ni kentoo-sasemasu.**
     shimasu ka. /bengoshi/

e)   **Dare ga Oosaka e shutchoo-shimasu ka.** **Hisho o shutchoo-sasemasu.**
     /hisho/

2 Transformation Practice

Example: Teacher: **Bengoshi ga keeyakusho o junbi-shimashita. /shachoo/**
                   "The lawyer prepared the contract." /the President/

            Student: **Shachoo wa bengoshi ni keeyakusho o junbi-sasemashita.**
                   "The President made the lawyer prepare the contract."

a)   **Tanaka-san ga kono zasshi o kaimashi-**   **Watakushi wa Tanaka-san ni kono zas-**
     ta. /watakushi/   **shi o kawasemashita.**

b)   **Kodomo ga sono hon o yomimasu.**   **Kanai wa kodomo ni sono hon o**
     /kanai/   **yomasemasu.**

c)   **Kenkyuushitsu ga robotto o shisaku-**   **Buchoo wa kenkyuushitsu ni robotto o**
     shimashita. /buchoo/   **shisaku-sasemashita.**

d) Yamada-san ga sono waapuro o tsu-kaimasu. /Buraun-san/

Buraun-san wa Yamada-san ni sono waapuro o tsukawasemasu.

e) Suzuki-san wa sono shorui o yomi-masen. /Ooyama-san/

Ooyama-san wa Suzuki-san ni sono sho-rui o yomasemasen.

3 Response Practice

Example: Teacher: **Itte kuremasu ka.**
"Will you go for me?"

Student: **Ee, ikasete kudasai.**
"Yes, please let me go."

a) Sekkeezu o kaite kuremasu ka.

Ee, kakasete kudasai.

b) Ashita mo kite kuremasu ka.

Ee, kosasete kudasai.

c) Buchoo ni renraku-shite kuremasu ka.

Ee, renraku-sasete kudasai.

d) Kawamoto-san ni atte kuremasu ka.

Ee, awasete kudasai.

e) Robotto o kenkyuu-shite kuremasu ka.

Ee, kenkyuu-sasete kudasai.

4 Response Practice

Example: Teacher: **Shachoo wa rainichi-suru deshoo ka.**
"Do you think the President will come to Japan?"

Student: **Ee, rainichi-suru rashii desu yo.**
"Yes, he is apparently coming (to Japan)."

a) Kikai no koshoo wa naotta deshoo ka.

Ee, naotta rashii desu yo.

b) Tanaka-san wa kyoo yasumu deshoo ka.

Ee, yasumu rashii desu yo.

c) Ano torihiki wa dame datta no deshoo ka.

Ee, dame datta rashii desu yo.

d) Husetsu no hiyoo wa takai deshoo ka.

Ee, takai rashii desu yo.

e) Ano hito wa gishi deshoo ka.

Ee, gishi rashii desu yo.

5 Transformation Practice

Example: Teacher: **Tokidoki Oosaka e ikimasu.**
"I sometimes go to Osaka."

Student: **Oosaka e iku koto ga arimasu.**
"There are times when I go to Osaka."

a) Tokidoki Nihon-ryoori o tabemasu.

Nihon-ryoori o taberu koto ga arimasu.

b) Tokidoki Takada-san ni aimasu.

Takada-san ni au koto ga arimasu.

c) Tokidoki yoku nemuremasen.

Yoku nemurenai koto ga arimasu.

d) Tokidoki waapuro o tsukaimasu.

Waapuro o tsukau koto ga arimasu.

e) Tokidoki kaisha o yasumimasu.

Kaisha o yasumu koto ga arimasu.

32/Service and Maintenance

6 Transformation Practice

Example: Teacher: **Keeyaku-shimasu. Yoku kenkyuu-shimasu.**
"We will make a contract. We will study (it) well."

Student: **Keeyaku-suru mae ni, yoku kenkyuu-shimasu.**
"Before making a contract, we will study (it) well."

a)   **Robotto o doonyuu-shimasu.**
Kumiai to hanashiaimashita.

Robotto o doonyuu-suru mae ni, kumiai to hanashiaimashita.

b)   **Mitsumori o todokemasu.**
Buraun-san ni misemasu.

Mitsumori o todokeru mae ni, Buraun-san ni misemasu.

c)   **Chuumon-shimasu.**
Nebiki no soodan o shimashoo.

Chuumon-suru mae ni, nebiki no soodan o shimashoo.

d)   **Kono kikai o seesan-shimasu.**
Tokkyo o totta hoo ga ii desu.

Kono kikai o seesan-suru mae ni, tokkyo o totta hoo ga ii desu.

e)   **Kooza o hirakimasu. Kee'ee-jootai o setsumee-shimashita.**

Kooza o hiraku mae ni, kee'ee-jootai o setsumee-shimashita.

7 Transformation Practice

Example: Teacher: **Kooji ga kansee-shimashita. Kikai o husetsu-shimasu.**
"Construction has been completed. We will install the machine."

Student: **Kooji ga kansee-shita ato, kikai o husetsu-shimasu.**
"After construction has been completed, we will install the machine."

a)   **Shachoo ni denwa-shimashita.**
Uchi e kaerimashita.

Shachoo ni denwa-shita ato, uchi e kaerimashita.

b)   **Mitsumori o kakimashita.**
Shain ni todokesasemasu.

Mitsumori o kaita ato, shain ni todokesasemasu.

c)   **Honsha ni toiawasemashita.**
Nebiki ni tsuite okotaeshimasu.

Honsha ni toiawaseta ato, nebiki ni tsuite okotaeshimasu.

d)   **Gijutsuteki na kentoo ga owarimashita.**
Moo ichido aimashoo.

Gijutsuteki na kentoo ga owatta ato, moo ichido aimashoo.

e)   **Robotto o kaihatsu-shimashita.**
Tokkyo o toru tsumori desu.

Robotto o kaihatsu-shita ato, tokkyo o toru tsumori desu.

8 Comprehension Practice

Directions: The teacher reads aloud the following passage and then asks the student questions about it.

Kyoo wa Buraun-san to Joonzu-san wa keeyaku mae no hanashiai no tame ni, Nissan no Ooyama-buchoo no jimusho e kimashita. Ooyama-san to soodan-shite, shiyoo-kikan wa san-kagetsu ni shimashita. Husetsu no dankai de wa, Yuu-esu-emu kara juu-nin gurai no senmonka ga kite, husetsu no tetsudai o shimasu ga, kooji ga kansee-shita ato wa unten no gishi to hoshu no gishi ga hitori zutsu nokoru koto ni narimashi-ta. Hoshoo-kikan wa ichi-nen de, sono kikan-chuu no koshoo wa subete Yuu-esu-emu no gishi ga naoshimasu ga, koshoo no gen'in ni yotte wa yuuryoo ni naru koto mo arimasu. Buraun-san wa hoshoo ni kansuru kitee ga kaite aru shorui o Ooyama-san ni agemashita. Ooyama-san wa sassoku sutahhu ni sono kitee o kentoo-saseru soo desu. Buraun-san mo keeyakusho no junbi ni torikakarimasu.

Questions:

1 Nan no tame ni Buraun-san to Joonzu-san wa Nissan e ikimashita ka.
2 Robotto no shiyoo-kikan wa dono kurai desu ka.
3 Yuu-esu-emu kara gishi wa nan-nin gurai kimasu ka.
4 Kooji ga kansee-shita ato mo gishi ga nokorimasu ka. Nan-nin desu ka.
5 Kono robotto no hoshoo-kikan wa dono kurai desu ka.
6 Koshoo wa dare ni naosasemasu ka.
7 Hoshoo-kikan-chuu no koshoo wa subete muryoo de naoshimasu ka.
8 Ooyama-san wa sassoku sutahhu ni nani o sasemasu ka.
9 Buraun-san wa nan no junbi ni torikakarimasu ka.

EXERCISES

Inform the teacher in Japanese that:

1 Apparently, Mr. Brown will start preparing the contract soon.
2 General Manager Ohyama is apparently opposing the terms concerning the warranty.
3 USM, Ltd. made Mr. Jones come to Japan for the negotiations with Nissan.
4 There are times when Mr. Brown goes back to America for meetings at the head office.
5 After consulting with Mr. Jones, Mr. Brown had the secretary type the contract.
6 Before starting the construction, you had better examine the cost once more.
7 According to the contract, an engineer will come to our factory to check the robots every six months.
8 Apparently, Mr. Brown will have Ms. Yamada go to Detroit.

Model Answers:

1 Buraun-san wa sassoku keeyakusho no junbi ni torikakaru rashii desu.
2 Ooyama-buchoo wa hoshoo ni kansuru kitee ni hantai-shite iru rashii desu.
3 Yuu-esu-emu wa Nissan to no kooshoo no tame ni Joonzu-san o rainichi-sasemashita (or **Nihon e kosasemashita**).
4 Buraun-san wa honsha no kaigi no tame ni, Amerika e kaeru koto ga arimasu.
5 Joonzu-san to soodan-shita ato, Buraun-san wa hisho ni keeyakusho o taipu-sasemashita.
6 Kooji ni torikakaru mae ni, moo ichi-do hiyoo o kentoo-shita hoo ga ii desu.
7 Keeyakusho ni yoru to, gishi ga rok-kagetsu goto ni uchi no koojoo ni robotto no tenken ni kimasu.
8 Buraun-san wa Yamada-san o Detoroito e ikaseru rashii desu.

BUSINESS INFORMATION

Maintaining the Long-Term Relationship

Japanese businessmen sometimes say that on a clear day, the American company can see forever–or at least through to the next quarter of the business year. Though spoken in jest, this quip underscores a real fear among the Japanese that Westerners do not share their own notions about lasting business relationships. Many think that Western companies are concerned only about short-term profits and if things go wrong, they would not hesitate to pull out of Japan leaving their customers in the lurch.

Japanese companies go through a lot of trouble every year to allay any such fears of sudden disruption. Following their example may help reassure your own clients that you are not just interested in a one-year stand but genuinely committed to long-term business in their country.

1 Year-Round Services: In Japan, "small service is true service." Companies invariably extend little favors and courtesies to one another in addition, and as a complement, to their actual business transactions. Such services of course vary from one industry to the next and include discounts on products, advance notice about–and preferential seating during–special events, etc. Companies also distribute a wide range of complimentary articles bearing their name and logo, such as calendars, diaries, umbrellas and notepads, which are usually of higher quality than the "give-aways" in other countries. Occasionally, firms even arrange special training sessions for the freshman staff of their clients. Banks, for example, will explain the ins and outs of savings accounts, while telephone companies may offer classes in over-the-phone courtesies, and so on. For foreign firms, it may be advisable to volunteer services that your Japanese competition cannot, e.g. assistance with English-language translations, or information about MBA and other educational programs back home. Whatever you do offer in terms of extras, however, you should remember that, in Japan, the term "service" or **saabisu** (サービス) *means* "free of charge." Any fee imposed on your extra favors will therefore be a contradiction in terms and no doubt also an insult.

2 Seasonal Gifts: In addition to their year-round services, Japanese businessmen have various seasonal obligations, such as sending year-end greetings or **nengajoo** (See *BUSINESS JAPANESE Business Information 1*), and giving traditional summer and winter gifts, or **ochuugen** (御中元) and **oseebo** (御歳暮), respectively. Choosing the right **ochuugen** and **oseebo** gifts for the right clients can be exceedingly complicated. Companies belonging to one trading or banking association take care not to present gifts produced by other companies within the same group, for example, and certain products may be appropriate for individual recipients though not for a whole company. In general, though, seasonal gifts consist of edible goods with long shelf-life, like spices or canned fruits, or useful daily household articles like towels and soap–in short, anything *but* cash. If you wish to give articles from the home country, you should take care to present them in attractive wrapping, and in sets of three, five or seven. Sets of four–a commonplace in the West–should be avoided at all cost since the pun on the Japanese word for four, or **shi**, is "death." It is also a good idea to keep a meticulous record of what you give and receive. This is partly so you will not accidentally repeat yourself the following year but also so you can upgrade your gifts gradually as your business relationship matures.

Foreigners sometimes complain that gift-giving in Japan is a vicious cycle since just about every gift entails an obligation to reciprocate in kind. To some visitors, moreover, **ochuugen** and **oseebo** smack of bribery. Actually, though, no gift–however elaborate–is expected to bring in new business. Overly generous gifts are in fact considered bad taste because of the return-obligation it forces upon the recipient. Instead, **ochuugen** and **oseebo** gifts are just tokens of appreciation for the business you received. Some people speculate that the usefulness of such gifts at one time symbolized the giver's own willingness to continue service in the future. Rather than blackmail or bribery, therefore, you should think of **ochuugen** and **oseebo** as signs of commitment and lubricants for a long-term business partnership.

3 Changing the Guard: More important than gifts are the formal visits to clients to announce changes in personnel. If you or anyone of your staff should resign, or if you are being recalled, you should do everything possible to assure your Japanese associates that, despite the changes, everything will be business as normal. It may in fact be advisable to take your cue from Japanese companies when it comes to changing the guard in your own. Whenever the Japanese shuffle their staff around–which they do frequently (See *BUSINESS JAPANESE II Business Information 28*)– the employee being transferred will visit all his personal clients, usually together with his superior or boss, and thank them for their past cooperation. He or his superior will also introduce his successor and ask for the client's continued support of the company. No matter how sudden your decision to resign, no matter how urgent the matter for which you are being recalled, you should at least take the time to go the rounds for **taishoku no aisatsu** (退職の挨拶, paying respects upon resignation) or **tenkin no aisatsu** (転勤の挨拶, paying respects upon transferral), as the case may be. Only then will you be able to reassure your client that, (to borrow from Tennyson) though faces come and faces go, your relationship goes on forever.

For your reference the following is a list of the articles that made the "Top Ten Most-Wanted List" of presents for **Ochuugen** and **Oseebo** in recent years.

Ochuugen: Top Ten*

1st	Place:	Gift Coupons
2nd	Place:	Beer Coupons
3rd	Place:	Coffee
4th	Place:	Cooking Oil
5th	Place:	**Nori** (Seaweed)
6th	Place:	Book Coupons
7th	Place:	Soap and Detergents
8th	Place:	Specialty Foods
9th	Place:	**Shiitake** (Mushrooms)
10th	Place:	**Yooshu** (Foreign Liquor)

32/Service and Maintenance

Oseebo: Top Ten**

1st	Place:	Gift Coupons
2nd	Place:	Spices, Seasonings, Cooking Oil
3rd	Place:	**Nori** (Seaweed)
4th	Place:	Coffee
5th	Place:	Sugar
6th	Place:	**Shooyu** (Soy Sauce)
7th	Place:	**Nihon Cha** (Green Tea)
8th	Place:	Dairy Products (Butter, Cheese)
9th	Place:	**Yooshu** (Foreign Liquor)
10th	Place:	Specialty Sweets

* The **Nikkei Ryuutsuu Shinbun**, 1984.
** Ajinomoto General Foods Survey, 1983.

Lesson 33

Planning a Celebration

OBJECTIVES

1   to report on the progress of business talks.

2   to express one's appreciation.

3   to discuss Japanese customs for entertaining guests.

4   to give polite advice.

5   to ask someone else's permission.

TARGET EXPRESSIONS AND PATTERNS

1   Why don't you do…   …**shitara doo desu ka.**
2   I think you should do…   …**shitara ii to omou.**
3   Please let me do…   …**sasete itadaku.**

SITUATION

Mr. Brown's endurance and·salesmanship are rewarded when, at long last, the contract with Nissan is finalized. Mr. Brown visits Mr. Takada at JETRO to report the good news.

33/Planning a Celebration

DIALOGUE

Brown   yesterday   **sakujitsu,** 昨日<ruby>昨<rt>さく</rt>日<rt>じつ</rt></ruby>

| 1 | Thanks to your (advice), (we) were finally able to finalize that robot contract yesterday [lit. That robot case, (we) were…]. | **Ree no robotto no ken desu ga, okagesa-ma de, sakujitsu keeyaku-dekimashita.** |

Takada

| 2 | Well, congratulations! You really worked hard for it. | **Sore wa omedetoo. Anata mo yoku gan-barimashita ne.** |

     big   **ookina,** 大<ruby>大<rt>おお</rt></ruby>きな
Brown   to succeed   **seekoo-suru,** <ruby>成<rt>せい</rt>功<rt>こう</rt></ruby>する

| 3 | Thank you. I'm also relieved to have succeeded in our first major transaction in Japan. | **Arigatoo gozaimasu. Watakushi mo Nihon de no saisho no ookina torihiki ga seekoo-shite, hotto-shite imasu.** |

     toast in celebration   **shukuhai,** <ruby>祝<rt>しゅく</rt>杯<rt>はい</rt></ruby>
     to raise   **ageru,** あげる
Takada   to raise a toast   **shukuhai o ageru,** <ruby>祝<rt>しゅく</rt>杯<rt>はい</rt></ruby>をあげる

| 4 | Then, how about a quick celebration tonight [lit. Shall we raise a toast in celebration right away tonight]? | **Jaa, konban de mo, sassoku shukuhai o agemashoo.** |

     favorite (bar)   **ikitsuke,** <ruby>行<rt>い</rt></ruby>きつけ
     bar   **sunakku,** スナック
     to take someone to   **annai-suru,** <ruby>案<rt>あん</rt>内<rt>ない</rt></ruby>する
Brown   to take someone to   **goannai-suru** (polite), ご<ruby>案<rt>あん</rt>内<rt>ない</rt></ruby>する

| 5 | Yes, that will be great. I'll take you to my favorite bar [lit. "Snack"]. | **Ee, ii desu nee. Watakushi no ikitsuke no sunakku e goannai-shimasu.** |

| | "karaoke" | karaoke*,　カラオケ |
| Takada | (the bar) where you do... | yatte iru tte iu no,　やっているっていうの |

| 6 | Is that the place where (they) say (you) are singing "*karaoke*" nowadays? | Sono mise desu ka, anata ga kono goro "karaoke" o yatte iru tte iu no wa. |

	tone-deaf	onchi,　音痴
	song	uta,　歌
Brown	to sing	utau,　歌う

| 7 | Oh no, I'm tone-deaf, but Jones sings quite often at that place. | Iie, watakushi wa onchi da kara, uta wa dame na n desu ga, Joonzu-san wa sono mise de, yoku utau yoo desu yo. |

	someplace	doko ka,　どこか
	to invite	maneku,　招く
	to invite	omaneki-suru (polite),　お招きする
	help, care	sewa, osewa (polite),　世話, お世話
Takada	to receive assistance	osewa ni naru,　お世話になる

| 8 | By the way, why don't you invite Mr. Ohyama of Nissan to someplace once? (He) will probably be helping you in the future, so ... | Tokoro de, Nissan no Ooyama-san o i-chi-do doko ka e omaneki-shitara, doo desu ka. Kongo mo iroiro osewa ni naru deshoo kara... |

| | to stay away | hikaeru,　控える |
| Brown | (I) should invite | omaneki-shitara ii,　お招きしたらいい |

| 9 | Oh, about that ... (I) heard something to the effect that Mr. Ohyama is cutting down on alcohol, so what sort of place should (I) invite (him) to? | Sore na n desu ga ... Ooyama-san wa ima osake o hikaete iru to ka kikimashi-ta no de, donna tokoro e omaneki-shitara ii deshoo ka. |

| | (you) should invite | shootai-shitara ii,　招待したらいい |
| Takada | passion for golf | goruhu-zuki,　ゴルフ好き |

| 10 | Is that right? Then, (I) think (you) had better invite (him) for golf. His passion for golf is well-known, so ... | Soo desu ka. Jaa, goruhu ni shootai-shitara ii to omoimasu yo. Kare no goruhu-zuki wa yuumee desu kara ... |

Brown	to hear a good thing	**ii koto o kiku,** いい事を聞く

11	Oh really? That's a good idea [lit. I heard a good thing]. (I)'ll arrange it right away.	**Soo desu ka. Ii koto o kikimashita. Sassoku tehai-shimashoo.**

	(golf) course	**koosu,** コース
	reservation	**yoyaku(-suru),** 予約(する)
Takada	and the like	**nanka,** なんか

12	(I) can help you with the course reservations, or with anything else.	**Koosu no yoyaku nanka, nan de mo tetsudaimasu yo.**

	to consult you	**soodan-sasete itadaku** (humble), 相談させていただく
Brown		

13	Thank you very much. If there is anything, (I)'ll ask your advice [lit. please let me ask…].	**Arigatoo gozaimasu. Nani ka attara, soodan-sasete itadakimasu.**

	reserve, hesitation	**enryo(-suru),** 遠慮(する)
	reserve, hesitation	**goenryo (-suru)** (polite), ご遠慮(する)
Takada	without reserve	**goenryo naku** (polite), ご遠慮なく

14	Yes, certainly. Don't hesitate anytime.	**Ee, itsu de mo goenryo naku.**

Brown

15	Thanks a lot [imp. I appreciate it].	**Yoroshiku onegai-shimasu.**

Takada

16	Oh, it's past 5 o'clock already. Let's start moving soon.	**Moo go-ji-sugi desu nee. Sorosoro dekakemashoo.**

* **karaoke** or "Empty Orchestra" is musical accompaniment recorded on cassette tape. Many bars and restaurants have *karaoke* equipment installed for customers who enjoy singing popular and traditional songs to the accompaniment of an orchestra [See *BUSINESS JAPANESE*, Lesson 14 *Business Information*].

174

JAPANESE WRITING

1　ブラウン：　例のロボットの件ですが、おかげさまで、昨日契約できました。

2　高　　田：　それはおめでとう。あなたも よく頑張りましたね。

3　ブラウン：　ありがとうございます。私 も 日本での 最初の大きな取引が成功して、ほっとしています。

4　高　　田：　じゃあ、今晩でも、早速祝杯をあげましょう。

5　ブラウン：　ええ、いいですねえ。私 の 行きつけのスナックへ ご案内します。

6　高　　田：　その店ですか、あなたがこの頃カラオケを やっているっていうのは。

7　ブラウン：　いいえ、私 は音痴だから、歌はだめなんですが、ジョーンズさんはその店で、よく歌うようですよ。

8　高　　田：　ところで、日産の大山さんを 一度どこかへ お招きしたら、どうですか。今後もいろいろ お世話になるでしょうから…

9　ブラウン：　それなんですが… 大山さんは いまお酒を控えているとか 聞きましたので、どんな 所へお招きしたらいいでしょうか。

10　高　　田：　そうですか。じゃあ、ゴルフに 招待したらいいと思いますよ。彼のゴルフ好きは 有名ですから…

11　ブラウン：　そうですか。いい事を聞きました。早速 手配しましょう。

12　高　　田：　コースの予約なんか、何でも手伝いますよ。

13　ブラウン：　ありがとうございます。何かあったら、相談させていただきます。

14　高　　田：　ええ、何時でもご遠慮なく。

15　ブラウン：　よろしく お願いします。

16　高　　田：　もう 5時過ぎですねえ。そろそろ出掛けましょう。

ADDITIONAL USEFUL EXPRESSIONS

1 A conversation between a foreign businessman and his Japanese friend

| A: | (Foreigner): (Doing) business in Japan is quite difficult. | **Nihon de no bijinesu wa taihen desu.** |

| B: | (Japanese): Why is that? | **Doo shite desu ka.** |

| | socializing, associating | **tsukiai, otsukiai** (polite), つき合い、おつき合い |

| A: | Besides business, there's socializing in the evening, so … | **Bijinesu no hoka ni, yoru no otsukiai ga arimasu kara nee.** |

33/Planning a Celebration

all the same, as well	**yahari,** やはり

B:	But that's a Japanese custom, so it's important all the same.	**De mo sore wa Nihon no shuukan desu kara, yahari taisetsu na n desu yo.**

Japanese-style party	**enkai,** 宴会
second-stage party	**ni-jikai,** 二次会
third-stage party	**san-jikai,** 三次会
every night	**maiban,** 毎晩
return to home	**kaeri,** 帰り

A:	But, after the party, there are second-stage and third-stage parties, right? I get home late every night, and my wife worries too, so ...	**Shikashi, enkai no ato ni, ni-jikai, san-jikai to tsuzuku deshoo. Maiban, kaeri ga osoku naru shi, kanai mo shinpai-suru no de ...**

to understand	**rikai-suru,** 理解する
must have (someone) understand	**rikai-shite morawanakereba ikenai,** 理解してもらわなければいけない

B:	Well, that's also for the job, so you must have your wife understand.	**Maa, sore mo shigoto no tame desu kara, okusan ni mo rikai-shite morawanakereba ikemasen ne.**

2 At the office

(Carefully observe the difference in speech levels between a superior and his staff.)

advice	**jogen(-suru),** 助言(する)
to fail	**shippai-suru,** 失敗(する)

A:	(Staff member): Mr. Brown of P & C really helped us a lot in this business. I think we would have failed, if he hadn't advised us.	**Kondo no torihiki de wa, Pii-and-shii no Buraun-san ni taihen osewa ni nari-mashita. Kare no jogen ga nakattara, shippai-shita to omoimasu.**

[lit.] to offer a reward	**oree o suru,** お礼をする

B:	(Superior): Then, we had better send him some token of our appreciation.	**Jaa, nani ka oree o shita hoo ga ii ne.**

	Japanese-style	Nihonteki/na/,	日本的(な)
	present, gift	okurimono(-suru),	贈 物(する)

A:	Yes, I'm thinking of some Japanese gift, but …	Ee, nani ka Nihonteki na okurimono o kangaete imasu ga …

B:	That's good. Then, please talk it over among yourselves and decide (on something).	Sore wa ii ne. Jaa, minna de soodan-shite, kimete kudasai.

A:	Then, we'll do so.	Jaa, soo shimasu.

3 A conversation between friends

A:	Thanks for introducing me to a good customer the other day.	Senjitsu wa ii okyakusama o shookai-shite kurete arigatoo.

B:	Did the business go well?	Torihiki wa umaku itta.*

	great success	daiseekoo(-suru),	大成功(する)
	large scale	ooguchi,	大口

A:	Thanks to you, it was a great success. We got a large order.	Okage de, daiseekoo. Ooguchi no chu-umon o moratta yo.

B:	That's wonderful. Congratulations!	Sore wa yokatta. Omedetoo.

	to treat (someone)	gochisoo-suru,	ごちそうする
	but	kedo,	けど

A:	And so, I would like to treat you to dinner today, but do you have time?	Sore de, kyoo wa gochisoo-shitai n da kedo, jikan wa aru.

* Pronunciation should be in question intonation.

33/Planning a Celebration

		don't need to do	shinakute mo ii,　しなくてもいい

B:	I've time, but you don't have to do that.	Jikan wa aru kedo, sonna koto wa shinakute mo ii yo.

		to accompany	tsukiau,　つき合う

A:	Oh, come on [lit. don't hesitate, and please accompany me today].	Enryo-shinai de, kyoo wa tsukiatte kudasai.

B:	Well, alright. [lit. let's do so].	Jaa, soo shimashoo.

REFERENCE

ryootee	料亭		Japanese-style restaurant
baa	バー		bar
kyabaree	キャバレー		cabaret
naito-kurabu	ナイトクラブ		night club
yokyoo	余興		parlor trick, entertainment
geesha	芸者		*geisha*
odori	踊り		dance
inshokuhi	飲食費		expenses for eating and drinking
saabisuryoo	サービス料		service charge
chippu	チップ		tip
zeekin	税金		tax

NOTES

1 Conditional + **doo desu ka**

A conditional + **doo desu ka** or **doo deshoo ka** literally means 'how is it if (someone) does such-and-such?' or 'how is it if (something) happens?' However, this combination may also be used to suggest something, and its English equivalent is 'why don't (you) do such-and-such?' or 'how about if (something) were such-and-such?'

Examples:　　a)　**Narubeku hayaku Ooyama-buchoo ni attara** *doo deshoo ka.*
　　　　　　　　"Why don't you meet General Manager Ohyama as soon as possible?"

　　　　　　b)　**Kono robotto o doonyuu-shitara** *doo desu ka.*
　　　　　　　　"How about installing this robot?"

c) **Watakushi ga mitsumori o todoketara *doo deshoo ka*.**
"How would it be if I delivered the estimate?"

2 Conditional + ii

A conditional + **ii** (**desu**) may likewise be used in a suggestion, and may be translated as '(someone) should do such-and-such' or '(something) should be such-and-such.' This construction is also used to ask someone else's advice.

Examples: a) **Konban honsha ni denwa-shi*tara ii* to omoimasu.**
"I think you should call the head office tonight."

            b) **Anata mo osake o hikae*tara ii* n desu ga ...**
"You too should stay away from alcohol, but ..."

            c) **Tokkyo no mondai ni tsuite dare ni soodan-shi*tara ii* deshoo ka.**
"Whom should I consult about the patent problem?"

3 Causative gerund + itadaku

A gerund of the causative verb + **itadaku** literally means '(the speaker or a member of the speaker's group*) does such-and-such through (someone else's) permission.' This combination is often used to request permission in an extremely polite way.

Examples: a) **Ashita otaku e ukagaw*asete itadakimasu*.**
"I would like to go to your house tomorrow [lit. I accept your letting me go to your house tomorrow]."

            b) **Mitsumori wa sugu hisho ni todoke*sasete itadakimasu*.**
"I'd like my secretary to immediately deliver the estimate to you [lit. I accept your letting my secretary deliver the estimate to you immediately]."

            c) **Anata o goruhu ni shootai-*sasete itadakemasen* deshoo ka.**
"May I invite you for golf [lit. Can't I have your permission to invite you for golf]?"

* Refer to *BUSINESS JAPANESE*, Lesson 6 *Business Information*.

4 Informal Speech

Informal speech is often used in conversations with subordinates or friends [See Additional Useful Expressions **2**, **3**. Refer also to *BUSINESS JAPANESE*, Lesson 6 *Business Information* for levels of formal and informal speech]. Some of the patterns used in informal speech are as follows:

A) Sentence ending in an informal verb:

         Jisho wa sono tsukue no ue ni *aru*.
"The dictionary is on that desk."

         Ano shoodan wa *shippai-shita* yo.**
"I failed in that negotiation."

** A sentence particle (i.e. **yo**, **ne**, **nee**, etc.) often occurs directly after the informal verb (i.e. **shippai-shita yo**).

B) Sentence ending in an adjective without the copula **da**:

> **Konna hoteru wa totemo *takai* yo.** *
> "This kind of hotel is very expensive."

> **Boku wa zehi kuruma ga *kaitai*.**
> "I really [lit. by all means] want to buy a car."

* In this case also, a sentence particle often follows the adjective.

C) Question ending without the question particle **ka**:

In informal speech, rising intonation may replace the interrogative particle **ka**. Thus,

> **Ashita Oosaka e iku.** **
> "Are you going to Osaka tomorrow?"

> **Kono wain (wa)***** **oishii.** **
> "Is this wine good [lit. delicious]?"

> **Kore (wa)***** **anata no hon.** **
> "Is this your book?"

 ** Pronunciation should be in question intonation.
*** In informal speech, certain particles are often omitted.

D) Question with particle **no**:

In informal questions, particle **no** is often used instead of the question particle **ka**.

> **Kono kuruma (o) kau *no*.**
> "Are you going to buy this car?"

> **Otaku (wa) tooi *no*.**
> "Is your house far (from here)?"

Note that a question with **no** is more gentle than a question with just a rising intonation.

5 Noun + **teki**

-teki added to certain nouns means 'like', 'similar', 'having to do with.' The nouns used in this pattern are **na** nouns, and therefore may be followed by the particle **na** when modifying another noun, e.g. **Nihon*teki* na okurimono** 'a Japanese-style present.'

Examples:	**keezai*teki***	'economic', 'economical' [lit. having to do with economy]
	rekishi*teki*	'historical' [lit. having to do with history]
	chinoo*teki*	'intelligent' [lit. having to do with intelligence]
	gijutsu*teki*	'technological' [lit. having to do with technology]

PRACTICE

1 Transformation Practice

Example: Teacher: **Ooyama-san o omaneki-shite kudasai.**
"Please invite Mr. Ohyama."

Student: **Ooyama-san o omaneki-shitara doo desu ka.**
"Why don't you invite Mr. Ohyama?"

a)	Honsha to soodan-shite kudasai.	Honsha to soodan-shitara doo desu ka.
b)	Ima mitsumori o kaite kudasai.	Ima mitsumori o kaitara doo desu ka.
c)	Atarashii kikai o kaihatsu-shite kudasai.	Atarashii kikai o kaihatsu-shitara doo desu ka.
d)	Doru-date de hanashi o susumete kudasai.	Doru-date de hanashi o susumetara doo desu ka.
e)	Moo sukoshi nebiki-shite kudasai.	Moo sukoshi nebiki-shitara doo desu ka.

2 Response Practice

Example: Teacher: **Donna tokoro e shootai-shimashoo ka. /goruhu/**
"What kind of place shall we invite (him) to?" /golf/

Student: **Goruhu ni shootai-shitara ii to omoimasu.**
"(I) think you should invite (him) for golf."

a)	Dare ni soodan-shimashoo ka. /Takada-san/	Takada-san ni soodan-shitara ii to omoimasu.
b)	Donna okurimono o agemashoo ka. /Nihonteki na mono/	Nihonteki na mono o agetara ii to omoimasu.
c)	Itsu shukuhai o agemashoo ka. /konban/	Konban shukuhai o agetara ii to omoimasu.
d)	Buraun-san o doko e annai-shimashoo ka. /ikitsuke no sunakku/	Ikitsuke no sunakku e annai-shitara ii to omoimasu.
e)	Nani o gochisoo-shimashoo ka. /sukiyaki/	Sukiyaki o gochisoo-shitara ii to omoimasu.

3 Transformation Practice

Example: Teacher: **Nani ka attara, mata soodanshimasu.**
"If anything comes up, I'll consult (with you) again."

Student: **Nani ka attara, mata soodan-sasete itadakimasu.**
"If anything comes up, I'd like to consult (with you) again [lit. I'll have you permit me to consult (with you) again]."

33/Planning a Celebration

a)	Ashita yasumimasu.	Ashita yasumasete itadakimasu.
b)	Amerika no uta o utaimasu.	Amerika no uta o utawasete itadaki-masu.
c)	Kono kikai no setsumee o shimasu.	Kono kikai no setsumee o sasete itadaki-masu.
d)	Minna de soodan-shite, kimemasu.	Minna de soodan-shite, kimesasete ita-dakimasu.
e)	Konban wa tsukiaimasu.	Konban wa tsukiawasete itadakimasu.

4 Level Practice

Example: Teacher: **Kyoo jikan ga arimasu ka.** (formal)
"Do you have time today?"

Student: **Kyoo jikan (ga) aru.** or **Kyoo jikan (ga) aru no.** (informal)
"You have time today?"

a)	Kare wa sake o hikaete imasu yo.	Kare wa sake o hikaete iru yo.
b)	Kono hon wa omoshiroi desu ka.	Kono hon (wa) omoshiroi.* or Kono hon (wa) omoshiroi no.*
c)	Are ga boku no kuruma desu.	Are (ga) boku no kuruma.*
d)	Takada-san wa paatii e kimasen yo.	Takada-san (wa) paatii e konai yo.
e)	Ano waapuro wa takakatta desu.	Ano waapuro (wa) takakatta.*
f)	Kinoo Buraun-san ni aimashita ka.	Kinoo Buraun-san ni atta.* or Kinoo Buraun-san ni atta no.*
g)	Moo okurimono o kimemashita ka.	Moo okurimono (o) kimeta.* or Moo okurimono (o) kimeta no.*
h)	Torihiki wa umaku ikimashita yo.	Torihiki (wa) umaku itta yo.
i)	Ooguchi no chuumon o moraimashita.	Ooguchi no chuumon (o) moratta.*
j)	Ooyama-san o doko e annai-shimasu ka.	Ooyama-san (o) doko e annai-suru.* or Ooyama-san (o) doko e annai-suru no.*

* Pronunciation should be in question intonation.

5 Comprehension Practice

Directions: The teacher reads aloud the following passage and then asks the student questions about it.

Nissan to no torihiki ga seekoo-shita no de, Buraun-san wa konban Takada-san to shukuhai o ageru koto ni shimashita. Buraun-san wa Takada-san o ikitsuke no sunak-ku e annai-shimasu. Sono sunakku de wa kono goro Joonzu-san ga karaoke de uta o utatte iru soo desu. Buraun-san wa onchi desu kara uta wa utawanai to iimashita ga, hontoo wa tokidoki utatte iru yoo desu. Buraun-san wa chikai uchi ni Ooyama-san o doko ka e shootai-shitai to omotte imasu ga, ima Ooyama-san wa osake o hikaete iru soo desu kara, ryooriya e shootai-suru no wa yoku nai to omoimasu. Buraun-san ga sore ni tsuite Takada-san ni soodan-shimashita. Takada-san wa Ooyama-san ga goru-hu-zuki da kara, goruhu ni shootai-shitara ii to oshiete kuremashita no de, Buraun-san wa soo suru koto ni shimashita.

182

Questions:

1   Doo shite Buraun-san to Takada-san wa konban shukuhai o agemasu ka.
2   Buraun-san wa Takada-san o doko e annai-shimasu ka.
3   Kono goro dare ga yoku karaoke de utatte imasu ka.
4   Buraun-san wa zenzen utaimasen ka.
5   Buraun-san wa doo shite Ooyama-san o ryooriya e shootai-shimasen ka.
6   Takada-san wa Ooyama-san wa nani ga suki da to iimashita ka.
7   Buraun-san wa Ooyama-san o doko e shootai-shimasu ka.

EXERCISES

a)   Give the following advice in Japanese to your friend:

1   Why don't you stay away from alcohol a little?
2   Why don't you introduce this kind of robot in your factory?
3   Why don't you study Japanese when (you) are in Japan?
4   Why don't you develop a new automatic machine tool?
5   Why don't you deliver the catalogue as soon as possible?

b)   Inform the teacher in Japanese that:

1   Mr. Brown invited Mr. Takada to his favorite Japanese restaurant in Ginza.
2   Mr. Brown thinks he should arrange the party right away.
3   If it weren't for Mr. Kawamoto's advice, Mr. Brown might have failed in the transaction this time [lit. If (he) didn't have Mr. Kawamoto's advice, ...].
4   Mr. Tanaka is grateful to Mr. Yamamoto for having introduced good customers.
5   President Smith decided to give a gift to Mr. Brown because he succeeded in this transaction.

Model Answers:

a)   1   Sukoshi osake o hikaetara doo desu ka.
2   Anata no koojoo ni konna robotto o doonyuu-shitara doo desu ka.
3   Nihon ni iru toki ni, Nihongo o benkyoo-shitara doo desu ka.
4   Atarashii jidoo koosakuki o kaihatsu-shitara doo desu ka.
5   Narubeku hayaku katarogu o todoketara doo desu ka.

b)   1   Buraun-san wa Takada-san o Ginza no ikitsuke no Nihon ryooriya e shootai-shimashita.
2   Buraun-san wa sassoku paatii no tehai o shitara ii to omotte imasu.
3   Kawamoto-san no jogen ga nakattara, Buraun-san wa kondo no torihiki ni shippai-shita ka mo shiremasen.
4   Tanaka-san wa Yamamoto-san ga ii okyaku o shookai-shite kureta no de, kansha-shite imasu.
5   Kono torihiki ni seekoo-shita no de, Sumisu-shachoo wa Buraun-san ni okurimono o ageru koto ni shimashita.

BUSINESS INFORMATION

Socializing

In Japanese professional circles, out of sight generally means out of mind. Businessmen therefore go out of their way to show their faces to customers and socialize with them on a scale, and with a frequency, unrivalled anywhere in the world.

1 Office Visits: Making "house calls" is a firmly entrenched custom in Japanese society. Friends visit one another at every opportunity, businessmen call on clients every week or so and salesmen regularly appear at homes and offices peddling everything from cosmetics to automobiles. Although door-to-door calls are of course costly and time-consuming, most Japanese companies would not dream of abandoning them for other, allegedly more efficient marketing tools like direct mail. For one thing, these visits provide a "personal touch" highly valued by the Japanese customer. Furthermore, visiting representatives can observe first-hand all the goings-on at their various clients' offices or homes, and so keep abreast of changes in company policy and staff as well as personal circumstances. They are thus in a better position to make sales-pitches that coincide with major events like promotions and bonuses, and to design all those extra little **saabisu** that do so much in Japan to foster brand loyalty and maintain smooth business relationships.

2 After-Hours Socializing: If you cannot regularly visit at your client's office, you should at least make an effort to socialize with him after hours. You should note, however, that appointments for after-hours socializing are arranged rather spontaneously in Japan, sometimes even at 5 p.m., or just as you are heading out the door. As much as possible, you should try to accept such last-minute invitations to show your willingness to accomodate even at short notice. Equally important, if you refuse, your caller may hesitate to impose on you in the future, with the result that you miss a potentially valuable opportunity to nourish your business partnership.

In contrast to the West, moreover, after-hours socializing in Japan is seldom a one-stop affair. Instead, businessmen migrate from one watering hole to another until the wee hours, or at least till 1 a.m. when the trains stop running. Most foreign businessmen agree that accompanying clients and staff to **ni-jikai** and **san-jikai** (second and third "stages") does enhance professional relationships, but you should not feel compelled to do so if you have other priorities. Your Japanese companions will not in any case expect you to go everywhere they do. If family life comes first, therefore, you can always retreat gracefully, as one foreign advertising executive does, by claiming an appointment with your "last client of the day."

3 Formal Entertainment: Business entertainment Japanese-style is hard to beat for service, style and expense. Meals can cost upward of $200 a head, while waitresses in kimonos attend to your every need, quite literally, on bended knee. Instead of trying to outdo your Japanese counterparts in local entertainment, most foreign businessmen recommend that you reciprocate with small courtesies while in Japan (See *BUSINESS*

JAPANESE II Business Information 32) and play the host in earnest only when your Japanese partners visit in your home country. Home entertainment, especially, is generally thought to be more meaningful in your country where the home is truly your own and not just company-provided, as it often is in Japan. Also, as some overseas businessmen feel, the disparity between your living standard and that of your Japanese associates will not be as apparent there, or as embarrassing. If you can afford to do so, therefore, you should wait until your Japanese business partners travel to your country to entertain them in style. In the meantime, just accept the "special guest" treatment, enjoy the wining and dining and, to be a good sport, learn at least one song for "**karaoke.**"

4 Golf: For those who do not drink—like Mr. Ohyama in the DIALOGUE—golf is a welcome alternative to **kaiseki** dinners and club-hopping in the Ginza. Golf is in fact easily the most popular sport in the Japanese business community. As of September 1985, there were over 1,500 courses in the country, patronized by an estimated 70 million people a year. All the major corporations and trading houses have club memberships; some also have staff who are regularly assigned to entertain—and sometimes lose graciously to—important clients on golf courses. Moreover, since patrons include over 48% of all male executives in the Tokyo metropolitan area as well as numerous business and government luminaries, golf clubs offer prime opportunities for forging important connections.

Playing golf in Japan does have certain disadvantages, however. First, it is not always the leisurely, relaxing sport it is elsewhere. Most courses are located at several hours' drive from the big cities so that a single game can entail a major weekend excursion. Second, golf courses are frequently crowded, with players lining up to tee off, and waiting right behind you for their turn at every hole. Long-time golfers in Japan in fact recommend that inexperienced players carry more extra balls around with them than usual so that they will not hold up the line if they happen to lose a ball in the rough. At times it may even seem as though you are being pursued relentlessly by impatient players from hole to hole. If on top of all this you have to accompany an uncongenial business partner, one can well imagine that what would normally be a pleasant afternoon in other countries can be a stressful time for all in Japan.

Perhaps the most stressful aspect of playing golf in Japan is the cost. Initiation fees in a run-of-the-mill club start from ¥3 million—or about half what an average white-collar worker earns a year—but can reach up to ¥30 million for top-of-the-line clubs where you also pay for the privilege of rubbing shoulders with government and business elite. The problem is compounded if you are seriously committed to your game. If you score a hole-in-one in Japan, for example, you should be prepared to host a party for all who played with you or distribute gifts to fellow club-members in commemoration of your own achievement. If you are an accomplished golfer, therefore, you would be well advised to down-play you skill since gratification of one's ego on the fairway is achieved only at the expense of one's wallet. In Japan, as one frustrated businessman put it, you need a hole-in-one like you need a hole in the head.

33/Planning a Celebration

How Japanese Businessmen Socialize After Hours

A. **Activities** [Source: Fukoku Insurance Survey, 1983]*

1.	Eating and drinking	82.0%
2.	Mahjongg	30.6%
3.	Sports	27.8%
4.	Chatting	24.8%
5.	Drinking coffee	23.4%
6.	"**Karaoke**"	17.6%
7.	"**Go**", "**Shoogi**"**	6.4%
8.	Discotheques	1.0%

B. **Frequency** [Source: Sanwa Bank Home Consultant Survey, 1983]

1.	2-3 days/week	38.2%
2.	once a week	30.2%
3.	1-2 days/month	17.6%
4.	4-5 days/week	7.4%
5.	once in 2-3 months	4.8%

C. **Companions** [Source: Sanwa Bank Home Consultant Survey, 1983]*

1.	Company peers	39.1%
2.	Company superiors	20.9%
3.	Company subordinates	14.1%
4.	Clients	9.9%
5.	Alone	9.6%

* Multiple responses were permitted.
** Traditional Japanese board games, similar to "Othello" and chess.

Lesson 34

Technical Trouble

OBJECTIVES

1   to make a complaint.

2   to discuss mechanical problems.

3   to use the Passive form.

TARGET EXPRESSIONS AND PATTERNS

1   <X> is (done) by <Y>.   <X> wa <Y> ni ...-sareru/-rareru.

2   to start to do ...   ...shihajimeru.

3   to do too much.   ...shisugiru.

4   before (such-and-such) (happens)...   ...shinai uchi (ni)

SITUATION

Upon completion of the transaction, the new USM robots are installed at one of Nissan's automobile assembly lines. However, after the trial period is over and the technicians have gone home, a mechanical problem arises. Mr. Ohyama calls Mr. Brown and asks him to look into the problem.

34/Technical Trouble

DIALOGUE

		to call	**yobu,** 呼ぶ
Ohyama		to be called	**yobareru,** 呼ばれる

1	The fact is, (I) was called to the factory yesterday, regarding the robots.	**Jitsu wa kinoo robotto no ken de, koojoo no hoo e yobaremashite ne.**

Brown	a problem occurs	**mondai ga okiru,** 問題が起きる

2	Has any problem occured?	**Nani ka mondai ga okimashita ka.**

	is not so... as to be called...	**...to iu hodo ja nai,** ⋯という程じゃない
Ohyama	bearings	**bearingu,** ベアリング

3	(It) is not so serious a problem [lit. as to be called a problem], but (it)'s about the bearings...	**Mondai to iu hodo ja arimasen ga, bearingu no koto de...**

Brown

4	Which is to say?	**To iimasu to.**

	check-up	**kensa(-suru),** 検査(する)
	periodical check-up	**teeki-kensa,** 定期検査
	to notice	**ki ga tsuku,** 気が付く
	to replace	**torikaeru,** 取り替える
	so ... that they need to be replaced	**torikaenakereba naranai hodo,** 取り替えなければならない程
Ohyama	to be worn out	**mametsu-suru,** 摩滅する

5	(They) said that last week, while doing a periodical check-up, they noticed it... but (the robot bearings) were so worn out that (they) needed to be replaced.	**Senshuu, teeki-kensa o shita toki ni, ki ga tsuita soo desu ga, moo torikaenakereba naranai hodo, mametsu-shite ita soo desu.**

		full-scale, real	honkakuteki/na/, 本格的(な)
Brown		to start using	tsukaihajimeru, 使い始める

6	It's only been 6 months since (you)'ve really started using (them), right? (I) shall ask USM to investigate this immediately.	Mada, honkakuteki ni tsukaihajimete kara, rok-kagetsu desu ne. Kore wa sugu Yuu-esu-emu ni choosa-sasemasu.

Ohyama		to endure, last	motsu, もつ

7	Yes, please do. According to USM's manual, (they) are supposed to last for a year, so...	Onegai-shimasu. Yuu-esu-emu no setsumeesho de wa ichi-nen wa motsu hazu desu kara...

		half a year	hantoshi, 半年
Brown		too soon	hayasugiru, 早すぎる

8	Half a year is too soon, isn't it?	Hantoshi de wa hayasugimasu ne.

		to check	shiraberu, 調べる
		to check why it happens	naze soo naru ka (o) shiraberu, 何故そうなるか(を)調べる
Ohyama			

9	Therefore, (we)'d like to have you check why this has happened and...	Desu kara, naze soo natta no ka shirabete moraitai to omoimashite...

Brown

10	Yes, because if an accident or something occurs, it would be awful.	Jiko de mo okitara, taihen desu kara ne.

Ohyama		as long as we don't know	wakaranai uchi, 分からないうち

11	Well, that probably wouldn't happen, but as long as (we) don't know the cause, (we)'ll be concerned, so...	Maa, sonna koto mo nai deshoo ga, gen'in ga wakaranai uchi wa, shinpai desu kara...

34/Technical Trouble

	counter measures	taisaku,	対策
Brown	to take measures	taisaku o toru,	対策を取る

12	Then, (I)'ll contact USM and take the necessary action within a few days.	De wa, Yuu-esu-emu ni renraku-shite, suujitsu-chuu ni taisaku o torimasu.

Ohyama

13	Please do so.	Yoroshiku onegai-shimasu.

JAPANESE WRITING

1 大山： 実は きのうロボットの件で、工場の方へ 呼ばれましてね。

2 ブラウン： 何か問題が 起きましたか。

3 大山： 問題という程じゃ ありませんが、ベアリングのことで…

4 ブラウン： と 言いますと。

5 大山： 先週、定期検査をした時に、気がついたそうですが、もう 取替えなければ ならない程、摩滅していたそうです。

6 ブラウン： まだ、本格的に使い始めてから、6か月ですね。これは すぐ ユー・エス・エムに 調査させます。

7 大山： お願いします。 ユー・エス・エムの説明書では 一年はもつはずですから…

8 ブラウン： 半年では 早過ぎますね。

9 大山： ですから、何故そうなったのか 調べてもらいたいと思いまして…

10 ブラウン： 事故でも 起きたら、大変ですからね。

11 大山： まあ、そんなこともないでしょうが、原因が分からないうちは、心配ですから…

12 ブラウン： では、ユー・エス・エムに連絡して、数日中に 対策を取ります。

13 大山： よろしくお願いします。

ADDITIONAL USEFUL EXPRESSIONS

1 A customer complaint (over the phone)

Imai:	This is P & C.	Pii-ando-shii desu.

Ishida	**Ishida,** 石田
Tokyo-Kikai, Co. (a company name)	**Tookyoo-kikai,** 東京機械

Ishida:	This is Ishida of Tokyo-Kikai, Co.	**Kochira Tookyoo-kikai no Ishida desu ga…**

Imai:	Good morning [lit. We're indebted to you every time]. This is Imai.	**Maido osewa ni natte orimasu. Imai de gozaimasu.**

to buy, install	**ireru,** 入れる

Ishida:	Oh, Mr. Imai, actually, it's (about) the machine we purchased last month, but somehow we can't use it very well.	**Aa, Imai-san, jitsu wa sengetsu ireta kikai desu ga, doo mo umaku tsukaenai n desu yo.**

person in charge	**kakari,** 係

Imai:	Is that so? Then, we'll send the person in charge immediately and have him check it.	**Soo desu ka. De wa, sassoku kakari o okutte, shirabesasemasu.**

Ishida:	Please do so as soon as you can. It's also a problem for our factory, so…	**Narubeku hayaku, onegai-shimasu. Koojoo no hoo mo komatte imasu kara…**

to understand	**shoochi-suru,** 承知する
responsibility	**sekinin,** 責任
to take responsibility	**sekinin o motsu,** 責任を持つ
to deal with	**shori-suru,** 処理する

Imai:	Yes, I understand. We'll take care of it [lit. with my responsibility].	**Hai, shoochi-shimashita. Sekinin o motte, shori-shimasu.**

34/Technical Trouble

2 At the office

	to be delivered	**todoku,** 届く

A:	The materials we ordered the other day haven't arrived yet.	**Senjitsu chuumon-shita genryoo ga mada todoite imasen.**

	complaint	**monku,** 文句
	to complain	**monku o iu,** 文句を言う

B:	It's too slow. You had better call and complain right away.	**Ososugimasu nee. Sugu denwa-shite, monku o itta hoo ga ii desu yo.**

A:	Then, I'll call them right now.	**Jaa, sugu denwa-shimasu.**

	to run short	**husoku-suru,** 不足する
	section	**ka,** 課

B:	It's our section's responsibility if materials run short in the factory.	**Koojoo de genryoo ga husoku-shitara, wareware no ka no sekinin desu kara ...**

3 At the office

	complaint, grievance	**kujoo,** 苦情
	to express a grievance	**kujoo o iu,** 苦情を言う

A:	Yesterday, I got a complaint [lit. was told a grievance] from a customer.	**Kinoo, otokuisama ni kujoo o iwaremashita.**

B:	What happened?	**Nani ga atta n desu ka.**

A:	Well, our products didn't make it on (the scheduled delivery date).	**Sore ga nooki ni ma ni awanakatta n desu.**

B:	Why didn't it make it on time?	**Doo shite ma ni awanakatta n desu ka.**

subcontractor	**shitauke,** 下請
fire	**kaji,** 火事
to obtain	**te ni hairu,** 手に入る

| A: | The subcontractor's parts-factory (caught) on fire and we couldn't get the parts. | **Shitauke no buhin-koojoo ga kaji de, buhin ga te ni hairanakatta n desu.** |

circumstances	**jijoo,** 事情
to apologize	**wabiru,** 詫びる
to apologize	**owabi-suru** (polite), お詫びする

| B: | Then, (you) can't help it [lit. there is no way of doing]. You should explain the circumstances to (them) and apologize carefully. | **Jaa, shikata ga arimasen ne. Yoku jijoo o hanashite, owabi-suru koto desu nee.** |

4 Giving an excuse

on the way	**tochuu,** 途中
to be caught in the rain	**ame ni hurareru,** 雨に降られる
to stop, cease	**yamu,** 止む
can get (a taxi)	**(takushii ga) tsukamaru,** (タクシーが)つかまる

| A: | (I)'m sorry. (I)'m late. (I) was caught in the rain on the way and tried to get a taxi, but... | **Doo mo sumimasen. Osoku narimashita. Tochuu de, ame ni hurarete, takushii ga tsukamaranakute...** |

| B: | That's too bad. Well, please, come this way. | **Sore wa taihen deshita nee. Maa, doozo kochira e.** |

NOTES

1 The Passive Form

Most Japanese verbs have passive forms meaning 'to be acted on (by something/someone)' or 'to be affected by (something/someone).' To form the passive:

A) Class 1 verb (or **-ru** verb): Drop the final **-ru** and add **-rareru.**
   Example: **taberu** 'to eat' — **taberareru** 'to be eaten'
B) Class 2 verb (or **-u** verb): Drop the final **-u** and add **-areru.**
   Example: **hanasu** 'to speak' — **hanasareru** 'to be spoken'

34/Technical Trouble

Note: In the case of **-u** verbs ending in two vowels (e.g. **tsukau**), drop the final **-u** and add **-wareru**.

   Example: **tsukau** 'to use' — **tsuka*wareru*** 'to be used'

C)   Class 3 verb (or **-aru** verb): No passive form.

D)   Irregular verbs:
   Examples: **kuru** 'to come' — ***korareru*** 'to be affected by (someone's) coming'*
   suru 'to do' — ***sareru*** 'to be done'

* In Japanese, even intransitive verbs have passive forms, as will be explained below.

In Japanese there are two kinds of passive forms: A) Direct Passive and B) Indirect Passive.

A)   Direct Passive:
   The direct passive is formed only with transitive verbs which are usually preceded by the direct object with particle **o**. This is similar to the English passive voice.

Subject	Object	Transitive Verb
Machida-san ga	**Ooyama-san o**	**yobimashita.**
Mr. Machida called Mr. Ohyama.		

Person acted upon	Person/Thing acting	Passive Verb
Ooyama-san ga	**Machida-san ni**	**yobaremashita.**
Mr. Ohyama was called by Mr.Machida.		

Examples: a)   **Wagasha no shihonkin wa rainen zooshi-*saremasu*.**
   "The capital of our company will be increased next year."

   b)   **Yuu-esu-emu wa Nihon de mo yoku shir*arete* imasu.**
   "USM, Ltd. is well known even in Japan."

B)   Indirect Passive:
   The indirect passive differs from the Japanese direct passive and the English passive. The subject of the indirect passive is not directly acted upon, but is merely *affected*, usually unfavorably, by the action of something or someone else. The indirect passive may be formed with either transitive or intrasitive verbs.

i) Transitive Verb:

Subject	Object	Transitive Verb
Otooto wa	**boku no wain o**	**nomimashita.**
My younger brother drank my wine.		

Person affected*	Person/Thing acting	Object	Passive Verb
Boku wa	**otooto ni**	**wain o**	**nom*aremashita*.**
My wine was drunk by my younger brother [impl. and I was annoyed]. [lit. I had my wine drunk by my younger brother].			

ii) Intransitive Verb:

Subject	Intransitive Verb
Ame ga	**hurimashita.**
It rained [lit. Rain fell].	

Person affected*	Person/Thing acting	Passive Verb
Watakushi wa	**ame ni**	**hur*aremashita*.**
It rained on me [imp. and I was inconvenienced]. [lit. I was rained upon].		

* Note that the subject of the indirect passive is usually animate, i.e. a person or animal.

Examples: a) **(Watakushi wa) hoka no kaisha no hito ni mitsumori o mi*rarete*, komatte imasu.**
"Our estimate was seen by another company's people and I'm annoyed [lit. I had our estimate seen...]."

b) **Buraun-san wa hisho ni yamer*arete*, komatte iru rashii desu.**
"Mr. Brown's secretary took leave, so he is apparently annoyed [lit. Mr. Brown was left by his secretary ...]."

2 -sugiru

A verb stem (i.e. the **masu** form minus **-masu**), adjective stem (i.e. the citation form minus **-i**) or **na** noun may be combined with **-sugiru** 'to exceed' to mean 'to overdo (such-and-such)' or 'to be too (such-and-such).' Thus,

> **taberu** 'to eat' — **tabe*sugiru*** 'to eat too much'
> **ookii** 'is big' — **ooki*sugiru*** 'is too big'
> **genki** 'cheerfulness' — **genki*sugiru*** 'is too cheerful'

Examples: a) **Senshuu hataraki*sugita* kara, konshuu wa yasumu tsumori desu.**
"I overworked (myself) last week, so I plan to rest this week."

b) **Moo oso*sugiru* kara, Ooyama-san ni wa ashita ai ni ikimashoo.**
"It is already too late, so let's go to see Mr. Ohyama tomorrow."

c) **Kono shigoto wa Buraun-san ni wa muzukashi*sugiru* to omoimasu.**
"I think this job is too difficult for Mr. Brown."

3 Verb stem + hajimeru

A verb stem + **hajimeru** means 'to begin doing (such-and-such).' Thus,

> **Ima tegami o kaki*hajimeta* tokoro desu kara, chotto matte kudasai.**
> "I have just begun writing a letter, so please wait for a while."

> **Mada ano shorui o kentoo-shi*hajimenai* n desu ka.**
> "Aren't you going to begin examining that document yet?"

4 Negative Verb + **uchi**

A non-past negative verb + **uchi** literally means 'while (such-and-such) does not happen' and may be translated as 'before (such-and-such) happens' or 'as long as (such-and-such) does not happen.' As with verb + **toki**, this combination may be followed by the particle **ni** or by **wa**, depending on the context of the sentence [Refer to *BUSINESS JAPANESE*, Lesson 20, Note **2**]. Thus,

> **Shachoo ga ko*nai uchi* wa kaigi wa hajimeraremasen.**
> "We cannot begin the meeting before the president comes." or
> "As long as the president doesn't come, we cannot begin the meeting."

> **Ame ga hurihajime*nai uchi ni*, uchi e kaerimashoo.**
> "Let's go home before it starts raining."

> **Ame ga yama*nai uchi wa*, kaeremasen.**
> "I cannot go back before it stops raining." or
> "I cannot go back as long as it does not stop raining."

> **Mondai ga ookiku nara*nai uchi ni*, kaiketsu-dekimashita.**
> "I solved the problem before it became serious [lit. big]."

Note that when the verb in the main clause is negative, the particle **wa** is usually used after **uchi**; when the verb in the main clause is not negative, the particle **ni** usually follows **uchi**.

5 **Hodo**

Hodo 'extent, level' is used after an informal verb or adjective to describe the extent of an action or condition. Thus,

> **Mondai to iu *hodo* ja arimasen** (DIALOGUE **3**).
> "It is not so serious as to be called a problem
> [lit. It is not the extent of saying a problem]."

> **Torikaenakereba naranai *hodo* mametsushite imasu** (DIALOGUE **5**).
> "(They) are so worn out that they need to be replaced."

As you see in the above examples, **hodo** in a phrase or clause can also be translated 'so (much) ... that ...'

Examples: a) **Kaenai *hodo* ja arimasen ga, kanari takai desu.**
        "It is not so (expensive) that I cannot buy it, but it's fairly expensive."

        b) **Senmonka ga naosenai *hodo* muzukashii koshoo deshita.**
        "The mechanical problem was so difficult that the specialist could not fix it [lit. It was a (level of) such difficult breakdown that the specialist could not fix it]."

PRACTICE

1 Transformation Practice

Example: Teacher: **Machida-san ga Ooyama-san o yobimashita.**
"Mr. Machida called Mr. Ohyama."

Student: **Ooyama-san wa Machida-san ni yobaremashita.**
"Mr. Ohyama was called by Mr. Machida."

a) **Ooku no hito ga sono hon o yomi-mashita.**   **Sono hon wa ooku no hito ni yomaremashita.**

b) **Shain wa shachoo no kangae o rikai-shimasen deshita.**   **Shachoo no kangae wa shain ni rikai-saremasen deshita.**

c) **Bearingu o torikaemasu.**   **Bearingu ga torikaeraremasu.**

d) **Takada-san wa Buraun-san o paatii ni shootai-shimashita.**   **Buaun-san wa Takada-san ni paatii ni shootai-saremashita.**

e) **Buraun-san ga Imai-san o yatoimashita.**   **Imai-san wa Buraun-san ni yato-waremashita.**

2 Transformation Practice

Example: Teacher: **Otooto ga wain o nomimashita. /boku/**
"My younger brother drank the wine." /I/

Student: **Boku wa otooto ni wain o nomaremashita.**
"(My) wine was drunk by my younger brother (and I was annoyed)."

a) **Tanaka-san ga sono tegami o yomi-mashita. /Kawamoto-san/**   **Kawamoto-san wa Tanaka-san ni sono tegami o yomaremashita.**

b) **Tomodachi ga yoru osoku kimashita. /Yamada-san/**   **Yamada-san wa yoru osoku tomodachi ni koraremashita.**

c) **Gaikokujin ga michi o kikimashita. /watakushi/**   **Watakushi wa gaikokujin ni michi o kikaremashita.**

d) **Buchoo ga shorui o naoshimashita. /Suzuki-san/**   **Suzuki-san wa buchoo ni shorui o naosaremashita.**

e) **Ginkoo ga jigyoo-naiyoo o shirabemashi-ta. /Tanaka-san no kaisha/**   **Tanaka-san no kaisha wa ginkoo ni jigyoo-naiyoo o shiraberaremashita.**

3 Response Practice

Example: Teacher: **Mada tsukaimasen ka.**
"Aren't you using it yet?"

Student: **Iie, moo tsukaihajimemashita.**
"Yes [lit. No, you're wrong], we've already begun using it."

a) Mada kentoo-shiteimasen ka.   Iie, moo kentoo-shihajimemashita.

b) Mada taisaku o torimasen ka.   Iie, moo (taisaku o) torihajimemashita.

c) Mada robotto o seesan-shimasen ka.   Iie, moo seesan-shihajimemashita.

d) Mada mitsumori o kakimasen ka.   Iie, moo kakihajimemashita.

e) Mada koshoo o naoshimasen ka.   Iie, moo naoshihajimemashita.

4 Response Practice

Example: Teacher: **Zuibun hayai desu ne.**
"It's very early, isn't it?"

Student: **Ee, hayasugimasu ne.**
"Yes, it's too early, isn't it."

a) **Zuibun takai desu ne.**   **Ee, takasugimasu ne.**

b) **Zuibun hatarakimasu ne.**   **Ee, hatarakisugimasu ne.**

c) **Zuibun tabemasu ne.**   **Ee, tabesugimasu ne.**

d) **Zuibun isogashii desu ne.**   **Ee, isogashisugimasu ne.**

e) **Zuibun robotto o huyashimashita ne.**   **Ee, huyashisugimashita ne.**

5 Transformation Practice

Example: Teacher: **Gen'in ga wakarimasen. Shinpai desu.**
"We don't know the cause. We are concerned."

Student: **Gen'in ga wakaranai uchi wa shinpai desu.**
"As long as we don't know the cause, we are concerned."

a) **Buchoo ga sansee-shimasen.**
Shoodan wa susumeraremasen.
Buchoo ga sansee-shinai uchi wa shoodan wa susumeraremasen.

b) **Kee'ee-jootai ga wakarimasen.**
Torihiki wa dekimasen.
Kee'ee-jootai ga wakaranai uchi wa torihiki wa dekimasen.

c) **Teeki-kensa o shimasen.**
Kono kikai wa tsukaemasen.
Teeki-kensa o shinai uchi wa kono kikai wa tsukaemasen.

d) **Shisetsu no kaizoo o shimasen.**
Robotto wa doonyuu-dekimasen.
Shisetsu no kaizoo o shinai uchi wa robotto wa doonyuu-dekimasen.

e) **Kaisha ga taisaku o torimasen.**
Kumiai wa shigoto o shinai deshoo.
Kaisha ga taisaku o toranai uchi wa kumiai wa shigoto o shinai deshoo.

6 Response Practice

Example: Teacher: **Mondai desu ka.**
"Is it a problem?"

Student: **Mondai to iu hodo ja arimasen.**
"It is not so serious as to be called a problem."

a)	Shinpai desu ka.	Shinpai to iu hodo ja arimasen.
b)	Takasugimasu ka.	Takasugiru to iu hodo ja arimasen.
c)	Kiken na sagyoo desu ka.	Kiken na sagyoo to iu hodo ja arimasen.
d)	Jiko desu ka.	Jiko to iu hodo ja arimasen.
e)	Torikaenakereba narimasen ka.	Torikaenakereba naranai to iu hodo ja arimasen.

7 Comprehension Practice

Directions: The teacher reads aloud the following passage and then asks the student questions about it.

Buraun-san wa kyoo Ooyama-san ni yobarete, Nissan e ikimashita. Ooyama-buchoo ni yoru to, robotto no bearingu ga torikaenakereba naranai hodo, mametsu-shite iru soo desu. Yuu-esu-emu no setsumeesho de wa bearingu wa ichi-nen wa motsu hazu desu. Mada honkakuteki ni tsukaihajimete kara rok-kagetsu desu kara, chotto hayasugiru yoo desu. Buraun-san wa sassoku Yuu-esu-emu ni renraku-shite, choosa-saseru koto ni shimashita.

Questions:

1   Buraun-san wa dare ni yobaremashita ka.
2   Ooyama-buchoo wa doo shite Buraun-san o yobimashita ka.
3   Setsumeesho ni yoru to, bearingu wa dono kurai motsu hazu desu ka.
4   Robotto o honkakuteki ni tsukaihajimete kara dono kurai desu ka.
5   Buraun-san wa doko ni renraku-shimasu ka.
6   Buraun-san wa Yuu-esu-emu ni nani o saseru tsumori desu ka.

EXERCISES

a)   Translate the following English sentences into Japanese, using the passive voice:

1   Mr. Jones was sent to Japan for negotiations with Nissan.
2   This kind of machine tool is used in American car factories.
3   Ms. Yamada was troubled because Mr. Imai used her typewriter.
4   P & C's statement of accounts was checked by the bank.
5   If I am invited to the party, I'll be glad to come.
6   Yesterday it didn't rain [lit. on me].
7   Where are cars produced in Japan [lit. Where are Japanese cars being produced]?
8   What necessary action [lit. counter measure] is being taken concerning the accident?

b)   Inform the teacher in Japanese that:

1   As long as the specialist does not come to Tokyo, Mr. Brown cannot explain the mechanical problem.
2   According to Mr. Ohyama, (they) don't seem to know the cause of the accident yet.

3 They noticed the mechanical problem while doing a periodical check-up.
4 The customer complained to Mr. Tanaka because the delivery of the new products was not on time [lit. Mr. Tanaka received complaints from a customer...].
5 Mr. Jones from USM said that the bearings should be replaced every six months.

Model Answers:

a) 1 Joonzu-san wa Nissan to no shoodan no tame ni Nihon e haken-saremashita.
2 Konna koosaku-kikai wa Amerika no jidoosha-koojoo de tsukawarete imasu.
3 Yamada-san wa Imai-san ni taipuraitaa o tsukawarete, komatte imashita.
4 Pii-ando-shii no kessan-hookokusho wa ginkoo ni shiraberaremashita.
5 Paatii ni shootai-saretara, yorokonde ukagaimasu.
6 Kinoo wa ame ni furaremasen deshita.
7 Nihon no jidoosha wa doko de tsukurarete imasu ka.
8 Jiko ni tsuite donna taisaku ga torarete imasu ka.

b) 1 Senmonka ga Tookyoo e konai uchi wa Buraun-san wa koshoo ni tsuite setsumee dekimasen.
2 Ooyama-san ni yoru to, jiko no gen'in wa mada wakaranai soo desu.
3 Teeki-kensa no toki ni, koshoo ni ki ga tsukimashita.
4 Shin-seehin no nooki ga ma ni awanakatta no de, Tanaka-san wa otokui-sama ni monku o iwaremashita.
5 Yuu-esu-emu no Joonzu-san wa bearingu wa rok-kagetsu goto ni torikaenakereba naranai to iimashita.

BUSINESS INFORMATION

Handling Problems

Problems in business are of course awkward in any country, but perhaps especially so in Japan where customers have such high expectations for quality and service, and where difficulties are compounded by language and cultural barriers. If problems ever occur between you and your clients or staff, the following guidelines may help you steer through to calmer waters.

1 Anticipate The Problem—"A Stitch in Time..." As much as possible, you should deal with problems before they actually happen. Whenever a new building is to be constructed in Japan, for example, the developers or owners will personally visit those in the neighborhood, apologize for the inconvenience they are about to cause and maybe even distribute gifts. Letting people know in advance of likely problems demonstrates how sincerely you regret troubling them—even if you haven't yet done so—and how sensitive you are to their circumstances. Also, of course, apologizing beforehand appeases those who might otherwise protest loudly later and so helps to avoid direct confrontation—and unnecessary delays in the construction project.

2 Shared Responsibility—"The Buck Stops Here": Whenever your firm makes a mistake, you should be prepared to shoulder full responsibility no matter how small or grave the error is, and no matter who in your staff was in fact directly responsible. In Japan, those in managing positions are expected to share the blame (or credit) for whatever transpires within their jurisdiction. It is not at all unusual for presidents of giant department stores to personally retrieve and replace defective merchandise, for example, or for the management of an airline to personally express **owabi** (お詫び, apologies) to passengers after a hair-raising flight. When problems occur due to an employee's oversight, therefore, you should never try to wriggle off the hook or make excuses. Simply accept the blame, apologize promptly to your client and try to rectify the situation without delay. Note also that, because of this notion of shared responsibility, it may be a good idea to assemble an appropriately large retinue to express formal apologies to clients for more serious mistakes. In general, the bigger the problem, the bigger the "**owabi** delegation."

3 No Attorneys—"Taking The Law In Your Own Hands": Even when serious difficulties develop, you should not attempt to resort to legal action. This suggests on the one hand that you care only for your own protection and, on the other, that you lack the confidence and inclination to work things out in private with your partner (See *BUSINESS JAPANESE II Business Information 27*). Also, taking one's problems to the law is generally considered **mittomonai** (みっともない, unbecoming) in Japan, like publicizing a domestic quarrel or airing dirty linen. If you hope to salvage anything of your business relationship for the future, therefore, you should try to iron out your own problems. Attorneys should be called in only when your partnership has deteriorated beyond repair —at which point they can only help to hasten its demise.

4 Staff Problems–"Keeping Cool": Even the most dedicated, workaholic members of your Japanese staff will occasionally make mistakes–perhaps serious ones. When this happens, you should take care not to lose your temper or scold them loudly for the entire office to hear. This is of course common courtesy in any country but it may be especially important in Japan where "loss of face" in front of colleagues and peers occasionally leads to resignation. If you must let off steam, therefore, you should do it out of earshot of other employees, or privately over lunch or drinks. A little respect for everyone's public "face" will go a long way to elevate your own status in the eyes of your Japanese subordinates, forestall unexpected staff departures and help maintain that all-important group harmony.

5 The Long-Term Perspective–"Business As Always": With both client and staff troubles, the important thing to remember in Japan is that long-range harmony usually outweighs short-term difficulties. Consequently, your first priority should always be to "normalize" your relationship, to regain your client's confidence and trust through personal apologies and visits–and *then* to tackle the problem at hand. Foreign consultants warn that sincerity in your attitude towards the problem is frequently as important as its actual solution, because each difficulty that arises is also an important testing ground for your views concerning the long-term relationship. You should therefore be prepared to devote personal attention to each and every snag in your relationship, no matter how trivial. Dispatching of "little" problems quickly and impersonally, as though they were a nuisance, might demonstrate professional competence but perhaps also indifference to the long-term. As a result, you may solve the problem efficiently this time–only to discover later that it was unfortunately also the last time.

Lesson 35

Clearing Up Misunderstandings

OBJECTIVES

1 to discuss mechanical problems.

2 to apologize for one's error.

3 to use the Passive Causative form.

TARGET EXPRESSIONS AND PATTERNS

1 \<X> is made to do …by \<Y>.   **\<X> wa \<Y> ni …saserareru.**
2 to be no more than \<X>.   **\<X> ni suginai.**
3 without doing…   **…sezu ni**
4 before doing…   **…suru made**

SITUATION

Notified by Mr. Brown of the technical problem at Nissan, Mr. Jones and several other engineers from USM fly to Japan. They investigate and correct the problem with the robot ball bearings. When all is clear, Mr. Jones drops in at Nissan to pay his respects to Mr. Ohyama before going home.

35/Clearing Up Misunderstandings

DIALOGUE

	again and again, often	**tabitabi,** 度々
Ohyama	thanks for your trouble	**gokuroo-sama,** ご苦労さま

1	Oh, Mr. Jones, thank you for coming out so many times.	**Iyaa, Joonzu-san, tabitabi shutchoo, gokuroo-sama desu.**

	trouble, inconvenient	**meewaku, gomeewaku** (polite), 迷惑, ご迷惑
	to give trouble	**meewaku o kakeru,** 迷惑をかける
	to give trouble	**gomeewaku o okake-suru** (polite),
Jones		ご迷惑をおかけする

2	Not at all. It is we who must apologize for having caused (you) this inconvenience.	**Tondemo gozaimasen. Kochira koso, gomeewaku o okake-shimashite, kyooshuku deshita.**

	to become clear	**hakkiri-suru,** はっきりする
Ohyama	to feel easy	**anshin-suru,** 安心する

3	But the cause (of the problem) has been clarified, so (I) feel easy now.	**De mo, riyuu ga hakkiri-shite, anshin-shimashita yo.**

	itself	**jitai,** 自体
	defect	**kekkan,** 欠陥
Jones	to be made to worry	**shinpai-saserareru,** 心配させられる

4	(I) am also relieved that (it) was not a defect in the product itself. (I) was really quite worried until (I) was actually at the site [lit. (I) was really made to worry until (I) saw the actual location].	**Watakushi mo seehin jitai no kekkan de wa nakatta node, hotto-shimashita. Genba o miru made wa zuibun shinpai-saseraremashita.**

	number	**suu,** 数
	number of hours	**jikansuu,** 時間数
Ohyama	not more than...	**...ni suginai,** に過ぎない

5	So, in the end, (it) was simply a problem of the number of hours in operation, right?	**Kekkyoku, unten-jikansuu no mondai ni suginakatta wake desu ne.**

Jones	inadequate	hubi /na/, 不備(な)

6	That's true, but (I) think our instruction manual was inadequate.	Sore wa soo desu ga, watakushidomo no setsumeesho ga hubi datta to omoimasu.

Ohyama	replacement	torikae, 取り替え

7	What (they) meant by a year without repair was in the case of an 8-hour working day, wasn't it [lit. ... in case (they) use it 8 hours a day]?	Ichi-nenkan, buhin no torikae ga iranai to iu no wa, ichi-nichi hachi-jikan tsukau baai datta n desu ne.

	system	see, 制
Jones	8-hour system	hachi-jikan-see, 八時間制

8	Yes, American factories are normally operated on an 8-hour basis, so...	Ee, Amerika no koojoo de wa hutsuu hachi-jikan-see desu kara...

	shift	kootai (-suru), 交替(する)
	two-shift system	ni-kootai-see, 二交替制
	without stopping	yasumazu ni, 休まずに
Ohyama	wear, damage	itami, 痛み

9	So, if (we) operate non-stop 16 hours a day with two shifts, the parts would naturally wear out faster.	Sore ga, ichi-nichi ni-kootai-see de, juuroku-jikan yasumazu ni unten-sureba, buhin no itami mo hayai wake desu ne.

Jones	anyway	tonikaku, とにかく

10	Anyway, (I) think it would have been better if our explanation were a little more detailed [lit. kind].	Tonikaku, setsumee ga motto shinsetsu dattara, yokatta to omoimasu.

Ohyama	misunderstanding	gokai (-suru), 誤解(する)

11	But, after all, it was (our) misunderstanding, so...	De mo, kekkyoku, gokai datta wake desu kara...

	to learn a lesson	**benkyoo ni naru,** 勉強^{べんきょう}になる
	Japan-oriented, for Japan	**Nihon-muke,** 日本向^{にほんむ}け
Jones	instruction manual	**kaisetsusho,** 解説書^{かいせつしょ}

12 We have also learned a good lesson. As soon as (I) return home, (I)'ll suggest that (we) prepare a special Japan-oriented manual. / **Watakushidomo mo ii benkyoo ni narimashita. Kikoku-shitara, sugu Nihon-muke no kaisetsusho o tsukuru teean o shimasu.**

Ohyama   idea   **kangae,** 考^{かんが}え

13 That's a good idea. Please do (your) best. / **Sore wa ii kangae desu nee. Doozo ganbatte kudasai.**

Jones

14 Thank you very much. (I) look forward to your continued cooperation. / **Arigatoo gozaimasu. Kongo tomo, yoroshiku onegai-shimasu.**

JAPANESE WRITING

1　大山^{おおやま}：　いやあ、ジョーンズさん、度々出張^{たびたびしゅっちょう}、ご苦労^{くろう}さまです。

2　ジョーンズ：　とんでもございません。こちらこそ、ご迷惑^{めいわく}をおかけしまして、恐縮^{きょうしゅく}でした。

3　大山^{おおやま}：　でも、理由^{りゆう}がはっきりして、安心^{あんしん}しましたよ。

4　ジョーンズ：　私^{わたくし}も製品自体^{せいひんじたい}の欠陥^{けっかん}ではなかったので、ほっとしました。現場^{げんば}を見^みるまでは ずいぶん心配^{しんぱい}させられました。

5　大山^{おおやま}：　結局^{けっきょく}、運転時間数^{うんてんじかんすう}の問題^{もんだい}にすぎなかったわけですね。

6　ジョーンズ：　それはそうですが、私共^{わたくしども}の説明書^{せつめいしょ}が不備^{ふび}だったと思^{おも}います。

7　大山^{おおやま}：　1年間^{ねんかん}、部品^{ぶひん}の取^とり替^かえが要^いらないというのは、1日8時間^{にちじかん}使^{つか}う場合^{ばあい}だったんですね。

8　ジョーンズ：　ええ、アメリカの工場^{こうじょう}では普通^{ふつう}8時間制^{じかんせい}ですから…

9　大山^{おおやま}：　それが、1日2交替制^{にちこうたいせい}で、16時間休^{じかんやす}まずに運転^{うんてん}すれば、部品^{ぶひん}の痛^{いた}みも早^{はや}いわけですね。

10　ジョーンズ：　とにかく、説明^{せつめい}がもっと親切^{しんせつ}だったら、よかったと思^{おも}います。

11　大山^{おおやま}：　でも、結局^{けっきょく}、誤解^{ごかい}だったわけですから…

12　ジョーンズ：　私共^{わたくしども}も いい勉強^{べんきょう}になりました。帰国^{きこく}したら、すぐ日本向^{にほんむ}けの解説書^{かいせつしょ}を作^{つく}る提案^{ていあん}をします。

13 大山： それはいい考えですねえ。どうぞ頑張ってください。

14 ジョーンズ： ありがとうございます。今後とも、よろしくお願いします。

ADDITIONAL USEFUL EXPRESSIONS

1 At the office

inferior products	**huryoohin,** 不良品

A:	According to the message [lit. contact] from the factory, there're a lot of inferior products in the parts we purchased this time.	**Koojoo kara no renraku ni yoru to, kondo katta buhin ni wa huryoohin ga ooi soo desu.**

agent, trader	**gyoosha,** 業者

B:	Is that so? That won't do. I'll call the agent immediately and have them replaced.	**Soo desu ka. Sore wa ikemasen nee. Sassoku gyoosha o yonde, torikaesasemashoo.**

inferior parts	**huryoo-buhin,** 不良部品
defective product	**kekkan-shoohin,** 欠陥商品

A:	In any case, if we use inferior parts, our products will also become defective, won't they?	**Tonikaku, huryoo-buhin o tsukattara, uchi no seehin mo kekkan-shoohin ni natte shimaimasu.**

trust	**shinyoo,** 信用
trust-problem	**shinyoo-mondai,** 信用問題

B:	We'll lose credit, so [lit. it'll become a trust-problem for our company].	**Wagasha no shinyoo-mondai ni narimasu kara nee.**

2 A conversation between friends

you	**kimi** (friendly), 君

A:	What kinds of things are you making at your factory now?	**Kimi no koojoo de wa ima donna mono o tsukutte iru n desu ka.**

35/Clearing Up Misunderstandings

| | for Europe | **Yooroppa-muke,** ヨーロッパ向け |
| | electrical product | **denki-seehin,** 電器製品 |

| B: | Mainly we make electrical products for Europe. | **Omo ni Yooroppa-muke no denki-see-hin desu.** |

| A: | Then you must be very busy these days. | **Jaa, saikin wa totemo isogashii n de-shoo.** |

| | oneself | **jishin,** 自身 |

| B: | Yes, (we've been pretty busy) since about 6 months ago. I myself am working 3,4 hours overtime everyday. | **Ee, rok-kagetsu gurai mae kara. Boku jishin, mainichi san, yo-jikan zangyoo-shite imasu.** |

	business world, industry	**gyookai,** 業界
	each and every company	**dono kaisha mo,** どの会社も
	half	**hanbun,** 半分

| A: | Our industry is in a slump, and each and every company is using only a-bout half of its production facilities. | **Wareware no gyookai wa hukeeki de, dono kaisha mo seesan-shisetsu no han-bun ga tsukawarete imasen.** |

| B: | That is terrible [lit. severe]. | **Sore wa kibishii desu nee.** |

REFERENCE

hyoojunhin	標準品	standard products
kikakuhin	規格品	standardized products
Jisu	ジス（JIS)	Japan Industrial Standard
Jasu	ジャス（JAS)	Japan Agriculture and Forestry Standard
kadoo-jikan	稼動時間	hours of operation
yuukyuu-shisetsu	遊休施設	idle facilities
seesan-kyootee	生産協定	production agreement
hukyoo-karuteru	不況カルテル	anti-depression cartel
shoomoohin	消耗品	consumable goods
hanseehin	半製品	half-finished goods

NOTES

1 The Passive Causative Form

Shinpai-saserareru is the passive causative of **shinpai-suru** 'to worry' and means 'to be made to worry.'

To form the passive causative:

A)   Class 1 verb (or **-ru** verb): Drop the final **-ru** and add **-saserareru**.
   Example: **taberu** 'to eat' —   **tabe*saserareru*** 'to be made to eat'

B)   Class 2 verb (or **-u** verb): Drop the final **-u** and add **-aserareru**.
   Example: **hanasu** 'to speak' —   **hanas*aserareru*** 'to be made to speak'

Note: In the case of **-u** verbs ending with two vowels (e.g. **tsukau**), drop the final **-u** and add **-waserareru**.

   Example: tsukau 'to use' — **tsuka*waserareru*** 'to be made to use'

C)   Class 3 verb (or **-aru** verb): The passive causative rarely occurs.

D)   Irregular verbs:
   Examples: **kuru** 'to come' — ***kosaserareru*** 'to be made to come'
   suru 'to do' — ***saserareru*** 'to be made to do'

Compare:

The Causative			
The person causing/acting	The person acted upon	Object	Causative Verb
Tanaka-san wa	**hisho ni**	**tegami o**	**kak*asemashita*.**
Mr. Tanaka had his secretary write a letter.			

and

The Passive Causative			
The person acted upon	The person causing/acting	Object	Passive Causative Verb
Hisho wa	**Tanaka-san ni**	**tegami o**	**kak*aseraremashita*.**
Mr. Tanaka's secretary was made to write a letter by Mr. Tanaka.			

Note: The subject of a passive causative, i.e. the person being acted upon, is followed by particle **wa** or **ga**; and the person/thing causing the action is followed by particle **ni**.

Examples: **a)   Yamada-san wa buchoo ni paatii no junbi o *saseraremashita*.**
   "Ms. Yamada was asked [lit. made] by the General Manager to prepare the party."

   b)   Raishuu Oosaka e ik*aserareru* ka mo shiremasen.*
   "Maybe I'll be asked [lit. made] to go to Osaka next week."

    c) **Ano kaisha de wa juugyooin ga maiban osoku made hataraka*serarete imasu.***

    "In that company, employees are being made to work until late every night."

    d) **Kinoo Buraun-san wa Joonzu-san ni biiru o takusan nom*aseraremashita* no de, kyoo wa atama ga itaku narimashita.**

    "Yesterday Mr. Brown was made to drink lots of beer by Mr. Jones, so he has a headache today."

* When the subject of the passive causative is the speaker, it is usually omitted.

2 Informal Negative Verb + **-zu ni** 'without (doing)'

When the **-nai** ending of the informal negative verb [Refer to *BUSINESS JAPANESE*, Lesson 19, Note **2**] is replaced by **-zu**, the combination may be translated as 'without (doing).' Thus,

    yasumu 'to rest'
        yasuma*nai* 'don't rest' — **yasuma*zu (ni)*** 'without resting'
    taberu 'to eat'
        tabe*nai* 'don't eat' — **tabe*zu (ni)*** 'without eating'
    kuru 'to come'
        ko*nai* 'don't come' — **ko*zu (ni)*** 'without coming'
    suru 'to do'
        shi*nai* 'don't do' — **se*zu (ni)***** 'without doing'

** The only exception to the formation rule above. Note that the **-zu** form is usually followed by particle **ni**.

Examples: a) **Buraun-san wa byooki da kara, nani mo tabe*zu ni* nete imasu.**
        "Mr. Brown is sick, so he is in bed without eating anything."

    b) **Buchoo wa nani mo iwa*zu ni* heya o dete ikimashita.**
        "The General Manager left the room without saying anything."

    c) **Jisho o tsukawa*zu ni*, kono eego o hon'yaku-shite mite kudasai.**
        "Please try to translate this English (passage), without using the dictionary."

3 Conditional + **sugu**

When a conditional verb is followed by **sugu** 'at once,' the sequence may be translated as 'as soon as (such-and-such) happens' or 'immediately after (such-and-such) happens.'

Examples: a) **Buchoo ga kitara, *sugu* dekakemashoo.**
        "As soon as the General Manager comes, let's go."

    b) **Honsha kara terekkusu ga haittara, *sugu* renraku-shite kudasai.**
        "As soon as you receive a telex from the head office, please contact me [lit. As soon as a telex comes...]."

    c) **Shachoo ga sansee-shitara,** *sugu* **keeyaku-shimasu.**
       "I'll make the contract immediately after the President approves it."

4 Verb + **made**

An informal non-past verb + **made** is used to mean 'before (doing)' or 'until (someone) does such-and-such.' When the subject of the verb is indicated in the sentence, it is usually followed by particle **ga**.

Examples: a) **Nihon e kuru** *made* **nihongo ga dekimasen deshita.**
            "I could not speak Japanese before coming to Japan."

           b) **Anata no setsumee o kiku** *made***, robotto ni tsuite zenzen wakarimasen deshita.**
            "I did not understand anything about the robot until I heard your explanation."

           c) **Shachoo ga sansee-suru** *made***, keeyaku wa matte kudasai.**
            "Please wait for the contract until the President agrees (to it.)"

5 Noun + **ni suginai**

A noun + **ni suginai** means 'no more than …' or 'only ….' Thus,

        Sore wa gokai *ni sugimasen* **deshita.**
        "That was no more than a misunderstanding."

        Sono hiyoo wa nijuu-man-en *ni sugimasen.*
        "That cost is only 200,000 yen."

PRACTICE

1 Response Practice

Example: Teacher: **Ikimasu ka.**
                 "Will you go?"

             Student: **Ee, ikaseraremasu.**
                 "Yes, I'll be made to go."

a) **Shinpai-shimasu ka.**   **Ee, shinpai-saseraremasu.**

b) **Tsukaimasu ka.**   **Ee, tsukawaseraremasu.**

c) **Hatarakimasu ka.**   **Ee, hatarakaseraremasu.**

d) **Yasumimasu ka.**   **Ee, yasumaseraremasu.**

e) **Kikimasu ka.**   **Ee, kikaseraremasu.**

f) **Yomimasu ka.**   **Ee, yomaseraremasu.**

g) **Kakimasu ka.**   **Ee, kakaseraremasu.**

h) **Shirabemasu ka.**   **Ee, shirabesaseraremasu.**

35/Clearing Up Misunderstandings

2 Transformation Practice

Example: Teacher: **Buchoo wa hisho ni tegami o kakasemashita.**
"The General Manager made his secretary write a letter."

Student: **Hisho wa buchoo ni tegami o kakaseraremashita.**
"The secretary was made to write a letter by the General Manager."

a) **Joonzu-san wa gishi ni kikai o shirabe-sasemashita.**   **Gishi wa Joonzu-san ni kikai o shirabe-saseraremashita.**

b) **Tanaka-san wa okusan ni kuruma o unten-sasemashita.**   **Okusan wa Tanaka-san ni kuruma o unten-saseraremashita.**

c) **Buraun-san wa Imai-san o asa hayaku kosasemashita.**   **Imai-san wa Buraun-san ni asa hayaku kosaseraremashita.**

d) **Ooyama-san wa Suzuki-san ni denwa o kakesasemashita.**   **Suzuki-san wa Ooyama-san ni denwa o kakesaseraremashita.**

e) **Shachoo wa Buraun-san o kikoku-sasemasu.**   **Buraun-san wa shachoo ni kikoku-saseraremasu.**

3 Transformation Practice

Example: Teacher: **Terekkusu ga hairimasu. Renraku-shite kudasai.**
"A telex comes in. Please contact me."

Student: **Terekkusu ga haittara, sugu renraku-shite kudasai.**
"Please contact me as soon as a telex comes in."

a) **Kikoku-shimasu.**
Joonzu-san ni aimasu.   **Kikoku-shitara, sugu Joonzu-san ni aimasu.**

b) **Ashita jimusho e kimasu.**
Kono tegami o taipu-shimasu.   **Ashita jimusho e kitara, sugu kono tegami o taipu-shimasu.**

c) **Koshoo o shirabemasu.**
Gen'in ga wakarimashita.   **Koshoo o shirabetara, sugu gen'in ga wakarimashita.**

d) **Keeyaku-shimasu.**
Noohin-shimasu.   **Keeyaku-shitara, sugu noohin-shimasu.**

e) **Kono robotto o doonyuu-shimasu.**
Seesansee ga koojoo-suru deshoo.   **Kono robotto o doonyuu-shitara, sugu seesansee ga koojoo-suru deshoo.**

4 Response Practice

Example: Teacher: **Itsu made machimasu ka. /Tanaka-san ga kuru./**
"Until when will you wait?" /Mr. Tanaka comes./

Student: **Tanaka-san ga kuru made machimasu.**
"I'll wait until Mr. Tanaka comes."

a) **Itsu made koko ni imasu ka.**
/Terekkusu ga hairu./   **Terekkusu ga hairu made koko ni imasu.**

b) Itsu made Nihon ni imasu ka.
/Shoodan ga seekoo-suru./

Shoodan ga seekoo-suru made Nihon ni imasu.

c) Itsu made sono kikai o shirabemasu ka.
/Gen'in ga wakaru./

Gen'in ga wakaru made, (kono kikai o) shirabemasu.

d) Itsu made koojoo de hatarakimasu ka.
/Shisetsu no kaizoo ga owaru./

Shisetsu no kaizoo ga owaru made koo-joo de hatarakimasu.

e) Itsu made kono kikai o tsukaimasu ka.
/Atarashii kikai ga kuru./

Atarashii kikai ga kuru made (kono kikai o) tsukaimasu.

5 Transformation Practice

Example: Teacher: **Yasumimasen. Unten-shimasu.**
"We don't rest. We operate (it)."

Student: **Yasumazu ni, unten-shimasu.**
"We operate it without stopping."

a) **Tabemasen. Hatarakimasu.** | **Tabezu ni, hatarakimasu.**

b) **Nemasen. Benkyoo-shimasu.** | **Nezu ni, benkyoo-shimasu.**

c) **Buchoo ni soodan-shimasen. Keeyaku-shimashita.** | **Buchoo ni soodan-sezu ni, keeyaku-shimashita.**

d) **Setsumeesho o yomimasen. Kikai o tsu-kaihajimemashita.** | **Setsumeesho o yomazu ni, kikai o tsu-kaihajimemashita.**

e) **Shinpai-shimasen. Matte ite kudasai.** | **Shinpai-sezu ni, matte ite kudasai.**

6 Response Practice

Example: Teacher: **Are wa gokai deshita ka.**
"Was that a misunderstanding?"

Student: **Ee, gokai ni sugimasen deshita.**
"Yes, (it) was no more than a misunderstanding."

a) **Sore wa Tanaka-san no kangae desu ka.** | **Ee, Tanaka-san no kangae ni sugi-masen.**

b) **Are wa buhin no mondai desu ka.** | **Ee, buhin no mondai ni sugimasen.**

c) **Hiyoo wa go-man-en desu ka.** | **Ee, (hiyoo wa) go-man-en ni sugimasen.**

d) **Sore wa Nihon no shooshuukan desu ka. ka.** | **Ee, Nihon no shooshuukan ni sugi-masen.**

e) **Ano kaisha wa dairiten desu ka.** | **Ee, (ano kaisha wa) dairiten ni sugi-masen.**

7 Comprehension Practice

Directions: The teacher reads aloud the following passage and then asks the student questions about it.

35/Clearing Up Misunderstandings

Robotto no bearingu no mametsu ga hayasugiru no de, choosa no tame ni, Joonzu-san ga shutchoo-shite kimashita. Iroiro shirabete kara, gen'in ga wakarimashita. Sore wa unten-jikan-suu no mondai ni sugimasen deshita. Yuu-esu-emu no setsumeesho ni yoru to, bearingu no torikae wa ichi-nenkan iranai koto ni natte imashita ga, sore wa ichi-nichi hachi-jikan unten-suru baai deshita. Desu kara, ichi-nichi ni-kootai-see de, juuroku-jikan-ijoo unten-suru Nissan no baai wa motto hayaku itamu hazu desu. Gen'in ga wakatta no de, Ooyama-san wa hotto-shimashita. Joonzu-san mo gen'in ga seehin no kekkan de wa nakatta kara, anshin-shimashita. Joonzu-san wa kikoku-shitara, sugu motto kuwashii setsumeesho o junbi-suru tsumori desu.

Questions:

1 Joonzu-san wa doo shite Nihon e shutchoo-shite kimashita ka.
2 Joonzu-san wa gen'in ga wakarimashita ka.
3 Yuu-esu-emu no setsumeesho wa doo natte imashita ka.
4 Kekkyoku, gen'in wa nan deshita ka.
5 Nissan de wa robotto o ichi-nichi nan-jikan gurai unten-shimasu ka.
6 Ooyama-san wa doo shite hotto-shimashita ka.
7 Joonzu-san wa naze anshin-shimashita ka.
8 Joonzu-san wa kikoku-shitara, nani o suru tsumori desu ka.

EXERCISES

Inform the teacher in Japanese that:

1 Mr. Jones was made to make a business trip to Japan.
2 Mr. Imai is made to work until about eight o'clock every day.
3 Mr. Brown has never been made to sell high-tech products.
4 As soon as the cause of the mechanical problem is known, Mr. Jones is supposed to inform his head office [lit. It has been arranged that Mr. Jones will inform ...].
5 Mr. Brown said that he cannot give a discount before consulting with USM, Ltd.
6 The fact that there are no Japan-oriented manuals was the cause of the misunderstanding.
7 In Nissan's car factory, the operating hours are 16 hours a day with two shifts.
8 USM, Ltd. is responsible for fixing all mechanical problems until the warranty expires [lit. ... has responsibility to fix all breakdowns until the warranty period finishes].

Model Answers:

1 Joonzu-san wa Nihon e shutchoo-saseraremashita.
2 Imai-san wa mainichi hachi-ji goro made hatarakaseraremasu.
3 Buraun-san wa hai-teku-seehin o uraserareta koto wa arimasen.
4 Koshoo no gen'in ga wakattara, sugu Joonzu-san ga honsha e shiraseru koto ni natte imasu.
5 Buraun-san wa Yuu-esu-emu to soodan-suru made, nebiki wa dekinai to iimashita.
6 Nihon-muke no kaisetsusho ga nai koto ga gokai no gen'in deshita.
7 Nissan no jidoosha-koojoo wa kadoo jikan wa ichi-nichi ni-kootai-see de 16-jikan desu.
8 Yuu-esu-emu wa hoshoo-kikan ga owaru made, subete no koshoo o naosu sekinin ga arimasu.

BUSINESS INFORMATION

Joining A Japanese Firm

As Japan becomes increasingly prominent in the world economy, businessmen from over-seas are preparing more Japan-oriented brochures and materials, as Mr. Jones in the DIALOGUE is. At the other end, Japanese companies are also hiring more and more foreigners as part- and full-time workers. For those looking to join a Japanese company, the following information may come in useful.

1 Contracts and Responsibilities: Employment contracts are rare in Japan. As in business, many Japanese feel that such agreements are not really necessary if employer and employee are sincerely committed to working together (See *BUSINESS JAPANESE II Business Information 27*). Contracts *are* drawn up for the benefit of foreign employees, but even these are seldom more than a certificate of employment for visa purposes. You should therefore not be surprised if your contract is vague about conditions and responsibilities. Also, do not expect the document to be binding. Many foreigners find that, once they have entered the Japanese corporation, they end up performing all kinds of chores that they had never bargained for. This is partly because the employer does not always have a precise idea about how to utilize your talents at the time he hires you. More important, he expects that once you have been accepted into the corporate family, you will voluntarily contribute in as many ways as possible to the organization, and not just within your narrow field of specialization (See *BUSINESS JAPANESE II Business Information 28*). Consequently, you should not think yourself exploited if you are asked to do more than you officially agreed to. Instead, just remember that you are now one of a great big family of *generalists*, and play your part accordingly.

2 Bonuses: Bonuses in Japan are negotiated as part of one's annual salary, and not necessarily awarded in recognition of meritorious performance. Most Japanese employees receive the equivalent of 2-3 months' salary in the form of a bonus in both June and December, so that their annual salaries actually amount to about 17 months' pay. The size of the bonus will normally be determined at the time you join the company. Foreigners may even be asked whether they want to be included in the Japanese bonus system or whether they want their annual salary divided evenly over 12 months, *without* bonus. While the whole system may seem unnecessarily complicated, many foreigners do prefer to have their wages dispensed in 14 payments with these two bonuses. As one grateful foreign employee explained, the bonus system may force you to live on a shoe-string for 10 months of the year, but it is the only way to assure systematic savings in a society of rampant consumerism.

3 Holidays: The Japanese employee has less vacation time than his counterparts in other industrialized countries. In contrast to the West Germans and Americans who are granted about 30.2 days and 19.5 days a year on holiday, respectively, the Japanese get an average of only 15. Even then, most Japanese are reluctant to take all they are entitled to. Not only is it considered unseemly to do so, but it is also safer to reserve some of these days for

215

emergencies and illnesses. Also, holidays in Japan are hardly the peaceful, relaxing times they are meant to be. What with the typically horrendous traffic jams and crowds and screaming children, many Japanese businessmen actually find returning to the hectic office a welcome relief after their "vacation." None of this will come as good news to the prospective foreign employee, of course, but you may derive some meager comfort from the knowledge that the Japanese do at least have more national holidays than most, i.e. 12 days a year as opposed to 8-11 in most of Europe and the U.S. (See *BUSINESS JAPANESE II Business Information 21*).

4 Office Relations: Foreigners working full-time in Japanese companies do not always have an easy time. They do not always fit into the corporate environment–or into the miniature desks, for that matter–and seldom receive the same feed-back and evaluation from superiors that they are accustomed to back home. And since they are not expected to become lifetime employees or remain in Japan forever, they may also be passed up for important positions. Occasionally, foreign employees may even find themselves paraded before clients as though they were token **gaijin** (外人, foreign persons)–or as proof of the company's cosmopolitan outlook. And finally, although foreigners normally do enjoy higher salaries, longer vacations and various other perks, this privileged status can at the same time generate resentment from among their Japanese colleagues.

Of course, you cannot help being different. Nor, unfortunately, is there much you can do to counter resentment or envy. The argument that expatriate businessmen of all nationalities are always given special privileges does not hold much water in Japan since Japanese employees sent abroad often do *not* get higher pay, nor do their companies necessarily help with the relocation. Instead, experienced businessmen in Japan offer the following advice: First, just be yourself. Don't go overboard trying to fit in or become Japanese because no one expects you to, and you won't succeed anyway. Second, do your job –and do it well. The only way to avoid being viewed as a token foreigner is to prove that you are more; the best way to handle resentment about special perks is to prove you deserve them. Last but not least, learn Japanese. Learning the language will help you understand the system you are now a part of. Understanding the system, in turn, can help assure that you are not always perched at its fringes but actively involved and contributing. And most important, as one businessman put it, learning the language "allows the people around you to become people, and not just co-workers."

Ganbatte kudasai!
Good Luck!

Appendix/Index

Appendix I

1. Verb Inflections 218
2. Suru Verbs Chart 222
3. Adjectives Chart 225
4. Copula Chart 225

Appendix II

1. Katakana 226
2. Hiragana 227
3. Kanji 229

Index 239

APPENDIX I

1. Verb Inflections

Citation Form	Verb Class	Meaning (Lesson)	Stem (-masu)	Gerund	Informal Past	Potential
agaru	(-u)	rise, 30	agari	agatte	agatta	agareru
ageru	(-ru)	raise, 33	age	agete	ageta	agerareru
azukeru	(-ru)	deposit, 26	azuke	azukete	azuketa	azukerareru
hakobu	(-u)	carry, 31	hakobi	hakonde	hakonda	hakoberu
hareru	(-ru)	clear up, 21	hare	harete	hareta	(harerareru)
heru	(-u)	decrease, 27	heri	hette	hetta	(hereru)
hikaeru	(-ru)	stay away, 33	hikae	hikaete	hikaeta	hikaerareru
hikidasu	(-u)	withdraw, 26	hikidashi	hikidashite	hikidashita	hikidaseru
hiraku	(-u)	open, 26	hiraki	hiraite	hiraita	hirakeru
hueru	(-ru)	increase, 22	hue	huete	hueta	(huerareru)
huku	(-u)	it is windy, 21	huki	huite	huita	(hukeru)
huru	(-u)	fall, 21	huri	hutte	hutta	(hureru)
huyasu	(-u)	increase, 27	huyashi	huyashite	huyashita	huyasareru
ireru	(-ru)	install, 34	ire	irete	ireta	irerareru
kakaru	(-u)	need, 24	kakari	kakatte	kakatta	(kakareru)
kakikomu	(-u)	write in, 26	kakikomi	kakikonde	kakikonda	kakikomeru
kariru	(-ru)	borrow, 31	kari	karite	karita	karirareru
kasamu	(-u)	expand, 27	kasami	kasande	kasanda	(kasameru)
ki ga tsuku	(-u)	notice, 34	ki ga tsuki	ki ga tsuite	ki ga tsuita	(ki ga tsukeru)
kimaru	(-u)	be decided, 27	kimari	kimatte	kimatta	(kimareru)
kimeru	(-ru)	decide, 27	kime	kimete	kimeta	kimerareru
kotaeru	(-ru)	answer, 21	kotae	kotaete	kotaeta	kotaerareru
kumoru	(-u)	become cloudy, 21	kumori	kumotte	kumotta	(kumoreru)
kuwawaru	(-u)	join, 30	kuwawari	kuwawatte	kuwawatta	kuwawareru
maneku	(-u)	invite, 33	maneki	maneite	maneita	manekeru
ma ni au	(-u)	be on time, 24	ma ni ai	ma ni atte	ma ni atta	(ma ni aeru)
mieru	(-ru)	come, appear, 28	mie	miete	mieta	(mierareru)
motsu	(-u)	endure, 34	mochi	motte	motta	(moteru)
mukaeru	(-ru)	meet, 21	mukae	mukaete	mukaeta	mukaerareru
nakunaru	(-u)	vanish, 27	nakunari	nakunatte	nakunatta	(nakunareru)
naosu	(-u)	fix, 32	naosi	naoshite	naoshita	naoseru
nasaru	(-u)	do, 24	nasa(r)i	nasatte	nasatta	nasareru
nemuru	(-u)	sleep, 22	nemuri	nemutte	nemutta	nemureru
neru	(-ru)	go to bed, 22	ne	nete	neta	nerareru
nokoru	(-u)	remain, 32	nokori	nokotte	nokotta	nokoreru
okiru	(-ru)	get up, 22	oki	okite	okita	okirareru
okonau	(-u)	perform, 23	okonai	okonatte	okonatta	okonaeru
oku	(-u)	place, 23	oki	oite	oita	okeru
okureru	(-ru)	be late, 24	okure	okurete	okureta	(okurerareru)
osu	(-u)	push, 26	oshi	oshite	oshita	oseru
sagaru	(-u)	go down, 30	sagari	sagatte	sagatta	sagareru
shiharau	(-u)	pay, 25	shiharai	shiharatte	shiharatta	shiharaeru
shiraberu	(-ru)	check, 34	shirabe	shirabete	shirabeta	shiraberareru
shiraseru	(-ru)	inform, 28	shirase	shirasete	shiraseta	shiraserareru
shitagau	(-u)	obey, 29	shitagai	shitagatte	shitagatta	shitagaeru
susumeru	(-ru)	progress, 25	susume	susumete	susumeta	susumerareru
susumu	(-u)	progress, 29	susumi	susunde	susunda	susumeru
tashikame-ru	(-ru)	confirm, 32	tashikame	tashikamete	tashikameta	tashikamerareru
todokeru	(-ru)	deliver, 24	todoke	todokete	todoketa	todokerareru
todoku	(-u)	arrive, 34	todoki	todoite	todoita	(todokeru)

Conditional	Provisional	Tentative	Causative	Passive	Passive Causative
agattara	agareba	agaroo	agaraseru	agarareru	agaraserareru
agetara	agereba	ageyoo	agesaseru	agerareru	agesaserareru
azuketara	azukereba	azukeyoo	azukesaseru	azukerareru	azukesaserareru
hakondara	hakobeba	hakoboo	hakobaseru	hakobareru	hakobaserareru
haretara	harereba	(hareyoo)	(haresaseru)	harerareru	(haresaserareru)
hettara	hereba	(heroo)	heraseru	(herareru)	heraserareru
hikaetara	hikaereba	hikaeyoo	hikaesaseru	hikaerareru	hikaesaserareru
hikidashitara	hikidaseba	hikidasoo	hikidasaseru	hikidasareru	hikidaserareru
hiraitara	hirakeba	hirakoo	hirakaseru	hirakareru	hirakaserareru
huetara	huereba	hueyoo	huesaseru	huerareru	huesaserareru
huitara	hukeba	(hukoo)	(kukaseru)	(hukareru)	(kukaserareru)
huttara	hureba	huroo	(huraseru)	hurareru	(huraserareru)
huyashitara	huyaseba	huyasoo	huyasasu	huerareru	huesaserareru
iretara	irereba	ireyoo	iresaseru	irerareru	iresaserareru
kakattara	kakareba	kakaroo	(kakaraseru)	(kakarareru)	(kakaraserareru)
kakikondara	kakikomeba	kakikomoo	kakikomaseru	kakikomareru	kakikomaserareru
karitara	karireba	kariyoo	karisaseru	karirareru	karisaserareru
kasandara	kasameba	(kasamoo)	(kasamaseru)	(kasamareru)	(kasamaserareru)
ki ga tsuitara	ki ga tsukeba	(ki ga tsukoo)	ki ga tsuka-seru	ki ga tsukareru	ki ga tsukaserareru
kimattara	kimareba	kimaroo	kimaraseru	(kimarareru)	(kimaraserareru)
kimetara	kimereba	kimeyoo	kimesaseru	kimerareru	kimesaserareru
kotaetara	kotaereba	kotaeyoo	kotaesaseru	kotaerareru	kotaesaserareru
kumottara	kumoreba	(kumoroo)	(kumoraseru)	kumorareru	(kumoraserareru)
kuwawattara	kuwawareba	kuwawaroo	kuwawaraseru	kuwawarareru	kuwawaraserareru
maneitara	manekeba	manekoo	manekaseru	manekareru	manekaserareru
maniattara	maniaeba	(maniaoo)	maniawaseru	(maniawareru)	maniawaserareru
mietara	miereba	(mieyoo)	(miesaseru)	mierareru	(miesaserareru)
mottara	moteba	motoo	motaseru	(motareru)	motaserareru
mukaetara	mukaereba	mukaeyoo	mukaesaseru	mukaerareru	mukaesaserareru
nakunattara	nakunareba	nakunaroo	nakunaraseru	nakunarareru	nakunaraserareru
naoshitara	naoseba	naosoo	naosaseru	naosareru	naosaserareru
nasattara	nasareba	nasaroo	(nasaraseru)	(nasarareru)	(nasaraserareru)
nemuttara	nemureba	nemuroo	nemuraseru	nemurareru	nemuraserareru
netara	nereba	neyoo	nesaseru	nerareru	nesaserareru
nokottara	nokoreba	nokoroo	nokoraseru	nokorareru	nokoraserareru
okitara	okireba	okiyoo	okisaseru	okirareru	okisaserareru
okonattara	okonaeba	okonaoo	okonawaseru	okonawareru	okonawaserareru
oitara	okeba	okoo	okaseru	okareru	okaserareru
okuretara	okurereba	okureyoo	okuresaseru	okurerareru	okuresaserareru
oshitara	oseba	osoo	osaseru	osareru	osaserareru
sagattara	sagareba	sagaroo	sagaraseru	sagarareru	sagaraserareru
shiharattara	shiharaeba	shiharaoo	shiharawaseru	shiharawareru	shiharawaserareru
shirabetara	shirabereba	shirabeyoo	shirabesaseru	shiraberareru	shirabesaserareru
shirasetara	shirasereba	shirasoo	shiraseru	shiraserareru	shirasaserareru
shitagattara	shitagaeba	shitagaoo	shitagawaseru	shitagawareru	shitagawaserareru
susumetara	susumereba	susumeyoo	susumesaseru	susumerareru	susumesaserareru
susundara	susumeba	susumoo	susumaseru	susumareru	susumaserareru
tashikame-tara	tashikame-reba	tashikame-yoo	tashikame-saseru	tashikame-rareru	tashikame-saserareru
todoketara	todokereba	todokeyoo	todokesaseru	todokerareru	todokesaserareru
todoitara	todokeba	todokoo	todokaseru	(todokareru)	(todokaserareru)

Citation Form	Verb Class	Meaning (Lesson)	Stem (-masu)	Gerund	Informal Past	Potential
toiawaseru	(-ru)	check, inquire, 27	toiawase	toiawasete	toiawaseta	toiawaserareru
torikaeru	(-ru)	replace, 34	torikae	torikaete	torikaeta	torikaerareru
torikakaru	(-u)	start, 32	torikakari	torikakatte	torikakatta	torikakareru
toritsukeru	(-ru)	mount, 32	toritsuke	toritsukete	toritsuketa	toritsukerareru
tsukaiha-jimeru	(-ru)	start to use, 34	tsukaihajime	tsukaihaji-mete	tsukaihajimeta	tsukaihajime-rareru
tsukaina-reru	(-ru)	be accustomed to using, 26	tsukainare	tsukainarete	tsukainareta	(tsukainare-rareru)
tsukamaru	(-u)	can get, 34	tsukamari	tsukamatte	tsukamatta	(tsukamareru)
tsukareru	(-ru)	be tired, 30	tsukare	tsukarete	tsukareta	(tsukarerareru)
tsukiau	(-u)	accompany, 33	tsukiai	tsukiatte	tsukiatta	tsukiaeru
tsuku	(-u)	arrive, 22	tsuki	tsuite	tsuita	tsukeru
tsureru	(-ru)	take along, 28	tsure	tsurete	tsureta	(tsurerareru)
tsuzuku	(-u)	continue, 21	tsuzuki	tsuzuite	tsuzuita	tsuzukeru
urikomu	(-u)	sell, 29	urikomi	urikonde	urikonda	urikomeru
utau	(-u)	sing, 33	utai	utatte	utatta	utaeru
wabiru	(-ru)	apologize, 34	wabi	wabite	wabita	wabirareru
yamu	(-u)	stop, cease, 34	yami	yande	yanda	(yameru)
yaru	(-u)	do, 30	yari	yatte	yatta	yareru
yasumu	(-u)	rest, 28	yasumi	yasunde	yasunda	yasumeru
yobu	(-u)	call, 34	yobi	yonde	yonda	yoberu
yokosu	(-u)	send, 32	yokoshi	yokoshite	yokoshita	yokoseru

* Verb forms indicated in parentheses are rarely used.

Conditional	Provisional	Tentative	Causative	Passive	Passive Causative
toiawasetara	toiawasereba	toiawaseyoo	toiawase-saseru	toiawaserareru	toiawasesaserareru
torikaetara	torikaereba	torikaeyoo	torikaesaseru	torikaerareru	torikaesaserareru
torikakattara	torikakareba	torikakaroo	torikakar-aseru	torikakarareru	torikakaraserareru
toritsuketara	toritsukereba	toritsukeyoo	toritsuke-saseru	toritsuke-rareru	toritsukesaserareru
tsukaihajime-tara	tsukaiha-jimereba	tsukaiha-jimeyoo	tsukaihajime-saseru	tsukaihajime-rareru	tsukaihajimesase-rareru
tsukainare-tara	tsukainare-reba	tsukainare-yoo	tsukainare-saseru	(tsukainare-rareru)	tsukainaresase-rareru
tsukamattara	tsukamareba	(tsukamaroo)	(tsukama-raseru)	(tsukama-rareru)	(tsukamarase-rareru)
tsukaretara	tsukarereba	tsukareyoo	tsukaresaseru	tsukarerareru	tsukaresaserareru
tsukiattara	tsukiaeba	tsukiaoo	tsukiawaseru	tsukiawareru	tsukiawaserareru
tsuitara	tsukeba	tsukoo	tsukaseru	tsukareru	tsukaserareru
(tsuretara)	(tsurereba)	(tsureyoo)	(tsuresaseru)	(tsurerareru)	(tsuresaserareru)
tsuzuitara	tsuzukeba	tsuzukoo	tsuzukaseru	(tsuzukareru)	tsuzukaserareru
urikondara	urikomeba	urikomoo	urikomaseru	urikomareru	urikomaserareru
utattara	utaeba	utaoo	utawaseru	utawareru	utawaserareru
wabitara	wabireba	wabiyoo	wabisaseru	wabirareru	wabisaserareru
yandara	yameba	(yamoo)	(yamaseru)	(yamareru)	(yamaserareru)
yattara	yareba	yaroo	yaraseru	yarareru	yaraserareru
yasundara	yasumeba	yasumoo	yasumaseru	yasumareru	yasumaserareru
yondara	yobeba	yoboo	yobaseru	yobareru	yobaserareru
yokoshitara	yokoseba	yokosoo	yokosaseru	yokosareru	yokosaserareru

2. Suru Verb Chart

In Japanese, there are many compound verbs consisting of some kind of noun plus the irregular verb **suru** 'to do.' For example, the noun **kentoo** 'examination' + **suru** is this kind of compound verb and it means 'to examine.' In this text, these kinds of nouns are indicated by the following (**-suru**). The inflections of these compound verbs are completely the same as those of the irregular verb **suru**.

The inflections of
·SURU:

Citation Form	suru
Stem	shi
Gerund	shite
Informal Past	shita
Potential	dekiru
Conditional	shitara
Provisional	sureba
Tentative	shiyoo
Causative	saseru
Passive	sareru
Passive Causative	saserareru

These kinds of nouns and compound verbs introduced in this text are as follows;

annai-suru (33)*	'to take someone to'
anshin-suru (35)	'to feel easy'
antee-suru (25)	'to stabilize'
bikkuri-suru (22)	'to be surprised'
chuukoku(-suru) (29)	'to advise'
daiseekoo(-suru) (33)	'to achieve great success'
doonyuu (-suru) (23)	'to introduce'
enryo(-suru) (33)	'to be reserved'
giron (-suru) (32)	'to argue'
goannai-suru (33)	'to take someone to (polite)'
gochisoo-suru (33)	'to treat (a person)'
goenryo(-suru) (33)	'to be reserved (polite)'
gokai (-suru) (35)	'to misunderstand'
haken-suru (29)	'to send (a person)'
hakkiri-suru (35)	'to become clear'
hanbai(-suru) (27)	'to sell'
hantai-suru (23)	'to oppose'
hatchuu-suru (24)	'to order'
henpin (-suru) (27)	'to return (goods)'
hookoku (-suru) (28)	'to report'
hoshoo (-suru) (32)	'to guarantee'
hoshu (-suru) (32)	'to maintain'
hotto-suru (32)	'to be relieved'
husetsu (-suru) (24)	'to install'
husoku-suru (34)	'to lack'
jidooka (-suru) (23)	'to automate'
jogen (-suru) (33)	'to advise'
kaitaku-suru (29)	'to develop'
kaizen-suru (30)	'to improve'
kaizoo (-suru) (27)	'to remodel'

kakunin-suru (25)	'to confirm'
kanri (-suru) (30)	'to manage'
kansee-suru (32)	'to complete'
kanshin-suru (30)	'to be impressed'
kee'ee (-suru) (25)	'to manage (a company)'
keekaku(-suru) (31)	'to plan'
kenbutsu (-suru) (21)	'to go sight-seeing'
kenkyuu-suru (23)	'to study, research'
kensa (-suru) (34)	'to check'
kiboo-suru (25)	'to hope, prefer'
kinen (-suru) (28)	'to commemorate'
kinoo (-suru) (23)	'to function'
kitai-suru (27)	'to expect'
kitee (-suru) (32)	'to prescribe' regulate'
kooji(-suru) (32)	'to construct'
koojoo-suru (30)	'to progress'
koonyuu(-suru)(27)	'to purchase'
kooritsuka(-suru) (23)	'to improve efficiency'
kootai (-suru) (35)	'to change shifts'
koshoo (-suru) (32)	'to be out of order'
koyoo (-suru) (28)	'to employ'
kuroo-suru (29)	'to have a hard time with'
kyooshuku(-suru) (27)	'to thank (you) very much'
mametsu-suru (34)	'to be worn out'
nebiki (-suru) (24)	'to discount'
noohin (-suru) (24)	'to deliver goods'
noonyuu-suru (32)	'to deliver'
okari-suru (31)	'to borrow (polite)'
okiki-suru (28)	'to ask, hear (polite)'
okurimono(-suru) (33)	'to present (something)'
omaneki-suru (33)	'to invite (polite)'
omatase-suru (32)	'to keep (someone) waiting (polite)'
ootomeeshonka-suru (31)	'to automate'
otazune-suru (27)	'to call on (polite)'
owabi-suru (34)	'to apologize (polite)'
oyobi-suru, (25)	'to call (you) (polite)'
rainichi-suru (21)	'to visit Japan'
reiohu (-suru) (23)	'to lay off'
rikai-suru (33)	'to understand'
riyoo-suru (31)	'to utilize'
sagyoo (-suru) (23)	'to work'
sansee-suru (23)	'to agree'
seekoo-suru (33)	'to succeed'
seekyuu-suru (24)	'to claim, request, charge'
seesan-suru (22)	'to produce'
setsuritsu (-suru) (22)	'to establish'
shippai-suru (33)	'to fail'
shisaku-suru (31)	'to manufacture for trial'
shitsumon (-suru) (21)	'to question'
shiyoo (-suru) (32)	'to put to trial'
shoochi-suru (34)	'to agree, understand'

shookyuu (-suru) (28)	'to have a salary raised'
shori-suru (34)	'to deal with'
shukka-suru (30)	'to dispatch, send'
shuuri (-suru) (32)	'to repair'
sookin-suru (26)	'to remit money'
sooritsu (-suru) (22)	'to establish'
teean (-suru) (23)	'to propose'
tehai-suru (32)	'to arrange'
tenken (-suru) (32)	'to check'
unten (-suru) (32)	'to operate'
yosoo-suru (24)	'to expect'
yoyaku (-suru) (33)	'to reserve'
zooshi-suru (22)	'to increase the capital'

* The number in parentheses indicates the lesson in which the noun or compound verb has been introduced.

3. Adjective Chart

Non-past	Meaning (Lesson)	Adverbial (-ku form)	Gerund	Conditional	Provisional
abunai	(is) dangerous (23)	abunaku	abunakute	abunakattara	abunakereba
akarui	(is) well-lit (30)	akaruku	akarukute	akarukattara	akarukereba
atatakai	(is) warm (21)	atatakaku	atatakakute	atatakakattara	atatakakereba
atsui	(is) hot (21)	atsuku	atsukute	atsukattara	atsukereba
hayai	(is) soon, early (21) (is) fast (30)	hayaku	hayakute	hayakattara	hayakereba
hidoi	(is) terrible (22)	hidoku	hidokute	hidokattara	hidokereba
hikui	(is) low (22)	hikuku	hikukute	hikukattara	hikukereba
ikenai	(is) not good (29)	ikenaku	ikenakute	ikenakattara	ikenakereba
karui	(is) light (23)	karuku	karukute	karukattara	karukereba
katai	(is) hard (31)	kataku	katakute	katakattara	katakereba
kurai	(is) dark (30)	kuraku	kurakute	kurakattara	kurakereba
mushiatsui	(is) muggy (21)	mushiatsuku	mushiatsukute	mushiatsukat-tara	mushiatsu-kereba
nagai	(is) long (32)	nagaku	nagakute	nagakattara	nagakereba
omoi	(is) heavy (23)	omoku	omokute	omokattara	omokereba
samui	(is) cold (21)	samuku	samukute	samukattara	samukereba
suzushii	(is) cool (21)	suzushiku	suzushikute	suzushikattara	suzushikereba
tadashii	(is) right (23)	tadashiku	tadashikute	tadashikattara	tadashikereba
tsumetai	(is) cold (29)	tsumetaku	tsumetakute	tsumetakattara	tsumetakereba
tsuyoi	(is) strong (31)	tsuyoku	tsuyokute	tsuyokattara	tsuyokereba
urayamashii	(is) envious (28)	urayamashiku	urayamashikute	urayamashi-kattara	urayamashi-kereba
yasashii	(is) gentle (29)	yasashiku	yasashikute	yasashikattara	yasashikereba
yawarakai	(is) soft (31)	yawarakaku	yawarakakute	yawarakakattara	yawarakakereba
yowai	(is) weak (31)	yowaku	yowakute	yowakattara	yowakereba
zurui	(is) cunning (29)	zuruku	zurukute	zurukattara	zurukereba

4. Copula Chart

	Non-past	Gerund	Past	Conditional	Provisional	Tentative
Informal	da	de	datta	dattara	nara	daroo
Formal	desu	deshite	deshita	deshitara	deshitaraba	deshoo

APPENDIX II   READING JAPANESE

1. Katakana

The **katakana** syllabary is used for writing words borrowed from foreign languages. It is also used occasionally for emphasis in writing native Japanese words.

The borrowed words are pronounced in a way that approximates the original pronunciation but are adapted to the Japanese sound system.

KATAKANA Chart

ア	カ	ガ	サ	ザ	タ	ダ	ナ	ハ	ファ	バ	パ	マ	ヤ	ラ	ワ
a	ka	ga	sa	za	ta	da	na	ha	fa	ba	pa	ma	ya	ra	wa
イ	キ	ギ	シ	ジ	チ	ヂ	ニ	ヒ	フィ	ビ	ピ	ミ		リ	ン
i	ki	gi	shi	ji	chi	ji	ni	hi	fi	bi	pi	mi		ri	n
ウ	ク	グ	ス	ズ	ツ	ヅ	ヌ	フ		ブ	プ	ム	ユ	ル	
u	ku	gu	su	zu	tsu	zu	nu	hu		bu	pu	mu	yu	ru	
エ	ケ	ゲ	セ	ゼ	テ	デ	ネ	ヘ	フェ	ベ	ペ	メ		レ	
e	ke	ge	se	ze	te	de	ne	he	fe	be	pe	me		re	
オ	コ	ゴ	ソ	ゾ	ト	ド	ノ	ホ	フォ	ボ	ポ	モ	ヨ	ロ	
o	ko	go	so	zo	to	do	no	ho	fo	bo	po	mo	yo	ro	

キャ	ギャ	シャ	ジャ	チャ	ヂャ	ニャ	ヒャ		ビャ	ピャ	ミャ		リャ
kya	gya	sha	ja	cha	ja	nya	hya		bya	pya	mya		rya
キュ	ギュ	シュ	ジュ	チュ	ヂュ	ニュ	ヒュ		ビュ	ピュ	ミュ		リュ
kyu	gyu	shu	ju	chu	ju	nyu	hyu		byu	pyu	myu		ryu
キョ	ギョ	ショ	ジョ	チョ	ヂョ	ニョ	ヒョ		ビョ	ピョ	ミョ		リョ
kyo	gyo	sho	jo	cho	jo	nyo	hyo		byo	pyo	myo		ryo

(Note: Long vowels in **katakana** are represented by ─ ,e.g. バー 'bar.')

Reading Practice

(1) アメリカ America, イギリス England, フランス France, ドイツ Germany, イタリア Italy, カナダ Canada, オーストラリア Australia, スイス Switzerland, スペイン Spain, メキシコ Mexico, ブラジル Brazil, ポーランド Poland, ソビエト Soviet (Union), シンガポール Singapore, チリ Chile

(2) アムステルダム Amsterdam, ベルリン Berlin, モスクワ Moscow, ローマ Rome, シカゴ Chicago, パリ Paris, ニューヨーク New York, ロンドン London, トロント Toronto, シドニー Sydney, イスタンブール Istanbul

(3) ビジネス business, ノート notebook, オフィス office, ペン pen, タイプライター typewriter, テーブル table, エレベーター elevator, ビル building, アポイントメント appointment, ハイテク high-tech

(4) コーヒー coffee, ケーキ cake, ランチ lunch, ステーキ steak, ビール beer, ワイン wine, ウイスキー whisky, カクテル cocktail, ジュース juice, パン bread, バター butter, アイスクリーム ice cream

(5) デパート department (store), スーパー・マーケット supermarket, マッチ match, ホテル hotel, レストラン restaurant, タクシー taxi, バス bus, チップ tip, サービス・チャージ service charge, ノー・タックス no tax

2. Hiragana

The **hiragana** syllabary is used for writing verb endings and adjectives, all forms of the copula **desu**, particles, and some Japanese words not written in kanji.

The particles 'e', 'o' and 'wa' are written by using the 「へ」、「を」 and 「は」 for historical reasons.

For example,

"Mr. Brown will come to a hotel in Tokyo tomorrow."

Buraun-san wa ashita Tookyoo no hoteru e kimasu.

ブラウン さん は あした 東京 の ホテル へ 来 ます。
  1   2   2   2   3   2   1   2 3   2

1=katakana, 2=hiragana, 3=kanji

HIRAGANA Chart

あ	か	が	さ	ざ	た	だ	な	は	ば	ぱ	ま	や	ら	わ
a	ka	ga	sa	za	ta	da	na	ha	ba	pa	ma	ya	ra	wa
い	き	ぎ	し	じ	ち	ぢ	に	ひ	び	ぴ	み		り	ん
i	ki	gi	shi	ji	chi	ji	ni	hi	bi	pi	mi		ri	n
う	く	ぐ	す	ず	つ	づ	ぬ	ふ	ぶ	ぷ	む	ゆ	る	
u	ku	gu	su	zu	tsu	zu	nu	hu	bu	pu	mu	yu	ru	
え	け	げ	せ	ぜ	て	で	ね	へ	べ	ぺ	め		れ	
e	ke	ge	se	ze	te	de	ne	he	be	pe	me		re	
お	こ	ご	そ	ぞ	と	ど	の	ほ	ぽ	ぽ	も	よ	ろ	
o	ko	go	so	zo	to	do	no	ho	bo	po	mo	yo	ro	

きゃ	ぎゃ	しゃ	じゃ	ちゃ	ぢゃ	にゃ	ひゃ	びゃ	ぴゃ	みゃ	りゃ
kya	gya	sha	ja	cha	ja	nya	hya	bya	pya	mya	rya
きゅ	ぎゅ	しゅ	じゅ	ちゅ	ぢゅ	にゅ	ひゅ	びゅ	ぴゅ	みゅ	りゅ
kyu	gyu	shu	ju	chu	ju	nyu	hyu	byu	pyu	myu	ryu
きょ	ぎょ	しょ	じょ	ちょ	ぢょ	にょ	ひょ	びょ	ぴょ	みょ	りょ
kyo	gyo	sho	jo	cho	jo	nyo	hyo	byo	pyo	myo	ryo

Reading Practice

(1) あい love, あう to meet, いい good, いう to say, いいえ no, あおい blue, おおい many, いえ house, おい nephew

(2) あかい red, えき station, きく to hear, ここ here, かく to write, かかく price, いく to go, くうき air

(3) がいこく foreign country, かいがい overseas, ぐあい conditions, えいが movie, かいぎ meeting, げき drama, ごかい misunderstanding

(4) あさ morning, あそこ there, すき to like, けさ this morning, さけ sake, すし sushi, せき seat, きそく regulation

(5) けいざい economics, ざいかい business world, かじ fire, きず injury, ぜい tax, かぞく family, かぜ wind, かず number

(6) たかい expensive, ちず map, つかう to use, て hand, と door, つき moon, まつ to wait, ちかい near, とかい cities

(7) だいがく university, どこ where, でかい huge, だす to put out, かど corner, かだい subject, そで sleeve

(8) なか inside, なに what, きぬ silk, あね sister, この this, なつ summer, かね money, きのう yesterday, にく meat

(9) はい yes, ひ day, ふかい deep, へた unskillful, ほか other, ふつう usual, ひどい terrible, はなし story, ふね ship

(10) ばあい case, くび neck, けいざいぶ Economic Section, かべ wall, ぼうえき foreign trade, ぶじ safety, そば near, べいこく America

(11) まち town, みぎ right, むこう over there, め eyes, くも cloud, なまえ name, みます to see, むすめ daughter, おもい heavy

(12) はらう to pay, かりる to borrow, きれい pretty, くろい black, きらい dislike, ひる daytime, れきし history, ひろい wide

(13) かわる to change, わかる to understand, わるい wrong, にわ garden

(14) ビールをのむ to drink beer, くるまをかう to buy a car

(15) ほん book, ひるごはん lunch, れんらく contact, ぶいん staff, てんき weather, でんわ telephone, げんきん cash

(16) こんや this evening, くすりや drugstore, ゆき snow, よる night, ゆうめい famous, よむ to read, やとう to employ, ふゆ winter

(17) きゃく guest, げっきゅう salary, きょうと Kyoto

(18) かいしゃ company, しょうしゅうかん business practice, ひしょ secretary

(19) おちゃ tea, ちゅうもん order, しゃちょう company president

(20) どうにゅう introduce, にょうぼう wife, こんにゃく a type of food (Japanese)

(21) ひゃっかてん department store, だいひょう representative

(22) りゅうこう fashion, りょかん inn, こうりょ consideration

Reading Exercises

Read the following sentences and translate them into English :

(1) おおやまさん は とても げんき です。

(2) こんばん やまださん が うち へ きます。

(3) ぼく は あたらしい くるま が かいたい ん です。

(4) あの ざっし は あなた の です か。

(5) らいげつ ロボット を どうにゅう します。

(6) ぶちょう は ウィスキー より ワイン の ほう が すき です。

(7) あした あめ が ふる そう です。

(8) だれ が この ワープロ を つかいますか。

Model Answers :

(1) **Ooyama-san wa totemo genki desu.** "Mr. Ohyama is very well."

(2) **Konban Yamada-san ga uchi e kimasu.** "Ms. Yamada will come to my house this evening."

(3) **Boku wa atarashii kuruma ga kaitai n desu.** "I want to buy a new car."

(4) **Ano zasshi wa anata no desu ka.** "Is that magazine yours?"

(5) **Raigetsu robotto o doonyuu-shimasu.** "We will introduce robots next month."

(6) **Buchoo wa uisukii yori wain no hoo ga suki desu.** "Our General Manager likes wine better than whisky."

(7) **Ashita ame ga huru soo desu.** "They say it will rain tomorrow."

(8) **Dare ga kono waapuro o tsukaimasu ka.** "Who uses this word processor?"

3. Kanji

Kanji 'Chinese Characters' have two kinds of readings: **on**-readings (Chinese readings) and **kun**-readings (Japanese readings). In this section, the **on**-reading is indicated with CAPITAL LETTERS and the **kun**-reading with lower-case letters.

When lower-case letters are enclosed in parentheses, it indicates endings of a verb or adjective.

For example, 来(る) ku (ru)　　大(きい) oo (kii)

Unit 1

Kanji		Readings	Meaning	Examples
1	一	ICHI, hito	one	一つ hito-tsu 'one unit'
2	二	NI, huta	two	二つ huta-tsu 'two units'
3	三	SAN, mi	three	三つ mit-tsu 'three units'
4	四	SHI, yo, yon	four	四つ yot-tsu 'four units'
5	五	GO, itsu	five	五つ itsu-tsu 'five units'
6	六	ROKU, mu	six	六つ mut-tsu 'six units'
7	七	SHICHI, nana	seven	七つ nana-tsu 'seven units'
8	八	HACHI, ya	eight	八つ yat-tsu 'eight units'
9	九	KYUU, KU, kokono	nine	九つ kokono-tsu 'nine units'
10	十	JUU, JU, too	ten	十キロ ju-k-kiro '10 km'
11	百	HYAKU	one hundred	百ドル hyaku-doru '$100'
12	千	SEN	one thousand	千ポンド sen-pondo '1,000 lbs'
13	万	MAN	ten thousand	一万 ichi-man '10,000'
14	日	NICHI, hi, ka	day	一日 ichi-nichi 'one day'
15	円	EN	yen	五十円 gojuu-en '50 yen'
16	人	NIN, JIN, hito, ri	counter for persons	三人 san-nin 'three people'

Reading Practice

(1) このパンを一つください。

(2) きょう 二人のともだちがうちへきます。

(3) ブラウンさんは三日にアメリカへかえります。

(4) そのタバコは二百四十円です。

(5) ちょっと、そのクリップを五つください。

(6) わたくしのかいしゃには、アメリカ人が六人います。

(7) うちからじむしょまで、七キロぐらいです。

(8) そのスポーツカーは八百万円ぐらいです。

(9) そのタイプライターは千九百ドルでした。

(10) あのしごとは九日ぐらいかかります。

(11) あのホテルは一日八十ドルです。

(12) あした 十一じに じむしょへきてください。

(13) スミスさんは千九百八十三ねんに にほんへきました。

(14) そのほんは四百五十ページぐらいあります。

(15) 六日から 十八日までりょこうします。

Kanji		Readings	Meaning	Examples
17	月	**GATSU, GETSU**	month	五月 **go-gatsu** 'May'
		tsuki	moon	来月 **raigetsu** 'next month'
18	年	**NEN**	year	一年 **ichi-nen** 'one year'
		toshi		来年 **rainen** 'next year'
19	時	**JI**	time	七時 **shichi-ji** 'seven o'clock'
		toki		時々 **tokidoki** 'sometimes'
20	分	**BUN, PUN**	minute	三十分 **sanjup-pun** '30 minutes'
		wa(karu)	understanding	分かる **wakaru** 'to understand'
21	本	**HON**	book	いい本 **ii hon** 'good book'
		moto	origin	日本 **Nihon** 'Japan'
22	大	**DAI**	big	
		oo(kii)		大きい **ookii** 'big'
23	会	**KAI**	meeting	会社 **kaisha** 'company'
		au		会う **au** 'to meet'
24	社	**SHA**	association	本社 **honsha** 'head office'
				社会 **shakai** 'society'
25	行	**KOO, GYOO**	going	
		i(ku)		行く **iku** 'to go'
26	来	**RAI**	coming	来日 **rainichi** 'visiting Japan'
		ku(ru)		来る **kuru** 'to come'

Reading Practice

(1) 来月カナダへ行きます。

(2) ブラウンさんは四年ぐらい日本にいました。

(3) あした八時三十分に会社へ来てください。

(4) この本はスミスさんのですか。

(5) 一月十日に本社へ行った時、ジョーンズさんに会いました。

(6) うちから会社まで五十分ぐらいかかります。

(7) ブラウンさんは来年アメリカへ かえります。

(8) きょうは十一時ごろ スミスさんの 会社に行くつもりです。

(9) あの大きいバスが ディズニーランドへ 行きますよ。

(10) きのうブラウンさんが 来ましたが、あなたは会いましたか。

(11) その本は二千円でしたが、あまりおもしろく ありませんよ。

(12) まいにち九時十五分までに 会社に来ます。

(13) あそこへ来る大きいアメリカ人は だれですか。

(14) 日本の会社は たいてい九時ごろからです。

(15) あの人のスポーツカーは 大きいですねえ。

Kanji		Readings	Meaning	Examples
27	何	**nani, nan**	what	何時 **nan-ji** 'what time?'
				何人 **nan-nin** 'how many people?'
28	山	**SAN**	mountain	大山 **Ooyama** (Family Name)
		yama		山本 **Yamamoto** (Family Name)
29	田	**DEN**	rice field	
		ta, da		田中 **Tanaka** (Family Name)
30	中	**CHUU, JUU**	inside	日本中 **Nihon-juu** 'throughout Japan'
		naka	middle	はこの中 **hako no naka** 'in a box'
31	小	**SHOO**	small	小さい **chiisai** 'small'
		chii(sai), ko		小山 **Koyama** (Family Name)
32	今	**KON**	now	今月 **kongetsu** 'this month'
		ima		今年 **kotoshi** 'this year'
33	前	**ZEN**	before	三時前 **san-ji mae** 'before three'
		mae	front	ホテルの前 **hoteru no mae**
				'(in) front of the hotel'
34	後	**GO**	afterward	その後 **sono go** 'after that'
		ato, ushiro	back	ホテルの後 **hoteru no ushiro**
				'back of the hotel'
35	午	**GO**	noon	午前 **gozen** 'morning, a.m.'
				午後 **gogo** 'afternoon, p.m.'
36	毎	**MAI**	every	毎日 **mainichi** 'every day'
				毎月 **maitsuki** 'every month'

Reading Practice

(1) 山田さん、今何時ですか。

(2) 大山さんは 毎日午前五時におきます。

(3) うちの会社は あのデパートの前に あります。

(4) スミスさんは 毎年八月に 日本へ来ます。

(5) 午後三時ごろ 田中さんに会いますが、その後、ブラウンさんのパーティへ 行きます。

(6) あのアパートの 後 にテニス・コートがあります。

(7) あなたは 何年何月に 日本へ来ましたか。

(8) あの小さい人が 田中さんで、大きい人が 中山さんですよ。

(9) 今月大山さんと山田さんがアメリカへ行っています。

(10) ぼくは毎日午前八時から 午後六時まで本社にいます。

(11) あしたは七時前にえきで 山田さんに会います。

(12) あなたの会社には 何人ぐらいはたらいていますか。

(13) あの田中さんの 後 にいる人は だれですか。

(14) その小さいスポーツカーは日本のですか。

(15) あなたは何年前に大山さんに会ったんですか。

Kanji		Readings	Meaning	Examples
37	間	**KAN**	interval	時間 **jikan** 'time'
		aida	between	
38	週	**SHUU**	week	一週間 **isshuukan** 'one week'
				毎週 **maishuu** 'every week'
39	高	**KOO**	expensive	
		taka(i)		高い **takai** 'expensive'
40	安	**AN**	cheap	
		yasu(i)		安い **yasui** 'cheap'
41	長	**CHOO**	long	社長 **shachoo** 'company president'
		naga(i)		長い **nagai** 'long'
42	聞	**BUN**	hearing	
		ki(ku)		聞く **kiku** 'to hear, ask'
43	新	**SHIN**	new	新聞 **shinbun** 'newspaper'
		atara(shii)		新しい **atarashii** 'new'
44	員	**IN**	member	社員 **shain** 'company employee'
				会社員 **kaishain** 'office worker'
45	同	**DOO**	same	
		ona(ji)		同じ本 **onaji hon** 'same book'
46	国	**KOKU, GOKU**	country	中国 **Chuugoku** 'China'
		kuni		国 **kuni** 'country'

Reading Practice

(1) 中国まで 何時間ぐらいかかりますか。

(2) 一週間ぐらい 山田さんに会っていません。

(3) このペンは高いですが、そちらのは安いんですよ。

(4) 大山さんの会社は デパートとホテルの 間にあります。

(5) 社長は何月に 中国へ行きますか。

(6) きょうの新聞は まだ来ませんか。

(7) あの会社は 社員が二千人ぐらいいます。

(8) スミスさんは長い 間 日本にいますねえ。

(9) この本とあの本は同じですか。

(10) ブラウンさんは何週間ぐらい デトロイトの本社にいっていますか。

(11) 田中さんも山田さんも 同じ会社の社員です。

(12) このへんに安くていいホテルはありませんか。

(13) あんな大きいスポーツカーは ずいぶん高いでしょうねえ。

(14) ジョーンズさんは ヨーロッパへ行っているそうですが、今どの国にいますか。

(15) そのニュースは だれから聞きましたか。

kanji		Readings	Meaning	Examples
47	出	**SHUTSU**	going out	
		de(ru)		出る **deru** 'to out'
48	入	**NYUU**	entering	入国 **nyuukoku** 'immiguration'
		hai(ru)		入る **hairu** 'to enter'
49	右	**U**	right	
		migi		右の方 **migi no hoo** 'right side'
50	左	**SA**	left	左右 **sayuu** 'left and right'
		hidari		左の方 **hidari no hoo** 'left side'
51	上	**JOO**	up, top	本の上 **hon no ue** 'on the book'
		a(garu), ue	going up	上がる **agaru** 'to go up'
52	下	**KA, GE**	down, under	本の下 **hon no shita**
				'under the book'
		sa(garu), shita	going down	下がる **sagaru** 'to go down'
53	方	**HOO**	direction	前の方 **mae no hoo** 'front part'
		kata	person	あの方 **ano kata** 'that person'
54	子	**KO**	child	子ども **kodomo** 'children'
55	男	**DAN**	male	
		otoko		男の人 **otoko no hito** 'male'
56	女	**JO**	female	男女 **dan jo** 'male and female'
		onna		女の子 **onna no ko** 'girl'

Reading Practice

(1) 社長 は何時に 出かけますか。

(2) あなたがあの会社に 入ったのは 何年前でしたか。

(3) 右の人が田中さんで、大山さんは 左 の方の人です。

(4) あなたのライターは あのテーブルの上に ありますよ。

(5) スミスさん、この子がわたくしの 上の男 の子です。

(6) あの 女 の方は ブラウンさんの 会社の社員でしょう。

(7) たいてい何時に うちを出て、何時ごろかえりますか。

(8) 子どもはここに 入ってはいけませんよ。

(9) あのパンフレットは その新聞の下 にあります。

(10) ヒルトン·ホテルは 右の方です。

(11) あの大きな男 は うちの会社の 新しい社員です。

(12) 本社の田中さんが来た時、わたくしは 出かけていました。

(13) スミスさんのオフィスは 左 の方ですよ。

(14) 上の子は 女 で、下の子が男 なんですよ。

(15) ブラウン社長 は 今右の方へ行きましたよ。

234

Unit 6

Kanji		Readings	Meaning	Examples
57	京	KYOO	capital	京都 Kyooto 'Kyoto'
58	東	TOO	east	東京 Tookyoo 'Tokyo'
		higashi		東アジア Higashi Ajia 'East Asia'
59	都	TO	metropolis	都会 tokai 'cities'
		miyako		
60	区	KU	ward	区長 kuchoo 'Chief of a ward'
61	央	OO	center	中央区 Chuuoo-ku 'Chuo Ward'
62	銀	GIN	silver	銀行 ginkoo 'bank'
63	座	ZA	seat	銀座 Ginza 'the Ginza'
64	丁	CHOO	town number	一丁目 itt-choome 'Chome No.1'
65	目	MOKU	eye	五目ソバ go-moku soba
				'a type of noodle dish' (Chinese)
		me		目方 mekata 'weight'
66	地	CHI, JI	land	地方 chihoo 'district, locality'
67	番	BAN	number	三番地 san-banchi 'house No.3'
68	図	ZU	chart	地図 chizu 'map'

Reading Practice

(1) 大山さんの会社は 東京 の銀座にあります。

(2) ブラウンさんは 来年 東 ヨーロッパへ 行くそうです。

(3) 東京都中央区には いろいろな会社の 本社があります。

(4) 田中さんの銀行は 銀座三丁目にあります。

(5) あなたは京都から来ましたか。

(6) オタワはカナダの 都 ですが、カナダにはもっと大きな都会がたくさんあります。

(7) この地図は番地がかいてありますから、べんりですよ。

(8) 山田さんの目は とてもきれいですねえ。

(9) 来月 中国の 東 の地方へ 行くことになりました。

(10) もっと大きいアメリカの地図がいりますが…。

(11) 中田さんの銀行は 東京都中央区銀座六丁目十七番地にあります。

(12) 山本さんの会社は 何区にありますか。

(13) あの方のうちは 分かりますが、番地はしりません。

(14) 東京には いくつの区がありますか。

(15) 何番目のお子さんが 銀行員になったんですか。

Kanji		Readings	Meaning	Examples
69	見	**KEN**	seeing	見学 **kengaku** 'field trip'
		mi(ru)		見る **miru** 'to see'
70	教	**KYOO**	teaching	教員 **kyooin** 'teacher'
		oshi(eru)		教える **oshieru** 'to teach'
71	学	**GAKU**	learning	大学 **daigaku** 'university'
		mana(bu)		学ぶ **manabu** 'to learn'
72	校	**KOO**	school	学校 **gakkoo** 'school'
73	部	**BU**	department	部長 **buchoo** 'general manager'
				学部 **gakubu** 'department of a university, college'
74	習	**SHUU**	learning	学習 **gakushuu** 'study'
		nara(u)		習う **narau** 'to learn'
75	主	**SHU**	main	主人 **shujin** 'husband'
		omo		主な **omona** 'main'
76	家	**KA**	house	家内 **kanai** '(my) wife'
		ie		ぼくの家 **boku no ie** 'my house'
77	内	**NAI**	inside	内部 **naibu** 'inside'
		uchi		社内 **shanai** 'in the company'
78	働	**DOO**	working	
		hatara(ku)		働く **hataraku** 'to work'
79	勤	**KIN**	working	
		tsuto(meru)		勤める **tsutomeru** 'to serve in'

Reading Practice

(1) ちょっと、その地図を見せてください。
(2) 山田さんは 毎日ブラウンさんに ワープロを教えています。
(3) うちの子は 来月学校に入ります。
(4) 大学を出てから、すぐ今の銀行に勤めました。
(5) 家内は毎週一日、ジャズ・ダンスを習っています。
(6) 田中さんは 四月からスミスさんの会社で 働くそうです。
(7) 部長 はいつも部員に いろいろ教えてくれます。
(8) ジョーンズさんは 今どこで 働いていますか。
(9) 山田さんのご主人は あの大学で教えています。
(10) 毎日八時ごろは テレビを見ています。
(11) この会社の主な社員は みな同じ大学を出ています。
(12) お子さんは 何を習っていますか。
(13) 家内は 午前十時から午後三時まで銀行で 働いています。
(14) 社長も部長も あしたは京都へ行きます。
(15) 家内も前は この会社の同じ部で 働いていました。

236

Unit 8

Kanji		Readings	Meaning	Examples
80	務	**MU**	work	
		tsuto(meru)		務める **tsutomeru** 'to work'
81	事	**JI**	matter	事務 **jimu** 'office work'
		koto	fact	大事 **daiji** 'important'
82	所	**SHO**	place	事務所 **jimusho** 'office'
		tokoro		
83	仕	**SHI**	serve	仕事 **shigoto** 'work'
		tsuka(eru)		仕える **tsukaeru** 'to serve'
84	全	**ZEN**	all	全部 **zenbu** 'all, whole'
		sube(te)		全て **subete** 'all'
85	作	**SAKU, SA**		作業 **sagyoo** 'work, operation'
		tsuku(ru)	making	作る **tsukuru** 'to make'
86	業	**GYOO**	operation	産業 **sangyoo** 'industry'
		waza	act	事業 **jigyoo** 'enterprise'
87	産	**SAN**	produce	日産 **Nissan** 'Nissan Motor Co.,Ltd.'
		u(mu)		産む **umu** 'to produce'
88	市	**SHI**	city	京都市 **Kyooto-shi** 'Kyoto City'
		ichi	market	市場 **shijoo** 'market'
89	町	**CHOO**	town	山下町 **Yamashita-choo** (place name)
		machi		田町 **Tamachi** (place name)
90	道	**DOO**	road	国道 **kokudoo** 'national road'
		michi		
91	場	**JOO**	place	作業場 **sagyoojoo** 'workshop'
		ba		場所 **basho** 'place'

Reading Practice

(1) ジョーンズさんの事務所は 山下町 にあります。

(2) これは大事な仕事ですから、全部わたくしがします。

(3) 京都市内には どんな産業 がありますか。

(4) あの会社は アメリカ市場のビジネスのために、ニューヨークに事務所を作りました。

(5) ヒルトン・ホテルへ行きたいんですが、道を教えてくださいませんか。

(6) 田中さんの 会社の作業場 は 事務所の後 にあります。

(7) 日産の本社は 中央区銀座六丁目十七番地にあります。

(8) この町には 大きな会社もとくべつな産業 もないので、仕事を見つけるのは むずかしいんですよ。

(9) 社長は 今新しい作業場を 作るために、場所をさがしています。

(10) 家内は 東京銀行で 事務の仕事をしていました。

(11) 中田さんは毎日、新聞を見て、仕事をさがしています。

237

(12) 大山さんの事業は 今とてもいいようです。

(13) この会社の作業時間は 午前九時から午後六時までです。

(14) ブラウンさんの事務所の事務員は 全て日本人です。

(15) 山中社長は 中国は後ですばらしい市場になるといいました。

Unit 9

Kanji		Readings	Meaning	Examples
92	金	**KIN**	gold, money	現金 **genkin** 'cash'
		kane		お金 **okane** 'money'
93	売	**BAI**	selling	売買 **baibai** 'trade'
		u(ru)		売る **uru** 'to sell'
94	買	**BAI, ka(u)**	buying	買う **ka(u)** 'to buy'
95	資	**SHI**	resources	資金 **shikin** 'capital'
				資料 **shiryoo** 'data'
96	言	**GEN, i(u)**	saying	言う **i(u)** 'to say'
97	話	**WA**	speaking	会話 **kaiwa** 'conversation'
		hana(su)		話す **hanasu** 'to speak'
98	電	**DEN**	electric	電話 **denwa** 'telephone'
99	料	**RYOO**	fee	料金 **ryookin** 'charge, fee'
			material	電話料 **denwaryoo** 'phone charge'
100	食	**SHOKU**	eating	食事 **shokuji** 'meal'
		ta(beru)		食べる **ta(beru)** 'to eat'

Reading Practice

(1) 部長は 電話で お金をもって来るように 言いました。

(2) スミスさんは 今の会社のビルを売って、新しい場所に ビルを買うつもりです。

(3) このホテルの 料金には サービス料も入っています。

(4) 社長は ロボットについての資料が 見たいと言っています。

(5) あの会社の資本金は 五千万だそうです。

(6) ブラウンさんは 日本の食事がすきで、何でも食られますよ。

(7) ジョーンズさんは 長い間シカゴで金の売買をしていたそうです。

(8) 大山さんの新しい会社の資金は 京都の銀行が出したんです。

(9) 本社に電話して、社長に 中国の産業について話しました。

(10) この事務所の事務員は たいてい十二時三十分ごろ食事をします。

(11) あした午後九時に デトロイトのジョーンズさんに電話してください。

(12) 田中さんは きのう日産のスポーツカーを買ったそうです。

(13) 来月から電話料金が 高くなるようです。

(14) ロボットを売るために、アメリカからセールス・エンジニアが来ます。

(15) 大きな仕事をするためには 大きな資本がいります。

INDEX

The number in parentheses indicates where the word appears for the first time in the book.

Example:

(21, 3)	Lesson 21, Dialogue **3**
(22, Ad. 1)	Lesson 22, Additional Useful Expressions **1**
(23, Ref)	Lesson 23, Reference

A

abunai (is) dangerous (23, 13)
agaru/-u/ to rise (30, 3)
ageru/-ru/ to raise (33, 4)
ahutaa-saabisu after-sale service (32, Ad. 2)
aikawarazu as usual (21, 3)
akaji deficit, loss, red figure (24, Ad. 3)
akarui (is) well-lit (30, 2)
ame rain (21, Ad. 2)
ame ni hurareru to be caught in the rain (34, Ad. 4)
Amerika ichi "No. 1" in America (22, 11)
Amerikajin American(s) (26, 12)
annai-suru to take someone to (33, 5)
anshin-suru to feel easy (35, 3)
antee-suru to stabilize (25, Ad. 1)
anzen/na/ safe, safety (23, Ad. 2)
anzensee safety (23, Ad. 2)
arashi storm (22, 3)
arimashitara if there is… (25, 4)
aru a certain (29, 2)
arubaito part-time job, side job (28, Ad. 1)
aru jidoosha-gaisha a certain automobile company (29, 2)
ashi leg (31, Ad. 1)
asu tomorrow (21, 4)
atama head (31, Ref)
atari per (24, 4)
atatakai (is) warm (21, Ref.)
atsui (is) hot (21, 3)
atsui hi hot day(s) (21, Ad. 1)
atsukau no handling (29, 4)
awasete in all (22, Ad. 1)
awatemono a hasty person (29, Ad. 2)
azukeru/-ru/ to deposit (26, Ad. 1)

B

baa bar (33, Ref)
baai case (24, 2)
bakari only (23, 13), about (23, Ad. 1)
Bank-obu-Amerika Bank of America (26, 8)
batterii battery (31, 7)
bearingu bearings (34, 3)
benkyoo ni naru to learn a lesson (35, 12)
bikkuri-suru to be surprised (22, 4)
buhin parts (31, 6)
buppinzee commodity tax (26, Ref)

C

chekku check (26, 12)
chihoozee local tax (26, Ref)
chikara power (23, Ad. 1)
chikara o ireru to make an effort (23, Ad. 1)
chikara-shigoto heavy labor (23, Ad. 1)
chinoo intelligence (23, 2)
chinoo-robotto intelligent robot (23, 2)
chippu tip (33, Ref)
chishiki knowledge (29, 5)
chokusetsuzee direct tax (26, Ref)
chooka-kinmu-teate overtime allowance (28, Ref)
chuujun the middle of a month (22, Ad. 2)
chuukoku (-suru) advice (29, 14)

D

daibu very much, quite (29, Ad. 1)
daijoobu/na/ sure, safe (32, Ad. 2)
daiseekoo (-suru) great success (33, Ad. 3)
daisuu number of units (27, 7)
dakara therefore (30, Ad. 1)
… dake de naku not only … (30, Ad. 1)
dankai stage, step (32, 10)
denki-seehin electrical product (35, Ad. 2)
denshin telegraph (26, Ad. 2)
doko ka someplace (33, 8)
dono kaisha mo each and every company (35, Ad. 2)
dono kurai about how much? (22, Ad. 1)
doo iu koto what (is it?) (27, 4)
dookan da to agree (30, Ad. 2)
doo ni ka naru can do something (27, 9)
doonyuu (-suru) introduction (23, 10)
doo okangae desu ka what do you think? (30, 6)
doo riyoo-suru ka ni tsuite about how to use (them) (31, 1)

E

en-daka higher yen quotation (25, Ad. 1)
en-date deshitara if it is in yen terms (25, 9)
enkai Japanese-style party (33, Ad. 1)
enryo (-suru) reserve, hesitation (33, 14)
en-yasu lower yen quotation (25, Ad. 1)
eru-shii L/C (25, 14)
eru-shii ichiran barai L/C at sight (25, 14)

G

geesha *geisha* (33, Ref)
gejun the last ten days of a month (22, Ad. 2)
genba actual place (30, Ad. 1)
gen'in cause (27, Ad. 1)
genryoo raw materials (30, Ad. 3)
genryoohi material costs (25, Ref)
gensen-chooshuu withholding (at source) (28, Ref)
genzai present (23, 5)
gimu duty (28, Ad. 1)
ginkoo-hurikomi bank transfer (26, 11)
ginkooin bank clark (26, 1)
girigiri at most (27, 10)
giron (-suru) argument (32, 3)
giron ga deru (an) argument takes place (32, 3)
gishi engineer (32, 9)
goannai-suru (polite) to take someone to (33, 5)
gochisoo-suru to treat (someone) (33, Ad. 3)
gochuukoku (polite) advice (29, 14)
gochuumon-nasaru (respectful) to order (24, 6)
goenryo (-suru) (polite) reserve, hesitation (33, 14)
goenryo naku (polite) without reserve (33, 14)
gokai (-suru) misunderstanding (35, 11)
gokansoo (polite) impression (30, 1)
gokiboo (respectful) hope (25, 7)
gokuroo-sama thanks for your trouble (35, 1)
gomeewaku (polite) trouble, inconvenient (35, 2)
gomeewaku o okake-suru (polite) to give trouble (35, 2)
goo village (29, 13)
goo-ten-go-paasento-biki 5.5% discount (27, 5)
goruhu-zuki passion for golf (33, 10)
goto ni every (32, Ad. 2)
goyooken (polite) business (26, 1)
gussuri (sleep) like a log (22, 6)
gyookai business world, industry (35, Ad. 2)
gyoosha agent, trader (35, Ad. 1)

H

ha tooth/teeth (31, Ref)
haa yes (25, 6)
hachi-jikan-see 8-hour system (35, 8)
hai-teku-seehin high-tech product (29, 4)
haitoo dividend (22, Ad. 2)
hajimete first time (29, 4)
haken-suru to send (29, 6)
hakkiri-suru to become clear (35, 3)
hakobu/-u/ to carry (31, 8)
hana nose (31, Ref)
hanbai (-suru) sale (27, Ad. 1)
hanbun half (35, Ad. 2)
handoru steering wheel (31, 7)

hanseehin half-finished goods (35, Ref)
hantai-suru to oppose (23, 10)
hantoshi half a year (34, 8)
hara belly (31, Ref)
hareru/-ru/ to clear up (21, Ad. 3)
has-shurui eight types (23, 4)
hatchuu-suru to order (24, Ad. 2)
hayai (is) early, soon (21, 10)
hayai (is) fast (30, 7)
hayasugiru too soon (34, 8)
hendoo-sooba-see floating exchange system (25, Ad. 1)
henpin (-suru) returns (27, Ad. 1)
heru/-u/ to decrease (27, Ad. 1)
hi day(s) (21, Ad. 1)
hidoi (is) terrible (22, 3)
hikaeru/-ru/ to stay away (33, 9)
hikidasu/-u/ to withdraw (26, Ad. 3)
hikui (is) low (22, Ad. 2)
hinshitsu quality (30, 4)
hinshitsu-kanri quality control (30, Ad. 1)
hiraku/-u/ to open (26, 2)
hiyoo cost, expense (24, 2)
hoka ni in addition (24, 2)
honkakuteki/na/ full-scale, real (34, 6)
honkyuu regular pay (28, Ref)
honsaiyoo official employment (28, 12)
honsha e no hookoku-sho report for the head office (28, 14)
hontai basic unit, body (24, 2)
hoojin corporation (26, 14)
hoojinzee corporate tax (26, 14)
hookoku (-suru) report (28, 14)
hookoku-sho written report (28, 14)
hoshoo (-suru) guarantee (32, 11)
hoshoo-kikan warranty period (32, 11)
hoshu (-suru) maintenance (32, 10)
hotondo almost (29, Ad. 1)
hotto-suru to be relieved (32, 4)
huantee/na/ unstable (28, Ad. 1)
hubi/na/ inadequate (35, 6)
hueru/-ru/ to increase (22, Ad. 2)
hukakachizee value added tax (26, Ref)
hukeeki/na/ bad business conditions (29, Ad. 1)
hukyoo business depression (29, Ad. 1)
hukyoo-karuteru anti-depression cartel (35, Ref)
huri/na/ disadvantageous (23, 12)
huru/-u/ to fall (21, Ad. 2)
huryoo-buhin inferior parts (35, Ad. 1)
huryoohin inferior products (35, Ad. 1)
husetsu (-suru) installation (24, 2)
husetsuhi installation cost (24, 4)
hushinsetsu/na/ unkind (29, Ref)
husoku-suru to run short (34, Ad. 2)
hutsuu-yokin ordinary deposit (26, 4)
huyasu/-u/ to increase (27, 5)
huzokuhin attachment (24, 2)
hyaku-en-dama 100 yen coin (26, Ad. 3)

hyaku-en-kooka 100 yen coin (26, Ad. 3)
hyoo list, chart (23, 4)
hyooban reputation (30, Ad. 1)
hyooban ga ii to have a good reputation (30, Ad. 1)
hyoojunhin standard products (35, Ref)

I

ichi position (23, 8)
ichi-man-en-satsu ten thousand yen note (26, Ad. 3)
ichi-nen-me the first year (24, Ad. 1)
ichi-oku one hundred million (24, Ad. 3)
ii koto o kiku to hear a good thing (33, 11)
ii tenki good weather (21, Ref)
ijoo more than (22, 13)
ika less than (22, Ad. 2)
ikenai (is) not good (29, 13)
ikisaki destination (31, Ad. 2)
ikitsuke favorite (bar) (33, 5)
ikutsuka no several (31, 11)
inkan seal (26, Ad. 1)
inshokuhi expenses for eating and drinking (33, Ref)
iraba (archaic) if one enters (29, 13)
irenakute mo ii it's alright (even) if you don't include (it) (24, 9)
ireru/-ru/ to buy, install (34, Ad. 1)
iro color (31, 5)
Ishida (Mr/Ms) Ishida (34, Ad. 1)
is-shu a kind (of), a type (of) (23, 2)
itadaite mo ii (humble) May I have (it)? (23, 9)
itami damage, wear (35, 9)
iu toori as (one) says (29, 8)
iya Oh, no (25, 2)
iya/na/ unpleasant (21, Ad. 1)
iya na tenki bad weather (21, Ref)

J

Jasu Japan Agriculture and Forestry Standard, JAS (35, Ref)
jidooka (-suru) automation (23, 5)
jidoo-koosakuki automatic machine tool (22, 9)
jidoosha car, automobile (23, 7)
jigyoo business (22, Ad. 2)
jigyoo-naiyoo business (results) (22, Ad. 2)
jijoo circumstances (34, Ad. 3)
jikankyuu hourly pay (28, Ref)
jikansuu number of hours (35, 5)
jiko accident (31, Ad. 1)
jinkenhi personnel expenses (25, Ref)
jishin oneself (35, Ad. 2)
Jisu Japan Industrial Standard, JIS (35, Ref)
jitai itself (35, 4)
jogen (-suru) advice (33, Ad. 2)
joobu/na/ durable (31, Ref)
joojun the first ten days of a month (22, Ad. 2)

Joonzu-shi Mr. Jones (21, 12)
Joonzu to iu hito person named Jones (21, 4)
jootai conditions (26, 13)
juugyooin employees (22, Ad. 1)
juu-mee ten persons (32, 10)

K

ka section (34, Ad. 2)
kabu stock, share (22, Ad. 2)
kabunushi shareholder (22, Ad. 2)
kabunushi-sookai general shareholders' meeting (22, Ad. 2)
kachi value (23, 5)
kadai goal, objective (23, 5)
kadoo-jikan hours of operation (35, Ref)
kaeri return to home (33, Ad. 1)
kaigai overseas, foreign country (24, 4)
kaihatsuhi development expenses (25, Ref.)
kaihatsu-shinakereba naranai must develop (31, 10)
kaisetsusho instruction manual (35, 12)
kaitaku-suru to develop, open (29, 3)
kaitaku-suru no opening (a market) (29, 3)
kaiteki/na/ comfortable (22, 2)
kaite shimau to finish writing (28, 14)
kaiun-suto shipping strike (30, Ad. 3)
kaizen (-suru) improvement (30, Ad. 2)
kaizoo (-suru) remodeling (27, 9)
kaji fire (34, Ad. 3)
kakari person in charge (34, Ad. 1)
kakaru/-u/ to cost (24, 2)
kakikomu/-u/ to fill out (26, Ad. 1)
kakuchi each place (32, Ad. 2)
kakunin-suru to confirm (25, 5)
... ka mo shirenai maybe (31, 11)
kanaboo iron stick (30, 9)
kangae idea (35, 13)
kankyoo environment (30, 4)
kanri (-suru) management (30, Ad. 1)
Kansai Kansai (Area name) (21, Ad. 2)
kansee-shita ato (de) after completing (32, 10)
kansee-suru to complete (32, 10)
kansetsuzee indirect tax (26, Ref)
kanshin-suru to be impressed (30, 2)
kansoo impression (30, 1)
kanzee custom duty (26, Ref)
kao face (31, Ref)
karada body (31, Ref)
karaoke "karaoke" (33, 6)
kariru/-ru/ to borrow (31, 11)
karui (is) light (23, 6)
kasamu/-u/ to expand (27, 9)
katachi shape (31, 5)
katai (is) hard (31, Ref)
kawase-sooba foreign exchange rate (25, Ad. 1)
kaze ga huku/-u/ the wind blows, It is windy (21, Ref)

kazoku-teate family allowance (28, Ref)
kedo but (33, Ad. 3)
kee'ee(-suru) management (25, Ad. 1)
keekaku(-suru) plan (31, 3)
keeyaku-suru mae (ni) before finalizing the contract (32, 5)
keezaisee economical efficiency (23, Ad. 2)
kega injury (31, Ad. 1)
kekkan defect (35, 4)
kekkan-shoohin defective product (35, Ad. 1)
kekkyoku after all, finally (32, 3)
kenbutsu(-suru) sight-seeing (21, Ad. 2)
kenkyuuhi research expenses (25, Ref)
kenkyuujo laboratory (30, 12)
kenkyuushitsu research department (30, 12)
kenkyuu-suru to study, do research (23, 5)
kensa(-suru) check-up (34, 5)
kentoo-saseru to have someone examine (32, 15)
keredo but (28, 10)
kessan settlement of accounts (22, Ad. 2)
kessan-hookokusho statement of accounts (26, 14)
ketsuron o dasu to conclude (32, Ad. 2)
kiboo-suru to hope for, prefer (25, 7)
ki ga tsuku/-u/ to notice (34, 5)
kikakuhin standardized products (35, Ref)
kikan period (32, 7)
kiken/na/ dangerous (23, Ad. 1)
kiken-teate (occupational) risk allowance (28, Ref)
kimaru/-u/ to be decided (27, 7)
kimeru/-ru/ to decide (27, Ad. 2)
kimi (friendly) you (35, Ad. 2)
kimijika/na/ impatient (29, 12)
kinaga/na/ patient (29, 11)
kinen(-suru) commemoration (28, 4)
kinkin before long (27, 2)
kinmuchi-teate service-area allowance (28. Ref)
kinoo(-suru) function (23, 2)
kinri interest (rate) (26, Ad. 1)
kiro kilogram, kg (31, 10)
kitai-suru to expect (27, 11)
kitee (-suru) regulations (32, 14)
kogitte check (26, 12)
kogitte no kooza checking account (26, 4)
kojin individual (26, 3)
kokuzee national tax (26, Ref)
konki this term (24, Ad. 3)
konna ni like this, to this extent (21, Ad. 1)
koodo high level (23, 2)
kooin factory worker (31, Ad. 1)
kooji (-suru) construction (32, 10)
koojoochoo factory manager (30, 13)
koojoo-shite kuru to have improved (30, 8)

koojoo-suru to improve, advance (30, 8)
kookyoo boom, period of prosperity (29, Ad. 1)
koonetsuhi utilities expenses (25, Ref)
koonyuu (-suru) purchase (27, Ad. 1)
kooritsu efficiency (23, Ad. 1)
kooritsuka(-suru) improvement in efficiency (23, Ad. 1)
koosaihi entertainment expenses (25, Ref)
koosu (golf) course (33, 12)
kootai (-suru) shift (35, 9)
kooza-bangoo account number (26, Ad. 2)
korareru can come (21, 9)
kore de with this, now (27, 14)
koshi lower back (31, Ref)
koshoo(-suru) out of order(32, 13)
kosuto cost (24, 6)
kotaerareru can answer (21, 7)
kotaeru/-ru/ to answer (21, 7)
(shita) koto ga aru to have ever (done) (26, 7)
(suru) koto mo aru may sometimes also (happen) (32, 14)
(suru) koto ni naru it is decided to (do) (25, 8)
koyoo (-suru) employment (28, 12)
koyoo-jooken employment terms (28, 12)
kubi neck (31, Ref)
kuchi mouth (31, Ref)
kujoo complaint, grievance (34, Ad. 3)
kujoo o iu to express a grievance (34, Ad. 3)
kumiaiin union member (23, 12)
kumitate assembly, assembling (23, 4)
kumitate-sagyoo assembling operations (23, 4)
kumoru/-u/ to become cloudy (21, Ad. 3)
kuni country (30, Ad. 3)
kurai (is) dark (30, Ad. 2)
kuroji surplus, black figure (24, Ad. 3)
kuroo-suru to have a hard time (29, 2)
kuukoo airport (21, Ad. 3)
kuwawaru/-u/ to join (30, 9)
kyabaree cabaret (33, Ref)
kyooshuku (-suru) thank you very much (27, 1)
kyuuka vacations (28, Ad. 1)
kyuu ni suddenly (27, 1)
Kyuu-shii-saakuru QC (quality control circles) (30, Ad. 1)

M_____

maa well, I dare say (31, 7)
maamaa so-so (29, 2)
madamada not yet, still more (29, 11)
maiban every night (33, Ad. 1)
mametsu-suru to be worn out (34, 5)

maneku/-u/ to invite (33, 8)
ma ni au/-u/ to be in time (24, Ad. 2)
matsu no waiting (29, 12)
mattaku certainly, really (21, 4)
me eye (31, Ref)
medatte significantly (30, 8)
-mee counter for people (32, 10)
meekaa to shite as a maker (22, 7)
meewaku trouble, inconvenient (35, 2)
meewaku o kakeru to give trouble (35, 2)
mendoo/na/ troublesome (26, 6)
mieru/-ru/ (polite) to come, appear (28, 3)
mimi ear (31, Ref)
misete itadaku to let us see (humble) (26, 13)
mitooshi prospect (22, 13)
mitsumori estimate (24, 7)
mitsumorisho written estimate (24, 10)
mondai ga okiru a problem occurs (34, 2)
monku complaint (34, Ad. 2)
monku o iu to complain (34, Ad. 2)
monogusa/na/ lazy (25, Ad. 2)
moo sukoshi a little more (25, 3)
mooke profit (27, Ad. 2)
motsu/-u/ to endure, last (34, 7)
mukae ni iku to go to meet (21, Ad. 3)
mukaeru/-ru/ to meet (21, Ad. 3)
mukashi old days (22, 7)
mune chest (31, Ref)
muryoo free of charge (32, 13)
mushiatsui (is) muggy (21, Ad. 1)

N_____

nado and others (26, 10)
nagai (is) long (32, 1)
nagai aida for a long time (32, 1)
... nagara while (doing ...) (25, 3)
naito-kurabu night club (33, Ref)
naiyoo contents (22, Ad. 2)
nakunaru/-u/ to vanish (27, Ad. 2)
nan-ji de mo anytime (23, Ad. 3)
nani mo ... nai not anything (28, 2)
nanka such things as (28, Ad. 1), and the like (33, 12)
nan-kagetsu mo for several months (29, 8)
naosaseru to have someone fix (32, 14)
naosu/-u/ to fix (32, 13)
Narita Narita (Airport) (21, Ad. 3)
narubeku hayaku as soon as possible (21, 10)
nasaru/-u/ (respectful) to do (24, 6)
naze soo naru ka (o) shiraberu to check why it happens (34, 9)
nebiki(-suru) to discount (24, 5)
nebiki-ritsu discount rate (27, 5)
nemuru/-u/ to sleep (22, 5)
nenkan per year (22, 12)
neru/-ru/ to go to bed (22, Ad. 3)
nesshin/na/ enthusiastic (30, 10)
nigate/na/ weak, weak point (29, 12)

Nihon-muke Japan-oriented, for Japan (35, 12)
Nihonteki/na/ Japanese-style (33, Ad. 2)
ni-jikai second-stage party (33, Ad. 1)
... ni kansuru concerning ... (32, 14)
nikkyuu daily pay (28, Ref)
ni-kootai-see two-shift system (35, 9)
ni, san two or three (32, 5)
... ni suginai not more than ... (35, 5)
... ni taisuru for ... (31, 5)
... ni tsuite about ... (31, 1)
... ni yotte depending upon ... (24, 4)
... ni yoru to according to ... (27, 5)
nokoru/-u/ to remain (32, 10)
nonki/na/ easy-going (29, Ad. 2)
noohin (-suru) delivery of goods (24, Ad. 2)
noonyuu-suru to deliver (32, Ad. 1)
nooritsu efficiency (30, 3)

O_____

odori dance (33, Ref)
odekake kudasai (polite) please come (30, 14)
okaerinasai welcome back (28, 1)
okage thanks to (30, 8)
okari-suru (polite) to borrow (31, 11)
okiki-suru (polite) to ask, hear (28, 13)
okiru/-ru/ to get up (22, Ad. 3)
okonau/-u/ to do, perform (23, 11)
oku/-u/ to place (23, 8)
oku 100 million (24, Ad. 3)
oku no ni in order to place (23, 8)
okureru/-ru/ to be late (24, Ad. 2)
okurimono (-suru) present, gift (33, Ad. 2)
omaneki-shitara ii (I) should invite (33, 9)
omaneki-suru (polite) to invite (33, 8)
omatase-suru (polite) to keep (you) waiting (32, 1)
omie ni naru/-u/ (respectful) to come, appear (28, 3)
omoi (is) heavy (23, 6)
onaka belly (31, Ref)
onchi tone-deaf (33, 7)
ongaku music (25, Ad. 2)
oni demon (30, 9)
onsen hot spring (28, Ad. 2)
ooguchi large scale (33, Ad. 3)
ookega serious injury (31, Ad. 1)
ookega o suru to be seriously injured (31, Ad. 1)
ookina big (33, 3)
ootomeeshonka-suru to automate (31, Ad. 1)
oree o suru [lit.] to offer a reward (33, Ad. 2)
osewa (polite) help, care (33, 8)
osewa ni naru to receive assistance (33, 8)
osu/-u/ to push (26, Ad. 1)
otaku your company (22, Ad. 2)
otazune-suru (polite) to call on (27, 2)

otenki (polite) weather (21, Ad. 2)
otokui customer (29, Ad. 1)
ototoshi the year before last (24, Ad. 3)
otsukare-sama thanks for your efforts (30, 1)
otsukiai (polite) socializing, associating (33, Ad. 1)
owabi-suru (polite) to apologize (34, Ad. 3)
oyobi-suru (respectful) to call (you) (25, 5)

P_____

pondo pound,lb (31, 10)

R_____

raigetsu next month (28, 12)
rainichi-suru to visit Japan (21, 4)
raku/na/ easy (29, 3)
rashii (it) seems (32, 3)
ree no that (28, 6)
reiohu (-suru) lay-off (23, 11)
renraku o toru to contact (25, 3)
rieki profit (24, Ad. 3)
rikai-suru to understand (33, Ad. 1)
rikai-shite morawanakereba ike-nai must have (someone) understand (33, Ad. 1)
rimawari yield, interest (22, Ad. 2)
ringisho in-house proposal, the *ringi* memorandum (29, 10)
rinji-yatoi temporary employment (28, Ad. 1)
ritsu rate (27, 5)
riyoo-suru to use, make good use of (31, 1)
riyuu reason (23, 14)
robotto no okage de thanks to robots (30, 8)
roodoo labor, work (23, 10)
roodoo-jooken working conditions (23, 13)
roodoo-kumiai labor union (23, 10)
ryootee Japanese-style restaurant (33, Ref)

S_____

saabisuryoo service charge (33, Ref)
sagaru/-u/ to go down (30, Ad. 2)
sagyoo (-suru) work, operation (23, 2)
saigo last (21, Ad. 2)
saikin recently (25, Ad. 1)
saisho first (22, 9)
saiteki/na/ ideal (31, 4)
sakan/na/ flourishing (30, Ad. 1)
sakuban last night (22, 5)
sakujitsu yesterday (33, 1)
samui (is) cold (21, Ref)
san-jikai third stage party (33, Ad. 1)
sanjup-pun shitara in/after 30 minutes (28, 14)
sansee-suru to agree (23, Ad. 2)

... (no) see de due to ... (30, Ad. 3)
see system (35, 8)
seekaku/na/ accurate (30, 7)
seekoo-suru to succeed (33, 3)
seekyuu-suru to claim, request charge (24, Ad. 1)
seerusu-enjinia sales engineer (21, 6)
seesan-suru to produce (22, 12)
seesan-kyootee production agreement (35, Ref)
seesansee productivity (30, 8)
seezoohi manufacturing expenses (25, Ref.)
seezoomoto manufacturer (29, 6)
sekinin responsibility (34, Ad. 1)
sekinin o motsu to take responsibility (34, Ad. 1)
sekkachi/na/ impatient, hasty (29, Ad. 2)
sen line, limit (27, 10)
senaka back (31, Ref)
sendenhi advertising expenses (25, Ref)
sen-en-satsu one thousand yen note (26, Ad. 3)
sengetsu last month (24, Ad. 2)
senmonteki/na/ specialized (29, 5)
sensaa sensor (23, 2)
setsubi facilities (30, Ad. 2)
setsuritsu (-suru) establishment (22, Ad. 1)
sewa help, care (33, 8)
(Joonzu)-shi Mr. (Jones) (21, 12)
shayoo for the company (26, 4)
shiharai payment (25, 13)
shiharau/-u/ to pay (25, 8)
shihonkin capital (22, Ad. 1)
shiito seat (31, 7)
shinakute mo ii don't need to do (33, Ad. 3)
shingata new type (23, 1)
shinpai-saserareru to be made to worry (35, 4)
shinsetsu/na/ kind (29. Ad. 2)
shinyoo trust (35, Ad. 1)
shinyoo-mondai trust-problem (35, Ad. 1)
shippai-suru to fail (33. Ad. 2)
shiraberu/-ru/ to check (34, 9)
shiraseru/-ru/ to inform, notify (28, 9)
shisaku-suru to manufacture for trial (31, 11)
shisetsu facilities (27, 9)
shishachoo manager of a branch (28, 1)
shitagau/-u/ to obey (29, 13)
shitauke subcontractor (34, Ad. 3)
shiten branch (26, Ad. 2)
shitsumon (-suru) question (21, 7)
... (shita) hoo ga ii (you) had better do (28, 9)
shiyoo (-suru) trial use (32, 7)
shiyoo-kikan trial period (32, 7)
shoobai-nesshin/na/ enthusiastic about business (30, 10)
shoochi-suru to understand (34, Ad. 1)
shookyuu (-suru) salary raises (28, 13)

242

shoomoohin consumable goods (35, Ref)

shoosho certificate (26, Ad. 1)

shooshuukan business practices (29, 4)

shootai-shitara ii (you) should invite (33, 10)

shori-suru to deal with (34, Ad. 1)

shotokuzee income tax (26, Ref)

shukka-suru to dispatch, send (30, Ad. 3)

shukuhai toast in celebration (33, 4)

shukuhai o ageru to raise a toast (33, 4)

shumi hobby (25, Ad. 2)

shurui kind, type (23, 4)

shuueki profit (30, Ad. 1)

shuukan customs (29, 4)

shuukyuu weekly pay (28, Ref)

shuuri (-suru) repairs (32, Ad. 2)

sono toori da that's it (29, 10)

sono uchi before long (25, Ad. 1)

soodan-sasete itadaku (humble) to consult you (33, 13)

sookin-suru to remit (money) (26, Ad. 2)

sooritsu (-suru) foundation (22, 8)

sora sky (22, 1)

sora no tabi flight (22, 1)

sore bakari de naku not only that (23, 13)

sore de and, then (24, Ad. 2)

sore ni moreover (21, 8)

sorezore each, respectively (32, 10)

sorosoro now, soon (30, 12)

subete all (25, 8)

sude ni already (31, 11)

sukkari completely (22, 6)

sunakku bar (33, 5)

susumeru/-ru/ to go ahead (25, 3)

susumu/-u/ to progress (29, 9)

suto strike (30, Ad. 3)

sutoraiki strike (30, Ad. 3)

suu number (35,5)

suu-dai-bun (work) for several units (23, 3)

suuryoo quantity (24, 5)

suzushii (is) cool (21, Ad. 1)

T

tabi trip (22, 1)

tabitabi again and again, often (35, 1)

tadaima I'm back. (28, 2)

tadashii (is) right, correct (23, 8)

taihuu typhoon (21, Ad. 3)

taisaku counter measures (34, 12)

taisaku o toru to take measures (34, 12)

taiya tire (31, 7)

tantoosha person in charge (29, 10)

... -tara sugu immediately after (doing) ... (32, Ad. 2)

tashikameru/-ru/ to confirm (32, 5)

tashika/na/ certain (28, 10)

teate nanka such things as allowances (28, Ad. 1)

teean (-suru) proposal (23, Ad. 2)

teeki-kensa periodical check-up (34, 5)

teeki-yokin time deposit (26, 15)

tehai-suru to arrange (32, Ad. 1)

tekisuru to be suitable, fit (31, 10)

te ni hairu to obtain (34, Ad. 3)

tenken (-suru) inspection (32, Ad. 2)

tenki weather (21, Ad. 2)

terebi TV (25, Ad. 2)

tesuuryoo charges, handling fees (24, Ad. 1)

Tii-kyuu-shii TQC (total quality control) (30, Ad. 1)

to when, if (27, 8)

tochuu on the way (34, Ad. 4)

todokeru/-ru/ to deliver (24, 10)

todoku/-u/ to be delivered (34, Ad. 2)

toiawaseru/-ru/ to check, inquire (27, 12)

... to iu hodo ja nai is not so ... to be called (34, 3)

to iu to does that mean? (27, Ad. 1)

... to ka iu to say something about ...(28, 3)

tokoro just, in the middle of (31, 3)

tokuchoo special characteristic(s) (23, 1)

toku ni particular (31, 5)

tonikaku anyway (35, 10)

toobun for the time being (29, 11)

toohoo our side (25, 9)

toohoo to shite wa as for us (25, 9)

too-koojoo this factory (23, Ad. 1)

Tookyoo-kikai Tokyo Kikai, Co. (34, Ad. 1)

toosha our company (21, 9)

tooza (-yokin) current, checking account (26, 5)

torihikisaki business partner (26, 10)

torikae replacement (35, 7)

torikaeru/-ru/ to replace (34, 5)

torikaenakereba naranai hodo so...that they need to be replaced (34, 5)

torikakaru/-u/ to start (32, 16)

torikeshi cancellation (27, Ad. 1)

toritsuke installment, mounting (31, 5)

toritsukeru/-ru/ to attach (23, 6)

... to shite mo for ... (27, 9)

tsukaihajimeru/-ru/ to start using (34, 6)

tsukainareru/-ru/ to be accustomed to using (26, 12)

(takushii ga) tsukamaru/-u/ can get (a taxi) (34, Ad. 4)

tsukareru/-ru/ to be tired (30, 1)

tsukiai socializing, associating, (33, Ad. 1)

tsukiau/-u/ to accompany (33, Ad. 3)

tsuku/-u/ to arrive (at) (22, 4)

tsumari that is, in short (23, 3)

tsume nail (31, Ref)

tsumetai (is) cold-hearted (29, Ad. 2)

tsureru/-ru/ to take along with (28, Ad. 2)

tsuuchoo bankbook (26, Ad. 3)

tsuukin-teate commuting allowance (28, Ref)

tsuyoi (is) strong (31, 9)

tsuyokereba tsuyoi hodo ii the stronger the better (31, 9)

tsuyoki/na/ firm stand, tough (27, Ad. 2)

tsuzuku/-u/ to continue (21, Ad. 1)

U

ude arm (31, Ref)

uketori receipt (26, 14)

uketorinin remittee (26, Ad. 2)

umi sea, beach (28, Ad. 2)

unten (-suru) operation (32, 10)

urayamashii (is) envious (28, Ad. 2)

uriage sales (22, 11)

urikomu/-u/ to sell, make a sale (29, 2)

urikomu no ni in order to sell (29, 2)

uta song (33, 7)

utau/-u/ to sing (33, 7)

W

wabiru/-ru/ to apologize (34, Ad. 3)

wagasha our company (23, 5)

wakaranai uchi as long as we don't know (34, 11)

wake da that means (23, 3)

wareware we (26, 12)

wariyasu/na/ comparatively cheap (24, 6)

Y

yahari all the same, as well (33, Ad. 1)

yama mountain(s) (28, Ad. 2)

yamu/-u/ to stop, cease (34, Ad. 4)

yarikirenai cannot stand (21, 4)

yaru/-u/ to do, perform (30, Ad. 1)

yasashii (is) gentle (29, Ad. 2)

yasumazu ni without stopping (35, 9)

yasumi day off, holiday (25, Ad. 2)

yasumi o toru to take (a) holiday(s) (28, Ad. 2)

yasumu/-u/ to rest, to go on holiday (28, Ad 2)

yatte iru tte iu no (the bar) where you do (33, 6)

yawarakai (is) soft (31, Ref)

yobu/-u/ to call (34, 1)

yobareru to be called (34, 1)

yokosu/-u/ to send (32, 9)

yokunakereba if (it) is not good (30, 4)

yoku ureru to sell well (32, Ad. 1)

yokyoo parlor trick, entertainment (33, Ref)

yooken business (26, 1)

Yooroppa-muke for Europe (35, Ref)

yooshi form (26, Ad. 1)

yosoo-suru to expect (24, Ad. 1)

yowai (is) weak (31, Ref)

yoyaku (-suru) reservation (33, 12)

yubi finger (31, Ref)

yuki ga huru/-u/ to snow (21, Ref)

yukisaki destination (31, Ad. 2)

yusoohi transportation expenses (25, Ref)

yuukyuu-kyuuka paid vacations (28, Ad. 1)

yuukyuu-shisetsu idle facilities (35, Ref)

yuumee/na/ famous, well known (22, 7)

yuuri/na/ advantageous (23, Ad. 2)

yuuryoku/na/ influential (29, Ad. 1)

yuuryoo charged (32, 14)

yuushuu/na/ highly qualified (29, Ad. 2)

Z

zaiko inventory (32, Ad. 1)

zaikobun goods in stock (32, Ad. 1)

zairyoo materials (31, Ref)

zeekin tax (33, Ref)

zenbu all (23, Ad. 1)

zenshateki/na/ throughout the company (30, Ad. 1)

zenzen...nai not at all (29, 9)

zooshi-suru to increase the capital (22, Ad.1)

zuibun very much (27, Ad. 1)

zurui (is) cunning, dishonest (29, Ad. 2)

zutsu each (32, 10)

zutto continuously (21, Ad. 2)